REDEMPTION IN POETRY
AND PHILOSOPHY

MCI

The Making of the Christian Imagination

Stephen Prickett
general editor

OTHER BOOKS IN THIS SERIES

Rowan Williams, *Dostoevsky*
Kevin J. Gardner, *Betjeman*
Fred Parker, *The Devil as Muse*
Ralph C. Wood, *Chesterton*
David Dickinson, *The Novel as Church*
Daniel Gabelman, *George MacDonald*

REDEMPTION IN POETRY AND PHILOSOPHY

Wordsworth, Kant, and the Making of the Post-Christian Imagination

Simon Haines

BAYLOR UNIVERSITY PRESS

Jacket Design by *the*BookDesigners
Jacket Image: Woman at dawn, Friedrich, Caspar David (1774–1840) / Museum Folkwang, Essen, West Germany / The Bridgeman Art Library

Library of Congress Cataloging-in-Publication Data

Haines, Simon, 1955–
  Redemption in poetry and philosophy : Wordsworth, Kant, and the making of the post-Christian imagination / Simon Haines.
    269 pages cm. -- (The making of the Christian imagination)
  Includes bibliographical references and index.
  ISBN 978-1-60258-779-3
  1. Wordsworth, William, 1770–1850--Philosophy. 2. Wordsworth, William, 1770–1850--Aesthetics. 3. Wordsworth, William, 1770–1850--Political and social views. 4. Kant, Immanuel, 1724-1804--Influence. 5. Redemption in literature. I. Title.
  PR5892.P5H35 2013
  821'.7--dc23

                                        2012043663

for Cathy and Will, who talked it all through with me
for Eddie, who always took my mind off it
for Jane, for everything

and in memory of my parents

SERIES INTRODUCTION
by Rowan Williams

The current rash of books hostile to religious faith will one day be an interesting subject for some sociological analysis. They consistently suggest a view of religion which, if taken seriously, would also evacuate a number of other human systems of meaning, including quite a lot of what we unreflectively think of as science. That is, they treat religious belief almost as a solitary aberration in a field of human rationality; a set of groundless beliefs about matters of fact, resting on—at best—faulty and weak argumentation. What they normally fail to do is to attend to what it is that religious people actually do and say—and also to attend to the general question of how systems of meaning, or "worldviews," work.

Systems of meaning—philosophies of life, if you must, though the term sounds immediately rather stale—seem to operate by allowing us to see phenomena in connected instead of arbitrary ways. But this means the capacity to see things in terms of other things: it means abandoning the idea that there is one basic and obvious way of seeing the world which any fool can get hold of (and which some people then insist on dressing up with unnecessary complications), and grasping that seeing the world and being able to talk about what it is that we encounter is something we have to learn, a set of skills that allows us to connect and to see one event or phenomenon through the lens of another. At the most severely pragmatic level, this leads to observational generalizations about laws; at a quite different but no less important level, it leads us into the world of metaphor. And in case anyone should think that these are radically separate, consider that "law" itself is a metaphor in the context of natural process. . . .

Metaphor is omnipresent, certainly in scientific discourse (selfish genes, computer modelings of brain processes, not to mention the magnificent extravagances of theoretical physics), and its omnipresence ought to warn us against the fiction that there is a language that is untainted and obvious for any discipline. We are bound to use words that have histories and associations; to see things in terms of more than their immediate appearance means that we are constantly using a language we do not fully control to respond to an environment in which things demand that we see more in them than any one set of perceptions can catch.

All of which is to say that no system of perceiving and receiving the world can fail to depend upon imagination, the capacity to see and speak into and out of a world that defies any final settlement as to how it shall be described. The most would-be reductive account of reality still reaches for metaphor, still depends on words that have been learned and that have been used elsewhere. So it should not be too difficult to see that a map that presents the intellectual world as a struggle between rival pictures, well-founded and ill-founded ways of describing things, literal and fanciful perspectives, or even natural and supernatural vision, is a poor one and one that threatens to devour itself in the long run, if the search is for the unadorned absolute. How shall we move the cultural discussion on from a situation in which religious perspectives are assumed to be bad descriptions of what can be better talked about in simpler terms?

This will involve the discipline of following through exactly what it is that the language of a particular religious tradition allows its believers to see—that is, what its imaginative resources are. When believers are engaged (as they routinely are, despite what may be assumed by the critics of faith) in society and politics and the arts in ways that are recognizable to nonbelievers, how are their perceptions actually and specifically molded by the resources of their tradition? This is not—*pace* any number of journalistic commentators—a matter of the imperatives supposedly derived from their religion. It is about what they see things and persons in terms of, what the metaphors are that propose further dimensions to the world they inhabit in common with nonbelievers.

Characteristically this repertoire of resources—in any religious tradition—is chaotically varied, not just a matter of a few leading ideas or doctrines. It includes the visual and the aural—what is sung and seen as well as said. It includes formative practices, rites, which leave their semantic traces in unexpected settings. And it includes the legacy of others who have engaged the world in the same ways, at various levels of sophistication. The forming of a corporate imagination is something that continues to be the more or less daily business of religious believers, and it needs to be acknowledged that this is a process immeasurably more sophisticated than the repetitive dogmatism so widely assumed to be the sole concern of those who employ religious language.

The way to demonstrate this is to lay out what it means in the practice of specific people; this series is an attempt to exhibit a common imagination at work—and in the process of further refinement and development—in the labors of a variety of creative minds. Because we are in danger of succumbing to a damaging cultural amnesia about what religious commitment looks like in practice, these books seek to show that belief "in practice" is a great deal more than following out abstract imperatives or general commitments. They look at creative minds that have a good claim to represent some of the most decisive and innovative cultural currents of the history of the West (and not only the West), in order to track the ways in which a distinctively Christian imagination makes possible their imaginative achievement. And in doing so, they offer a challenge to what one great thinker called the "cultured despisers" of Christian faith: in dismissing this faith, can an intellectually serious person accept confidently the simultaneous dismissal of the shifts, enlargements, and resources it has afforded the individual and collective imagination? What, finally, would a human world be like if it convinced itself that it had shaken off the legacy of the Christian imagination? The hope of the authors of these volumes is that the answer to that question will be constructively worrying—sufficiently so, perhaps, to make possible a more literate debate about faith and contemporary culture.

CONTENTS

Preface   xiii

Acknowledgments   xix

Introduction: The Making of the Post-Christian Imagination   1

1   Concepts, Metaphors, and Wordsworth   21

2   "Tintern Abbey"—*Restoring the Soul*   37

3   Spontaneity in Kant and Wordsworth   73

4   Wordsworth and Political Redemption I—*Paradise*   133

5   Wordsworth and Political Redemption II— *Paradise Lost*   185

Conclusion   215

Notes   221

Bibliography   237

Index   243

PREFACE

Often the most pressing ethical question is not how to live, but how to go on living. The more famous question usually starts to present itself only after we have already been living for a while, and so have acquired moral burdens, debts, errors, senses of our own inadequacy or fallibility, occasions for shame or guilt. Those who know or think they know how to live are generally the ones (maybe the lucky ones) who are just doing it, or still doing it. Those who might ask the famous question are generally the ones who have become aware that they do not know, or have not always known, how to live. And that means they feel some burden of past error: of not living well now, or not having lived well before. To them it may often seem that the way forward is blocked by that past error, so that living well is impossible without removing the block, without acquitting or redeeming the debt. How much better we would feel if only we could somehow *not* have done that thing: had been brave enough to do that other thing: have spent those years in *that* way and not *that*. If only we had done the things we ought to have done, and had not done the things we ought not to have done. If only we could pay off those debts, somehow, *then* we might be able to afford to live fully in the present. We cannot change or somehow jettison the past, but maybe we can change our sense of it, its value for us, so that it doesn't weigh on us: so that, perhaps, it seems like an asset, not a liability. "How to live" must surely include within its ethical scope *all* the living we have done and not done, not just how we live now, or want to live in the future; we feel there is a balance sheet of some kind. What it would be, then, not just to pay off the old debts but to see them as investments: not just to cast off our old chains but recast them as armor or ornaments. How much new energy we would have. We would be saved, restored, free to go on living.

This would not be just a matter of forgiveness or absolution: of finding someone, or everyone, to whom we might say "forgive us our trespasses": and then being forgiven. Our *propensity* to sin, our sinfulness itself, is what we would need to feel freed or saved from. Knowing how to go on living would imply a sense not just of being forgiven for what we had done, but also of being so changed that we, the new "we," would not do it anymore: indeed could hardly even remember what it was like to be the kind of person who *did* do it. We would be redeemed.

As the language of the last paragraph has already implied, for much of its duration and in many of its aspects Western civilization has approached such questions in a broadly Christian way (although of course much of humanity has not). The burden of sin was and will be lifted, the debt paid, all humanity changed, by a single Redeemer. Many people still believe this. But for many others that long process of dismantling the Christian faith, which began with the seventeenth- and eighteenth-century Enlightenment, has left them looking else- where for some kind, some analogue, of redemption: some secular, self-decontaminating rebirth into guiltless and shameless authenticity.

This book is about two of the earliest and greatest writers to sense this need, a poet and a philosopher, both of them writing on the cusp of Enlightenment and Romanticism. Many other writers might have been chosen; indeed most great writers since these two have wor- ried at it, one way or the other. One might point to Dostoevsky or Kierkegaard *versus* Nietzsche; or Eliot *versus* Wittgenstein; or Hei- degger *and* Musil; or Proust *and* Joyce. On the other hand only one great writer on the subject preceded both of our two: Rousseau was both a philosopher and a poet. So in a sense this is a book about the first consequences of Rousseau—about the earliest redemptive writers of Rousseauan modernity. How did they point the way for those many writers who followed them, whose experience of "sin," or its various secular transgression-analogues, also drew directly or indirectly from

Christian sources: and thus for the many readers they and all those successors quite clearly intended to point the way for?

Most of the book is about William Wordsworth. Poetry broadly conceived (including novels and plays) is life-writing. Poets write about how to live, or how to go on living, more urgently, essentially, and (in a broad sense) morally than anyone else. They are the masters of writing as a metaphorical and rhetorical analogue of life. In their writing, how to live and how we *do* live, value and fact, are all but indistinguishable. Wordsworth was not just a poet but also a poetic autobiographer, and he carried through the redemptive life-writing project more rigorously and coherently, if not more influentially, than his master Rousseau. Philosophy, on the other hand, is concept-writing, the conceptual analogue of life, and it has too often insisted on the separation of fact and value. The master of modern philosophy is Kant, perhaps Rousseau's greatest disciple, and the subject of an essential but much smaller part of this book, intended to sketch for nonphilosophical readers a highly suggestive convergence in the understanding of the auto-redemptive self between German Enlightenment philosophy and English Romantic poetry. Between them, following Rousseau, these two writers did much to set the stage and define the terms for the modern enterprise of secular redemption through writing.

In doing so, however, and without intending to, although not without some awareness of this outcome, they exposed the sheer difficulty of the enterprise. Secular literary redemption turns out, at least on the evidence of their writing, to be almost self-contradictory, either as an alternative to Christian redemption or as a return to some pre-Christian equivalent. To redeem ourselves *after* Christianity must imply, among other things, redeeming ourselves *from* Christianity: that is, from a faith that has determined, and that has largely defined itself in terms of, what redemption is. Secular *non*-literary redemption, of course, is another matter entirely, a matter of doing, not just writing and reading, and thus beyond the scope of any mere book. The question for us is: what if poetry and philosophy, which are the two essential modes of thinking with language (as opposed to just using it), made it their mission and central function to redeem us, and having believed them we turned to them to do exactly this—and then they failed? What might that mean, for writers or for readers?

It would mean, presumably, that those who cannot give up on their need for a sense of redemption must (a) give up looking for it in writing and reading, or (b) return to Christianity, or (c) both. On the other hand it might mean that (d) we should give up on redemption. In any case it would mean that (e) philosophy and poetry should give up on redemption too. People who take up Buddhism, move to mountain cabins to raise llamas, or try to help orphans in slums, are all doing (a). Many people still do (b). Some also do (c). Many again manage perfectly well with (d), while still more, most of humanity in fact, do not need to give up on something they never had (although, as the opening paragraphs of this preface imply, redemptive need in some form probably extends far beyond the Christian world). The issue for books like this is really (e), and should eventually, but not in this book, have to do with the various other directions in which post-Romantic poetry and philosophy have evolved, and the ways in which they have represented the modern self and its senses of being. But the salient point about the enterprise represented by Kant and Wordsworth is how determinative it has been of the modern secular consciousness, or at least the intellectual consciousness, of the West. In both of these enormously influential writers some ghost of the redemptive disposition haunts and even vitiates their thought at its very core.

One might say, isn't this just Nietzsche's point in so much of his work, the point of so much of it, from *The Birth of Tragedy* to *Thus Spake Zarathustra* and beyond? Namely, that Enlightenment writers, still haunted by Christian *ressentiment*, had mistakenly seen philosophy and art as redeeming life by acts of aesthetic cognition, whereas true secular redemption is something else entirely? Yes: but Nietzsche's inauguration of a new kind of redemption was actually anticipated by some of the very writers he was criticizing, including Kant and Rousseau: while being at the same time no less haunted by the older redemptive ghost. He was for all his polemical brilliance less original than they, still engaged in the same enterprise that they initiated but that (according to him) they understood so inadequately (compared with him): that of understanding the self in terms of the displacement of faith and virtue by will. Aquinas had achieved a vast and enduring synthesis of Aristotelian virtue and Christian faith, the two ethics that had long before displaced the ancient eye-for-an-eye systems of, respectively, Homeric honor and Old Testament theophany (although these also still endure in some cultures, and in some parts of all cultures). But Aquinas had in turn been displaced and disintegrated by the Enlightenment: above all, belatedly, by Rousseau. Wordsworth and Kant were two of the first writers to sense this and to try to chart, to find a path through, the . . . what? ruins? wasteland? earthly paradise? brave new world? How to go on living in *this* world: that is their question. How to make a post-Christian imagination.

S. H.
Bologna 2009—Charing 2012

ACKNOWLEDGMENTS

Most of the work on this book was made possible by a two-year research grant from the General Research Fund of the Hong Kong University Grants Committee. I am most grateful to the UGC for the grant and to the anonymous readers of the GRF proposal for their suggestions. During 2009 the University of Bologna and the Chinese University of Hong Kong kindly granted me, respectively, a senior research fellowship at the Institute of Advanced Studies and a period of research leave to work on the book.

A much earlier version of chapter 2 was published in *The Critical Review*, no. 31. I am grateful to the editor, Richard Lansdown, for his permission to use some of this material. An earlier version of chapter 3 was published as a chapter in *English Now* in 2008. My thanks to Marianne Thormahlen, the editor of the book, for permission to publish this revised version. Versions of various parts of the book were presented as papers at the IAUPE Conference in Lund, 2007; at the conference "Romanticism and the Tyrannies of Distance" held by the Romantic Studies Association of Australasia, 2011; and at seminars at the University of Hong Kong (2010), Princeton University (2010), and the University of Utrecht (2011). I am grateful for (and often felt chastened by) the range and breadth of the suggestions made on these occasions.

Thanks also to staff at the Bodleian Library and at the libraries of the University of Bologna, the Australian National University, and the

Chinese University of Hong Kong, for their advice and help. As the general editor of this series, Stephen Prickett read through the whole manuscript and made many crucial suggestions. So too did the reader for Baylor University Press. I am deeply grateful to both. The book's numerous remaining flaws are entirely my responsibility, needless to say.

I would also like to thank both Stephen and Richard for many years of support, encouragement, and friendship. I am grateful for the friendship and intellectual companionship of my colleagues in the English Department at CUHK and the School of Humanities at ANU, and of many others elsewhere, including Jane Adamson, Serena Baiesi, Will Christie, Lilla Crisafulli, Keir Elam, Richard Freadman, John Gillies, Chris Miller, Anna Molan and Marianne Thormahlen. Especial thanks to Fred Langman, who has been thinking about Wordsworth for far longer than I, and who first inspired me to try to write about him—indeed to read English literature at university to begin with. I, like many others, owe him a great deal. Also warm thanks to David Parker, for so many entirely congenial conversations on so many subjects over so many years: and for the opportunities he has given me.

INTRODUCTION
The Making of the Post-Christian Imagination

Romantic Redemption

Suppose we think of redemption not in its rich and complex Christian sense, as a "buying back" of humanity from sin by a Redeemer who is divine but must nevertheless, by God's grace, still pay the price of his own very human life to save us all; but more broadly, in thinner, secular terms, as any kind of saving, cleansing, absolving, or restoring of the erring or transgressing human spirit by the making of some great personal sacrifice. (I am not suggesting that redemption is *the* central concept of Christianity: but it is *a* central one.) Much is inevitably changed in this translation of redemptive into neo- or quasi-redemptive activity. To whom, for example, would this sacrifice, this payment, now be made? For whose sake would it be made? Could one person possibly make it for his own sake? From a prior position of Christian faith, this would be to think of redemption as being enacted not by God in Christ—that is, not through the agency of some inscrutable grace, first permissive and divine, then sacrificial and incarnate—but by man himself, for himself. Yet the very fact that a man (or woman) might or should presume to do this for himself (or herself), or even for others, especially for others, would be the first and greatest sin he needed absolving from, because to do this, of all things, for himself, would be to make himself into his own Redeemer *and* his own God. To presume to do it for others would be an act of possibly even

I

greater pride than to do it for himself. From the prior position of faith all this would be a sin almost beyond comprehension. "Father, forgive them," says the Redeemer at the moment of sacrifice. But just to start with, how could you possibly forgive *yourself*? Surely forgiveness, like gratitude, or grace, implies an outward movement of feeling toward another? And if self-forgiveness is unfathomable, how much harder it must be to understand self-redemption. Who could think of himself as sinner, self-sacrificer and divinity, all at once?

Of course this prior position, together with the unanswerable questions it raises, has already been occluded or forgotten in many Western societies; and yet the redemptive need and response do nevertheless still arise, in damaged or troubled spirits that would formerly have been consoled or even healed, in a Christian society, by their faith. Under these circumstances the damage or trouble must be at some unconscious level partly a recognition of that displacement. This makes the predicament specifically *post*-Christian; it can arise only in a society which was once Christian.[1] The faith can no longer offer itself, even to the memory or the imagination, as a sufficient response, and yet the redemptive reflex is still there: the sense that one has erred, that we all do, and that the only way to repair one's spirit, to atone for what we all do to ourselves and each other, is by paying a great price, on behalf either of others or of oneself.[2] Nor is this just a matter of making amends; redemption is not reparation. The price to save a soul may still be a life.

So how to express this quasi-redemptive or post-redemptive reflex? What kind of agency, what coinage, might be available to such post-Christians, when the redemptive turn appears to be the only way to relieve their painful consciousness of uncleanness, crookedness, evil— including their own? How can they come to terms with committing this "sin," in the terms of an old faith still perhaps operative at some deep level in their minds, by which they make themselves the redeemers of sin? Assuming that to propose oneself as the redeemer (really the Second Redeemer) of others' sins is an act of pride of satanic proportions:, then how are we at least to convert "I know that my Redeemer liveth" into a more modest and secular "I must redeem myself"?

Jesus paid with his life; that was his coinage. Of course, even for a non-Christian, something like that has always been possible. Many

have indeed paid like this, or with comparable forms of personal sacrifice, so that others may have morally better lives, or be somehow
redeemed from their wrongdoing. Socrates died partly so that Crito
and Phaedo might understand how much those great concepts, Justice, Truth, and Beauty, really meant: how transcendently important
they were to, and in, all lives. But if there is no Christ any more, if his
divinity and hence his unique redemptiveness are no longer credible,
then what is lost in a post-Christian society may be something that no
pre-Christian or non-Christian sacrifice can compensate for. Perhaps
the mode of the story has changed in a fundamental way. Socrates died
because he believed in the transcendent truth of the concepts he had
lived by. He showed his friends and countless others since them how
to do this: how to live and die not for Athens or honor, but for justice
or truth. And yet, for that very reason, he did not die *for Crito and
Phaedo*, or for the rest of us. He would have had to be Attis or Osiris
as well as Socrates to do that (as Attis or Osiris would also have had to
be Socrates: Jesus was no Corn King). Instead Socrates died *for himself*,
acting out of the conceptual self he lived by. Can some such proto-
Stoic attitude offer a model for post-Christian redemption? Above all,
can a post-Christian imagination ever really dispel the shadowy trace
or cultural memory of that unique sacrifice?

Christianity, and therefore redemption, required not only the
Christ, the sacrificial figure, but also a Mark, a Paul, even a Milton,
to make the cross morally so "crucial." Yes, one might say, but surely
its secular analogue also required a Phaedo, a Plato. There always has
to be some kind of witness. Someone has to suffer the sacrifice, and
someone *else* has to tell the story. The Gospel is what we read, how we
know about redemption, and so is part of the redemptive agency itself;
what would it mean to say that Christ redeemed us all *but noone knew?*
The Gospel is what Mark did, not what Christ did. And so, continuing the analogy, it was Plato, not Socrates, who wrote the Dialogues:
they, not the voice of Socrates himself, may console or inspire us in our
own lives. It was the witnesses and writers who made these two great
redemptive and quasi-redemptive events of our civilization into its two
great constitutive narratives.

But about 250 years ago, as the Enlightenment tipped over into
Romanticism, one of these two narratives started to lose its potency,

principally under assault from the other one (Voltaire and Hume were Socratists of a kind). By the same impulse, the witness-writer had started to seem as important as the redeemer. In fact the witness now *was* the redeemer. Autobiography was displacing biography. Rousseau's 1782 *Confessions*, not Boswell's 1791 *Life*, provided the model for the modern European literary self, in which the autobiographer witnesses not only his own sin, or perhaps just his ephemerality, but also his own redemption, his own redemptiveness: and witnesses them in the act of writing itself. Even though the Socratic life seemed to offer a post-Christian model of self-sacrifice, it now had at its core a space left empty by the second death of the redemptive Jesus: a space inevitably filled, an attitude inevitably adopted, by the writer himself. The Romantic self-redeemer, even when he is a philosopher (Rousseau, Kant, Hegel, Kierkegaard, Nietzsche, Heidegger . . .), is more an amalgamation of Jesus and Mark than of Socrates and Plato (although Wittgenstein may be an illuminating exception).

To repeat: modern or post-Christian redemption had to be reflexive. One can only presume to redeem oneself, now that Jesus has gone. (The Socratic attitude reinforces this reflexiveness by demanding only that each of us be true to certain concepts discovered within himself or herself.) Given one's own sin or weakness the proper attitude to others is one of atonement, not redemption. To atone is to make amends to the one you have injured. There are only two parties to this transaction, and furthermore only one of them is active. And it *is* a transaction: a balance is restored. To redeem, on the other hand, requires a third party to atone for or take on the burden of an injury she did not inflict, a sin she did not commit; it requires, that is, two active parties, sinner and redeemer. And it is not just a balancing of accounts; the price paid is incommensurable with the reward gained. The redeemer has to pay in a strange coin. An atonement can be transacted without pride by the single active party; a redemption can be so transacted only if the two active parties are the same person.

Under all these circumstances the strange coinage, the only possible coinage, surely, is language. When the Word made flesh can no longer redeem us, then only the written or spoken word can. The conclusion of this strange process of elision is that the writer of Gospels,

Epistles, epics or Confessions (but not of Dialogues or Investigations) can be both sinner in his life and redeemer in his writing.

But what of the injured, passive party, the one whose losses the atoner caused and then reimbursed, and the redeemer did not cause but nevertheless made his own (Antonio's melancholy in *The Merchant of Venice* as a faint echo of his Redeemer's at Gethsemane)? And, to return to the first question asked in this introduction, what of the One to whom this sacrifice must be made, the One who must be placated or persuaded? In the post-Christian language-world both are now the same person. Reader, this means You. All of us. Those who are supposed to be saved by this New Gospel are also those who have to decide whether to accept the sacrifice, whether the writer has redeemed himself. If the writer is both sinner and redeemer, the reader is both saved and God. But, as we saw, the injured party is passive, almost negligible, in this story: while as God, the reader has merely become the witness of, the mirror held up to, the sacrifice being made by the writer, whose own redemption is the true drama. Indeed it is equally arguable that the trinity of sinner-writer-redeemer is now the real God.

The thinning or hollowing out of the rich Christian *metaphor* of redemption into a post-Christian *concept* of sacrifice, cleansing, restoration and health went hand in hand with a (perhaps temporary) narrowing of focus or reference—of experience, indeed. One's own life is all that one can really presume to save. But if only the writer, the artist, perhaps only the autobiographer, can save himself, and if his real business is only to save *himself*, then who will save the rest of us? At the same time the urgent impulse to use language alone as an agent of redemption, to conscript it into a function performed for so long and until very recently by just one unique *life*, may have led, temporarily at the very least, to the impoverishment of language itself. How to save *that*?

One final consideration: in the Christian model redemption happens only by God's grace. He permits it; he offers his own son for sacrifice. That grace, like creation itself, comes out of some ineffable source beyond our comprehension. As we shall see, this conception of a mysterious source, from which salvation, redemption, and creation all spring, also lingers on, but now with an inexplicable aspect, in more secular models of the self.

Concepts, Metaphors, and Wordsworth

We have now reached the beginning of chapter 1. The rest of this introduction is an interpretative summary of the rest of the book, a short parallel narrative, in the light of what has just been said about redemption. Explicit references to Christian redemption in the rest of the book are in fact relatively rare, just because redemption is translated by Wordsworth, particularly, into the secular language of saving, cleansing, restoring, and so on: what I have called a quasi-redemptive language. But what has just been said should constantly be kept in mind.

First, then, if only language can redeem us now, what *kind* of language must it be? Chapter 1 of this book suggests that there are only two kinds of thinking *with* language, of thinking in which language is a medium of thought's expression, an air that thought breathes, not just an instrument of thought—two ways, that is, of reshaping the self in language, making experience our own by mixing language-thought with it. This is what would be required to absolve, cleanse, restore, or undo: to redeem. The first kind is broadly metaphorical; let us call it poetry. The second is broadly conceptual; let us call that one philosophy. Only broadly, though: each form has within it elements of the other.

The chapter further suggests that during the Romantic period, for the first time in history, some poets actually started to think of what they wrote as redemptive. But for the poetry to feel redemptive, strangely, it had to become less metaphorical and more conceptual: less poetic and more philosophical: less representational and more propositional: not so much how *we* live as how *to* live. More like an Epistle of Paul than a Gospel of Mark. Or so the chapter argues. Of course not all poetry was like this. There was another path for it to take, a non-redemptive, metaphorical, or richly conceptual one. But the more influential model was the former. And its principal and most influential exponent in English poetry, for at least a century and a half, maybe still, was William Wordsworth.

Wordsworth's poetry, says chapter 1, above all else pleads for conversion. Explicitly and urgently it sets out to change our hearts and minds so as to deliver us from evil. It also wants, therefore, to convert us *to poetry*, as the only mode of thought that can change us like this.[3] The irony is that in the very act of setting itself these two goals, making these two claims, the poetry also makes itself less like poetry, which is a fundamental, non-tendentious metaphorizing of experience: and more like a kind of ethico-religious case study, in which the poet's own life manifests and proves the conversion in him. The conversion is quite literal: outer objects, rocks, rivers, landscapes, are converted in Wordsworth's poetry into moral dispositions. This sounds metaphorical enough, surely; but the metaphor is used instrumentally, not experientially, as the servant of an idea that is primarily conceptual. "This is a picture of redemption/salvation," the poem is saying about itself.

But redemption means the suffering that buys salvation from sin. It is not the same as conversion, not the same as salvation, any more than it is the same as atonement, reparation, or forgiveness. Wordsworth consciously saw poetry as a means of conversion and salvation: but at some deeper level writing it was, *for him*, redemptive. This was the language, or language was the medium or coin, in which he bought back his spirit from sin, such that he, and we, his readers, could be saved—and also such that we could recognize him as redeemed.

In the following chapters, to return to what was said a moment ago, redemption, or redemptiveness, sacrifice for the sake of that saving, cleansing or healing process which will restore meaning to a self-damaged life, is always the unseen gravitational force influencing the thought, even when those various consequences are the thought's more explicit purposes, and the book's more explicit subjects. Chapters 2 to 5 deal with three redemptive modes: the aesthetic, the spontaneous, and the political. It might be argued, indeed, that these are *the* three redemptive modes proposed by a secular modernity in which consciousness of sin is still operative in some form.

"Tintern Abbey"

The poem proposes restoring the soul through the beauty of landscape. In recognizing a familiar natural scene we recognize ourselves, and in this double recognition the scene comes to have not just meaning but also *value* for us. This is our own personal *paysage moralisé*. The private language in which it speaks to us, its solipsistic seclusion, is deeply consolatory, and peculiarly fragile. We fear that it may have no wider value, even as we draw strength from its value for us—which is our love for it. At some level we fear that there may be no God in it, that the still small voice is only our own. There's a strange hesitancy in the poetry here, a metaphorical stumbling, that seems to express these misgivings. For the observer of such a familiar landscape it may seem that its value *is* its beauty, that the landscape is beautiful *because* it has this self-affirming value. But at a deeper level the process works the other way around. This is an aesthetic situation already turning itself into a moral case. The underlying claim is that a form of beauty can become a form of good; the landscape will restore our souls *and* our characters. If this scene is a picture of the mind, then the mind itself is an aesthetic form, graspable as a matter of sensuous perception, before it is a moral one. How we feel as a matter of aesthetics is indistinguishable from how we feel as a matter of morals. The pleasures of beauty can cause us to act well.

The poetry aspires, surely, to much more than the observation that, as a mere matter of appetite, satisfaction causes benefaction. A profounder insight is proposed, we feel: into virtue as well as value. But this insight is never quite articulated. The landscape makes us *feel* better, yes, but does it really *make* us better? If the poetry could show this, what a poetry it would be. And yet its real strength seems to consist in *claiming* this, rather than showing it—leaving us with the impression that showing it may, after all, be impossible. The aspiration seems greater than the language. There are wonderful moments, certainly, when the poem does seem about to modulate into a kind of hedonistic eudaimonism, a profound account of habituated virtue as enabled by aesthetic joy. And yet it always steps back from this fulfillment. In the end the metaphors break down; the virtues are just concepts.

This happens, finally, because *eudaimonia*, virtue, real joy in goodness, requires other people. The poetry wants to redeem us all, starting with the poet: but it never gets *beyond* the poet. Indeed the human world seems to him unintelligible, and at the heart of the unintelligibility is something dreadful (God is not in this part of the picture). The poet must flee the human world, abandon it, perceive it henceforth only as a far-off noise muffled by the forms of beauty rather than ordered by them; and yet in doing so he becomes the human flaw, the terrifying alien presence, in the very restorative landscape he loves. Indeed the act of fleeing is both a restoration and a desertion. It seems that one deals with suffering by thinking about it in another way, but this is just dealing with one's own suffering as caused by others' suffering. The poet needs to be redeemed from this kind of redemption.

The poem's other, complementary Presence is a kind of God, a Being far more deeply interfused. But the way in which the poem raises the possibility that such a Being might be the final ground of value, the court of appeal for redemptive activity, seriously undermines its purposes. First, it suggests that the Presence might actually be the emanation of the poet's own mind. One figure would then be sinner, redeemer, and divinity all at once, which as we saw at the start of this introduction is what secular redemption may imply—but by re-introducing God like this, Wordsworth risks exposing secular redemption as the merest simulacrum of the other kind. Secondly, if the rest of humanity is reduced to "noises off," his readers have the choice of identifying with him, which means knowingly making the same retreat: or identifying with the rest of humanity. And since, as we saw earlier, humanity in this secular model is the new God, then this God is not going to feel very sympathetic to a redemptive proposal based largely on exile from him.

This is particularly relevant in the poem's final paragraph, which in effect turns its back on human relationship, except in so far as it is a source of comfort and reassurance to the poet. The redemptive form of the poem stands revealed as that of a promise, not a delivery. The gap between beauty and good is actually the source of the poetry. The very fact that the poem exists shows that the gap cannot be closed. Aesthetic redemption is inadvertently declared impossible by the very poetry that claims to provide it.[4] And the implications of this are far-reaching, for if this poetry cannot do *that*, what *can* it do? A deep anxiety about human relationship and the metaphors in which it is best represented feeds into one about poetry itself. But only such a magnificent inaugural failure as this can show us the risks involved in aestheticism when it aspires to a redemptive status: as, since Wordsworth, it so often has, from the Romantic through the Modernist eras of thought.

Kant, Wordsworth, and Spontaneity

We now turn to our second mode of redemption. Kant inherited a Cartesian and Rousseauan model of the self, especially the ethical self, with a heterogeneous punctual "core" made, essentially, of good will.[5]

The first *Critique*, analyzed in some detail here in a fashion intended to be helpful for non-philosophers as well as apropos for philosophers, slowly winds itself in toward such a core, exposing it chiefly in the "Transcendental Deduction." The moment of judgment, the "critical moment," is the one in which we recognize ourselves in knowing the world *for* ourselves (a close analogue of the Wordsworthian recognition in "Tintern Abbey"). The understanding is "the legislation for nature," but also the making of us. And yet for all the painstaking assemblage of concepts and discriminations that make up the book's apparently exhaustive account of how we have experience, this critical moment is finally inexplicable. Out of nowhere, out of some deep place, we just *do* it, "spontaneously." This spontaneity *is* the core of the self, and in some mysterious way we both know and do not know it. And spontaneity is a moral source, not just an epistemological one. Out of that mysterious core comes "causality through freedom." The critical moment is not just one of knowing, but one of willing.

But the concept of spontaneity or *spontaneität* itself has a history, and this book takes the internal history of words more seriously than the modern structuralist, anti-philological turn in linguistics and literary theory would allow. Etymology is an undervalued tool now. The literal translation of the Greek *etumos logos* is either "the truth of words" or the "science of truth." With an unfashionable diachronicity that connects any poet's use of a word to both its earlier and its later senses just as closely as to its contemporary ones, etymology takes us to the metaphors still living, invisibly but inextricably, within apparently fossilized or sterile concepts. A poet should feel the existence of such micro-metaphorical life in his very bones, and exploit it; but, as chapter 2 shows, Wordsworth did not often think in that way.

As for a philosopher, the existence of such a life in words can subvert his thought utterly, especially if, like Kant, he devotes all the power of an exceptionally powerful, systematizing intellect to eliminating it. *Spondere* is "to bind, engage, or sacredly pledge," and the spontaneous act is a holy commitment, a pouring out of the self in recognition of God. Without reference to an external God, however, the model becomes one of a quasi-divine source at the core of the self, endlessly pouring out its libation, its self-caused causality, the only force in the universe that is not just mechanistically natural. Without this spontaneous self-generative activity of the will, we would have no idea of freedom. But even more fundamentally, this activity of the will happens under the influence of respect for a certain idea of reason— namely, *law*. We do not know where the will comes from, but it does so according, as it were, to the shape of the spout it pours out of. This reason-directed, self-legislating will is the only really *holy* thing in the world, says Kant. It has replaced God's grace in the moral world.

The purpose of the first two Critiques is to carve out this space for freedom of the will in a world of natural causality, rather than of divine creation. But the freedom is in the end just as much a matter of faith as God's grace was. We cannot know it; we know only that it happens—just as we cannot know the reality behind our world of appearances: only that it must be there. In both cases there is a "something," but that is all we can know. At the core of the self is a self-making good will, creating freedom *ex nihilo*. God created the universe; Kantian humanity creates itself, out of some impenetrable black box, a moral singularity in a mechanical universe.

Kant wanted philosophy to save us from nature, not deliver us from evil or restore our souls. But the redemptive model underlying this quest for salvation is even more startling than in the case of Wordsworth's aestheticism. If the self becomes the holy spontaneous creator of itself, then the space of creation is the space where God was. We can redeem ourselves from the specter of a soulless, in effect a godless, mechanical universe only by constant self-creation. In this model the "sin," the error, would lie in seeing the universe as merely mechanical. The philosopher is the redeemer. What is sacrificed, although Kant explicitly denies this, is God himself, who becomes no more than a necessary concept underpinning the moral law. The critical philosophy was supposed to deny reason in order to make room for faith. It actually does the opposite.

This book is primarily about a poet, not a philosopher. Still, the implications of these claims about Kant are far-reaching—out of all proportion to the space devoted to them here—for all modern literary thought, whether philosophical or poetic. Wordsworth, for his part, knew little of Kant (although Coleridge knew a great deal); and yet spontaneity figures in his work as prominently and suggestively as it does in Kant's own. We turn, then, back to Wordsworth: to the moment of spontaneity that constitutes the poem "Simon Lee." For most of the poem nothing happens at all. Life just goes on, more or less pointlessly. But then, out of nowhere, comes a moment of Kantian good will, a spontaneous overflow of powerful feelings, and we sense that the old huntsman has been redeemed. His affective life is regained, and the implication is that ours is too, in so far as we understand the poem. Apparently the redeemer is the narrator, the one who chops through the root of the old tree, who mourns on behalf of all unkind or grateful humanity, and who then writes the poem too, so that its readers can be saved. This is one of the purest pieces of secular redemption in Wordsworth, clearly a bridge between the Christian model and its modern secular equivalents. And yet the poem falters at the very end: for the redeemer's own agony displaces the sinner's. The focus is on the former, not the latter. The autobiographer is also the redeemer. The hidden depths of his own spontaneous grace, not Simon's suffering, become the mystery of Wordsworth's poem.

Something similar happens in "The Two April Mornings" and "Michael," where religious moments, singularities, occupy the centers of the two poems, and are presented by Wordsworth as *the* meanings of the lives they belong to. The rest of life would go on pointlessly without them. In these two cases the narrator is not at the center of the mystery, which strengthens the poems; but the overall redemptive cast of the thought is much the same. Meanwhile the whole of *The Prelude*, where of course the narrator is very much at the center, orients itself around such moments of sudden spontaneous connections with a kind of deity, with Being. In all these places spontaneity produces meaning or value out of nothing. Lives are given new meaning, which is to say redeemed, purged of that mechanical emptiness or triviality which seems to have become the modern, secular equivalent of the experience of sin. Equivalent, not duplicate: "sin" is hardly a term to which modern secular lives have much recourse. And yet we do not have to be either Kierkegaardian existentialists or chronically depressed to feel that we may be partly to blame for the world's apparent insignificance or unintelligibility, its visionary dreariness. Is it not our responsibility to supply the meaning, and so our fault if we have not done so, or even just cannot? Is it not something in us, some dead weight we should have tried harder to shrug off, some reprehensible incapacity that is preventing us from supplying it? Just because there is no longer a God or a Redeemer occupying that place in the imagination from which redemption formerly seemed to come, its source must be seen as within man himself, which is even more of a mystery, as well as a burden, possibly a shameful one.

The chapter argues, in conclusion, that Coleridge's "The Ancient Mariner" is likewise a poem of spontaneity (and a much better anticipation of modern redemptiveness than Coleridge's conventional prose passage on redemption in his 1825 *Aids to Reflection*). Both the fatal shot and the saving spring of love come out of nowhere, some deep inner place full of blessing and grace. The mariner, who is the sinner, is also the one required to sacrifice himself forever, placating the ice-demon or God under the sea so that others, his listeners, all of us, may be redeemed. Salvation and redemption, again, occupy that space within ourselves formerly occupied by God, but because God is not there any more they become our responsibility—and yet these are essentially religious conceptions, so that in trying to live up to this divine responsibility we must always fail. Romanticism (including, importantly, Kant's own prefiguring of it) inaugurates this modern dilemma: indeed modernity to a large degree *is* this dilemma.

Wordsworth and Political Redemption

The third mode of redemption to be considered here is the political. Rousseau and Hegel are perhaps the two modern thinkers for whom politics is most obviously and fundamentally redemptive, but this book's scope permits only the first of them to be discussed here. Godwin, in Rousseau's shadow, and Burke, his great adversary, are also considered. But the bulk of these two chapters is about books 9 and 10 of the 1805 *Prelude*.

The Prelude can on one level be thought of as an argument in Wordsworth's mind between a redemptive Rousseauan model of politics and a transmissive or inheritive Burkean model. In the early 1790s, he would have thought of himself as unquestionably Rousseauan, whereas by 1804 his conscious allegiance had shifted. And yet the Burkeanism was already there much earlier, while the Rousseauism persisted much later. The complex, palimpsestic self represented in the poem is consistently ambivalent.

Rousseau stood for a conception of politics driven by a secular version of original sin as a fall into inequality, and a model of the social contract as an artificial general will to good, redeeming us from that fall. We are all sinners, but collectively we *are* the single Redeemer of all our fallen selves. God, as for Kant and indeed for Wordsworth, is an insipid Divine Being, a politely postulated but, except in sublime landscapes, practically invisible benevolent intelligence (for Milton and Locke, briefly considered here, he is more of a presence, but still a hollow one). Burke, on the other hand, sees human nature as collaborative, political agency as entailed and agential, government as a "convenience" not a savior, and God as "He [who] willed . . . the state," the one to whom it is still consecrated.[6] Burke could not possibly see humanity as self-redemptive; politics for him is what we do together *under* God.

The first of the two central arguments of these chapters is that Wordsworth came, for a crucially formative but all too short period in his early twenties, to see cities, polities, political societies not just as noisy, chaotic hives of triviality and iniquity—as infernal pits—but also as cooperative activities, in which furthermore he could assume some sort of leadership. This process of realization culminated in his experience in France in 1792, when he briefly understood political constitution not as a born-again, proto-Rousseauan emanation from some general will (as he was at first excitedly, even zealously, inclined to think) but as the archetype of all human activity, with the self as essentially participative, collaborative, and agential. This was emphatically not a redemptive view.

The roots of this understanding lay in an upbringing simultaneously egalitarian and aristocratic, or romance-chivalric. This odd mixture was eventually, and paradoxically, to produce Wordsworth's much more redemptive conception of a few elevated, imaginative "minds truly from the Deity": including of course his own. Indeed from the start he was rather inclined to think of "humanity" like this, *de haut en bas*, rather than as a particularized collection of ordinary individuals with himself as just another one. We see this tendency in chapter 2, and we see it again here in "The Old Cumberland Beggar," in some rather Burkean ways as morally profound as anything he ever wrote, in other ways utterly insensitive.

The non-redemptive political understanding was deepened by his 1792 friendship with the aristocratic revolutionary Michel Beaupuy. (His contemporary experiences with Annette Vallon and their daughter Caroline were more or less irrelevant to it, or indeed to him.) In the *Prelude*, Beaupuy is presented as a knight-errant from story-book romance, and the romance genre itself as deeply formative of Wordsworth's own character. His truest friends were Robin Hood or Gil Blas. He sees great poets, by contrast, as his rivals. They write that which as a romance bard writing for ordinary people he must remake (Hazlitt speaks of his "levelling muse").

But the real task is political. Beaupuy, Wordsworth, and others like them are presented as the best hope of revolution: progressive and chivalrous all at once. And what is more, in the poetry's best moments their virtues are seen as communicable to the "rudest men," to everyone, no matter how poor or uneducated. At its less impressive moments the poetry still remains addicted to an idealist or redemptive zealotry, but these moments are overshadowed by one of the poem's most famous passages, a kind of hymn to politics. The chapter argues that the "Bliss was it in that dawn" passage, or at least the insight reported in it, was nothing less than the source of Wordsworth's entire poetic career: an epiphany utterly different in kind from any of the "spots of time." Here he experiences not a punctual Rousseauan connection with a general human will, a quasi-divine force, but a collective Burkean human exercise. Politics is a collective, shaping activity carried out in the space between genuine equals, and its practice is bliss, true heaven on earth, the only paradise we will ever know.

This was the paradise Wordsworth lost. The second central argument of these chapters is that when the non-redemptive Burkean understanding of politics he so briefly attained in the early 1790s was shaken and then destroyed by later events, he abandoned the political and social world for a regressively redemptive understanding of the self. He became a poet in the spirit of his failure as a politician.

He suffered a double "moral shock" when he fled from France in late 1792. For him this shock was the true revolution, since his earlier understanding had grown steadily out of his upbringing, his previous experience, and reading. He found himself in Britain completely out of sympathy with the government and most public opinion, while he was horrified by news of the Terror from France. He felt as if his very self was changed and unrecognizable. He was in a kind of spiritual limbo, more distressing in some ways than the idea of the physical inferno across the Channel. Worse than this, he felt himself *to blame*, something like a sinner, unable to defend or justify his earlier understanding. Maybe people like him had *caused* these horrors. Maybe what he was fleeing from was himself.

The final blow came from his own attempt to justify himself intellectually for his political failure, to talk himself conceptually out of this spiritual limbo. He turned to a thin, radical, materialist language of the self deriving from the French *philosophes*, and more immediately from Godwin. This was also a skeptical language, constantly seeking mathematical proof and certainty in moral questions, where they are not to be found. At first Wordsworth thought that this thin concept language would indeed allow him to redeem himself from his awful condition. Under the auspices of the God, Reason, he would be able to buy back political reform from the sinners and doubters in England and France, maybe even redeem *them*. But on the contrary, the language dragged him, he felt later, even deeper into error, into an inhuman abstraction or mechanical theorism: ever further from the rich dynamic self he had discovered in France. This language was no substitute for that activity.

Wordsworth now felt that he had to find a richer language of the self in which to justify or represent his life. He had to redeem himself, and he had to do it in language; but since philosophy apparently could not do the job, only poetry could. His new language had to be a form of beauty, a form of good *and* a form of life, as well, of course, as a form of words. Nothing less could replace what had been lost.

But the replacement still had to retain at least some of what had been lost. This meant that Wordsworth could not entirely leave Godwin or Rousseau behind. There are distinct Godwinian—and indeed Kantian—overtones in the "spots of time" concept, for example, with Imagination replacing Reason at the center of the self. The Rousseauan Supreme Being remained a strong presence in Wordsworth's Nature. His poetry had to remain dedicated to reform in some way; it was, in fact, fated to be a perpetual stand-in for that greater political fulfillment which was now lost. That fulfillment had *not* been redemptive in itself. It had been if anything anti-Rousseauan and anti-Godwinian.

But now that it was lost it seemed misguided. Events seemed to have proved this. On the other hand a redemptive politics, a Godwinian transcending of the state, a Rousseauan remaking of political humanity, now seemed equally unsatisfactory.

What happened to Wordsworth was that he turned to poetry as a post-political substitute language: to language itself as a substitute for political activity. Politics was not after all redemptive in itself; once it failed him, it became that which he needed to redeem himself, and humanity, *from*. It drove him to the redemptiveness he could express only in poetry. Politics was the non-redemptive origin of his redemptive conception of poetry. But poetry became the price he paid for having lost politics. It was his strange coin. He became a kind of Mariner, condemned to atone forever in speech for what he had culpably done, or not done, in action.

His final address to Coleridge in book 10 reminds us of the parallel address to Dorothy in "Tintern Abbey." Wordsworth could not "do" character, and remained oddly imperceptive about other lives, as so many critics have argued. This was why France had been so exciting: he had glimpsed, briefly, a collaborative way out of himself (this *is* exciting, for introverted minds like his). But now there remained only that meliorative or therapeutic kind of poetry, which would appeal to those who, like John Stuart Mill, felt themselves to have passed beyond political and social satisfaction and now needed some deeper source of fulfillment, of joy, to cater to that ancient need for cleansing, salvation, absolution, renewal—for redemption or its equivalent. The paradox is that in Wordsworth this redemptive language replaced a non-redemptive politics, masking the truly originary experience he had enjoyed in that blissful French dawn.

Redemption and the Modern Self

Kant and Wordsworth are two of the seminal thinkers of modernity. Kant's sphere of influence is much larger, of course: far larger than can be properly reflected in this book. But Wordsworth is also deeply representative, and constitutive, of an important cast of mind in the English-speaking world, including in ways on which an understanding of Kantian spontaneity can shed new light. This book is part of a larger argument about modernity, the modern self, as it was represented and constituted in poetry and philosophy from the 1780s to the middle of the twentieth century. These must be, at least for an English-speaking audience, two of the key figures in that argument.

Both of them have at the very core of their conception of the self an absence or space: the one where God used to be. This book considers that absence in these two writers in terms of the three crucial aspects of the concept of redemption in its post-Christian function mentioned above: aesthetic, spontaneous and political. Aesthetic redemption or redemptiveness assumes that forms of beauty, natural forms to start with, can also be forms of good. Looking at nature can make us morally better. But this means that the artistic forms in which this claim is made can make us better too. Art itself becomes redemptive.[7] Political redemption or redemptiveness, meanwhile, assumes that human nature can be remade, a new humanity created, in political association. Doing politics can make us not just better but also new.[8] Finally, spontaneous redemption or redemptiveness assumes that a better self will mysteriously just emerge out of some deep place in us, like a kind of divine grace.[9] We are seen as essentially ineffable, auto-redemptive beings.

In all three of these aspects modern secular redemptiveness carries traces of its older Christian function, which at its deepest level is also punctual and spontaneous. Christ's life as written by Mark and the others is a successful metaphorizing of what became the concept of redemption; God's grace, on the other hand, is a conceptual mystery. But there is a more fundamental dichotomy at work here.

Poetry and philosophy in the Graeco-Christian West, as I tried to show in an earlier book,[10] oscillate between metaphorical and conceptual understandings of human experience. We are seen by poets and philosophers alike as either realist lives or romantic souls. The concept-self or "romantic" self, in the terminology of that book, is dualist, centered on a heterogeneous, punctual, or dimensionless core. This model has been more influential: through Plato, St. Paul, Augustine, Virgil, Dante, Luther, Milton, Descartes, Nietzsche, and more recently Yeats and Heidegger. Its rival, a more "realist," metaphorical, and homogeneous model, transmitted through Aristotle, St. Mark, Aquinas, Machiavelli, Shakespeare, Hume, Austen, Keats, and lately T. S. Eliot and Wittgenstein, has certainly not been without influence of its own, including a lengthy period of predominance from the twelfth to the sixteenth centuries. But since the Enlightenment and Romanticism its star has waned.

What we find in Kant, Wordsworth and many of their successors is that the durable punctual model is especially vulnerable to subversion by decayed or suppressed Christian concepts. Redemption is a leading example. Uprooted from the rich metaphorical Gospel soil, where it flourished as a key (not of course the only) meaning of Christ's life, the concept is transplanted into the vacant or still-unreplenished core of the post-Christian self, where it brings forth the free-floating sense that we need to save ourselves from our own "sins," purge and cleanse ourselves, restore ourselves to an earlier better state, remake ourselves, attain some better future state—by art, by immersion in nature, by politics, by tapping into some deep inner source or space. This has been and so far remains a damaging impulse, sometimes an extremely destructive one. At its heart, always, is an absence, a loss, a space to be filled, a discontinuity, rather than (or not yet) a presence: dynamic, continuous, homogeneous, and inherited.

I

CONCEPTS, METAPHORS, AND WORDSWORTH

Poetry, Philosophy, Romanticism

In one form of thinking with language—let us call it poetry—moral life, the life of character, behavior, and value, of emotion and virtue, is *primarily* rendered metaphorically. In this form of thought (and its *form* is essential to it: meter in verse, for example, or rhetorical qualities in general, perform a distinctly metaphorical function), general moral terms or concepts such as courage, wisdom, envy, anger, patience, or pride, vital (in both senses) as they are in the development of character, in the activity of recognizing oneself or one another *as* something (though not as some *thing*), are still no more than enhancing, equivalent sub-organisms, constantly evolving or morphing within the fuller life they help to sustain, enrich or realize. "My heart's subdued / Even to the very quality of my lord," says Desdemona; but even "jealousy" itself is subdued to Othello's quality (as "anger" is subdued to the quality of Achilles). The poetry resists our reductive, Iago-like inclination to over- or pre- or mono-conceptualize. Indeed even Iago, having planted the dangerous conceptual seed ("beware, my lord, of jealousy"), immediately metaphorizes it, emphasizing this rhetorical shift through his insistent rhythms ("it is a green-eyed monster"). Othello says at the end of the play that he is "not easily jealous." This can be seen as a conceptual point as well as a moral and psychological one. He is not easily or straightforwardly *made* jealous, constructed simply as "jealous";

indeed criticism has notoriously found it unsatisfactory to pigeonhole him in this way. When he goes on to say that "being wrought" he was "perplexed in the extreme," it is as if jealousy itself has been "wrought" or "perplexed" by the play, by its metaphors and by other concepts (including perplexity), into something richer and stranger. This particular concept is one focus of the play's thought, not, as it has too often been made to seem, its source. (The same might be said of modern master-concepts such as "race" and "gender," by the way, which nowadays too often occlude thought about the play and the thought of the play, while having little or no purchase within its own language.) Enriching or perplexing, the concept is part of the play's achievement. So with Anne Elliot, in the final chapter of *Persuasion*: "She had not mistaken him. Jealousy of Mr Elliot had been the retarding weight, the doubt, the torment." She comes, the novel has come, to recognize Wentworth in the concept as much as the concept in Wentworth, but character and novel still metaphorize it at once, or rhetorically and accumulatively distribute its weight across other concepts, as they have throughout: not quite as a monster but still as an internal eating-away or weighing-down . . . a doubt . . . a torment. Anne makes sense of the concept in this metaphorical way, enables herself to think it, to assimilate it. This is "life with concepts," as Cora Diamond puts it.[1] They enrich moral life, they enable it, especially in large numbers: but they are not identical with it. This is life *with* concepts. They play their leavening role in an otherwise metaphorical dough, but the dough is life itself, malleable into the same shapes as our human clay.

Such concepts are still necessary elements in this kind of moral life with language, as characters, like the real people they plausibly and metaphorically emulate, navigate between their raw feelings and their tangential, analogous words: something they can do only from within their language practice. (This is why we are in the territory of the humanities, where to think is also to participate: not of the social sciences,[2] where the thinker stands aloof from the material.) But here, in poetry, the concepts do not govern the thought in their own mode; they do not set its style. One might say that in such an environment the concepts (*con-capere*, "taking to oneself," grasping the mass of appearances *as* something) themselves start to behave somewhat like metaphors (*meta-pherein*, "bearing across," analogical transfers or migrations of meaning away from the literal) as they become acclimatized. This metaphorical and rhetorical environment affects them, notably, even as they come into conflict with, or just approximate, each other, and especially as they proliferate. In multiple approximation they change. Jealousy plus doubt equals a third state not identical to the sum of its parts and articulable only metaphorically. One could say that in such circumstances concepts merge or *metabolize* (*meta-ballein*, "throwing across," is close cousin to *meta-pherein*), instead of commensurating. "This virtuous maid subdues me quite," says Angelo. His heart is subdued even to her very quality; erotic love subdues his virtue. Isabella's virtue, on the other hand, almost subdues her filial love. Virtue and love of various kinds (law and grace in Pauline terms) cannot be commensurated in *Measure for Measure*, a play whose very title invokes mensuration only to dissolve it; but the conflict, the very concept of virtue or love, is, like the dyer's hand, "subdued to what it works in": to poetry. One might go so far as to say that this poetic metabolizing, subduing or multiplying of concepts is essential to moral life and thought *outside* poetry. We need both to have the concepts, in large numbers, and to subdue them. But we often and damagingly confuse all moral life with a few basic moral concepts. The same is true with political life and political concepts.

We do this because the human instinct to simplify and then reify, to find a dominant concept, word, or idea and then turn it into a thing or quasi-material object, is very strong, even in the greatest poets. Sometimes the concept does become the basic entity, the governing node of thought, even in their work. *Pietas* in Aeneas, *amor* in Dido, disdain, despair, and envy in Milton's Satan, a number of virtues and vices in *The Faerie Queene* (or allegory in general), even the deeper infiltration of lives by concepts in Dante, where the determinative and exemplary passions of an Ugolino or a Francesca are essentially instrumental, for all their power: all this represents a strain paradoxically both aberrant and dominant in European poetry. Lives are frequently represented in it either as single, determinative, non-evolving concepts, recognition-stoppers governing the rest of the self (Aeneas); or as accumulative but non-reactive clusters of such nuclear concepts (Satan).[3] Needless to say readers of both kinds of poetry fall into the same trap, looking for conceptual accounts (generally ideological ones, nowadays) even of non-conceptual poetry. Yet the fabric (including the formal dress) of this aberrant strain of poetry is still metaphorical, even if it is often or determinatively warped or distorted by a few conceptual black holes.

Now there is another form of thinking with language—let us call it philosophy—that *primarily*, in its very fabric, renders the moral life in terms of small numbers of concepts. Here such general concepts as those listed earlier are indeed treated as the fundamental constituents of character and value, whether at individual or social levels (again, ideology has since Marx, or even Hegel, become important in this treatment: history as idea). Indeed in this form of thought selected concepts, not lives, are typically seen as foundational entities, as basic units of being. Exploring the presumably hard-and-fast relationships between *them*, not the fluid and dynamic ones between lives, is the paramount business of the thought. The impulse to reduce and then reify is now almost irresistible. This is still an essential form of thinking in language about the moral life, of purifying and enabling our thinking about it, but its conceptualism prevents that engagement with the fuller life which can only be supplied by metaphor's cross-dimensional associativeness, its capacity to accommodate and metabolize large numbers of concepts or to bear the mind across from concepts to passions and sensations and then back again, its resistance to concept-reification, and its congeniality with malleable rhetorical forms. Plato is the great ancient exponent of this conceptual way of thinking. At the foundation of all the major dialogues is a concept or small group of concepts (love, justice, excellence), and also a technique (*elenchos*) for collapsing every other aspect of character, value, emotion, and virtue, or every other maverick concept, back into that same handful of granular, irreducible components. Descartes is the great modern exponent. Beneath *mens, animus, ratio, ce moi,* or *l'âme* is a dimensionless and single-qualitied inner "I" underwritten only by an equally punctual external God. The Kantian self, as we shall see later, is also strongly conceptual.

This form of thinking with language has its own aberrant strain, although it might be seen as a pity that the aberration is not so dominant in this case. Whereas in the case of poetry the aberration behaves like philosophy, in the case of philosophy the aberration does not behave like poetry. Instead it treats concepts as always in need of clarification, not metaphorization. But it also avoids reification: it clarifies not with ever more foundational concepts, but just with other equal concepts, in a widening circle, reinforcing though not fusing or metabolizing. And all the concepts together are regarded as clarifying (by an *aisthêsis*, a grasping and conceiving that is experiential as much as it is conceptual), yet not finally or fully defining lives, values, objects, and appearances. Aristotle is the first master of this school, and Aquinas, Hume, and Wittgenstein are later ones. The school tends to respect and even on occasion defer to the power of metaphor and of moral emotion (though hardly ever to form, meter, or rhetorical device in general—the antithesis of concept).

Indeed, to conclude, these two forms of thinking with language, which we have called poetry and philosophy, are the *only* two forms of thinking *with* language. They are the only forms in which the language itself is put in question, is an intrinsic part of the thought itself, is itself reshaped, is the medium of thought, not just its vehicle (you might call this the center of the humanities). Any other form of thinking using language is not, strictly speaking, *thinking* in language at all, and is therefore less radical to our self-knowledge insofar as that is a linguistic activity. History, or history-writing, the third principal kind of literary thought, is the best example. Thucydides is a philosopher when he searches for the concepts to clarify the Athenian predicament, a poet when he describes their plight in plague or quarry. But he is neither of these when he sees facts and events as having some causative, collective shape. Here his sense of cause and effect, his empirical, almost pre-articulate grasp of the pressure of events on individuals and vice versa, is certainly thought, and is certainly in language—it is just not, primarily, thought *with* language. Nor is it, strictly speaking, narrative. It is at the mercy of reality, subordinating itself to reality, not shaping it (whatever the schools of Derrida or Foucault may say). It is more like an engineer's or builder's feel for how materials will behave under stress, or maybe a scientist's instinct or hunch for an underlying physical conformation or process. This empirical sense of mass or movement is not essentially linguistic—though in the world of art it might

very well be musical, sculptural, pictorial, or architectural. It is certainly not the essentially conceptual kind of thought to be found in the
tradition of Hegel.

So if concept and metaphor are the two fundamental modes of
thought with language, that is, of actually changing experience, making it our own by mixing language-thought with it, as Locke said the
earth is changed into property (literally made *proprius*, our own earth)
when labor is mixed with it; if philosophy is the archetype of concept-
clarifying while poetry is the archetype of language-metabolizing
(history-writing at its purest being a kind of leaving *un*changed, a pure,
transparent, empirical observation—and if this is impossible then
there is no such thing as truly historical thought at all); then what I
want to propose is that one era in modern literary history is of unique
and continuing importance to our thinking with language, in that it
witnessed a fundamental change in the balance of power between metaphor and concept. And I also want to propose that because of the
experiential nature of these modes of thought this change was not just
linguistic but also ethical, political and above all, religious. It is of the
greatest importance for us, even today.

Literary Romanticism in Britain (not so much in Germany, where
philosophy predominated) can be seen as the first conscious, sustained
attempt by European poetry not just to register but to alleviate, to buy
back, to redeem, a devastating spiritual loss—not only to replace God
in its capacity to deliver the soul from evil, its own and others', but also
to deliver it precisely from its sin in denying God's own capacity to do
this any more and offering itself in his place. This loss had in large part
happened in language, taking the form, at least since Descartes, of a
skeptical, reductive conceptualizing of the self and of God. It was a
loss of metaphor or of metaphorical understanding, of connectedness,
closely followed or accompanied by an equally damaging (rationalizing,
punctualizing) loss of concepts. Poetry was offering to save both language and lives here, seeing itself, seeing metaphorical activity, for the
first time as *immediately* moral and religious, as opposed to expressive
of some deeper truth, or analogically representative, or "merely" linguistic, or ornamentally figurative. This meant that language-thinking
was now for the first time professedly, not just presumptively, supposed
to change lives outside language. Of course making such a claim was

itself a belated, perhaps a too-late recognition that language itself, our life with language, might also have suffered a great loss; maybe it *was* after all "only" analogical. But some forms of language might still be less analogical, more redeemable, than others. Poetry could be such a form. Even if it could not re-metaphorize the self and (or as) God, could not revive language itself, perhaps it might at least insert many new concepts into our lives (the aberrant strain of poetry trying to behave like the aberrant strain of philosophy).

A forerunner of this new poetic enterprise was Vico's philological response of the 1720s to Descartes' philosophical challenge of the 1630s and 1640s, a response in which poetry was offered and language genealogized in precisely this way. Vico claimed that all concepts were born as metaphors; that language was radically poetic, not, as Descartes, Hobbes, and company had tried to demonstrate, radically philosophical. Even Vico, however, did not think of reversing the process, of turning concepts back into metaphors. On the contrary, his genealogy insisted on its own irreversibility. The tree of language can grow only upward, he thought: away from its metaphorical roots and toward its conceptual crown. Modernity's progress is one with the decline of poetry. Peacock said all this again in 1820, tersely and ironically.[4] Many of his contemporaries, though not all, showed in their practice that he and Vico might indeed be right, in that it did not occur to them to try to reverse the process, even though they were poets themselves. Indeed "romantic"-type poets (the aberrant strain) ever since Virgil, since Augustine, since Dante, had tried to work their way down through layers of metaphor toward a blazing, nuclear conceptual core, confirming Vico's genealogy (my awkward reversal of direction notwithstanding). This core had always been essentially religious in its reference. *Pietas, voluntas, amor*: all looked upward as well as inward—to look in *was* to look up. And now Descartes and the rest of the new philosophers and *philosophes*—Bayle, Voltaire, Rousseau, Hume—had driven a stake through the core by substituting new, stronger, non-religious concepts:("reason" and the *moi* looked in but *not* up. So the question of how you thought with language was now impossible to separate from the question of faith or belief. Was it possible to have a religious-type concept at the core of a poetry any more? Or, if not that, then any concept at all: a secular, humanistic, ethical, or political type? Or, worse still, if not even that, then could one have any poetry at all? Was that genre of thought indeed moribund? Wouldn't this have momentous consequences for how we all thought about ourselves?

Milton's answer to Descartes and Hobbes was stronger, earlier, and less friendly to metaphor than Vico's. He said yes to the first of the questions just posed. His God and Satan were his conceptual answers. Over a century later some of his most influential Romantic heirs were still trying to perform the second-best maneuver by putting non-religious concepts, especially the concept of "poetry" itself, in the space where Milton's religious (or, strictly, pseudo-religious) concepts, now destroyed by the Enlightenment, had once been. Second-best: one inescapable fact about these concepts was that they were *not* religious, but only occupying a previously religious space, an empty church. The sense of loss or absence was unavoidable. Thinkers who need concepts usually seek first a smaller group and then an ur-concept, the source of all the others, the one true Concept (or Word), some *logos*. Those who live by the concept must die by it too, or go on looking for it until they die. But what concepts really required was not replacing or updating, but massive proliferation and cross-fertilization. Even more, it was not concepts that required reviving, but metaphors. The deepest division in Christianity is between St. Mark's metaphorizing of the life of Jesus—that is, his making an idea of God into a human life—and St. Paul's conceptualizing of it, making the life of Jesus into an idea of God. In the Romantic era it was poetry itself that required re-thinking.

Among the poets of the age Blake may be thought to have come the closest to achieving this. The manacles and cages forged by the mind for itself in the *Songs of Experience* are made essentially of concepts, while the counterpart self of the *Songs of Innocence* not only dissolves them but also claims that this dissolving is essential to human relationship. But Blake was inaudible for a century, and the *Songs* are few and still oddly conceptual ("Mercy, Pity, Peace and Love . . ."); while the great Miltonic and Satanic figures of Urizen, Los and the rest represent precisely the Romantic fall into an inevitably compensatory or substitute humanism (rather than a genuinely new one). Wordsworth's insistence that poetry needed a deep rethinking of some sort was no more radical or courageous, but in the sheer ordinariness of its subjects and language (his lives may not really be very ordinary, but they are a lot more so than Enitharmon's) the poetry showed more accessibly how much had been lost to how many; and, more poignantly, how conflicted was the attempt to recover it. Hazlitt and Keats understood this, though Coleridge did not, nor did Byron, nor Shelley. (I know this sounds like old-fashioned "big six" thinking, but then these were precisely the poets who at that time thought biggest, remade life-with-language most consciously, radically and durably—in English verse, at least. Ordinary life with language was of course also being reasserted and perhaps more durably remade in the novel, by Jane Austen and to a much lesser extent Maria Edgeworth, *contra* the Romantic Gothic of Walpole, Radcliffe, Scott and indeed Byron—or even Wordsworth, as we shall see, briefly, in the third section of chapter 2. But Austen's—and the novel's—very great importance and significance in this story, in the end completely eclipsing that of verse, deserve a book in themselves.)

Romantic poetry was captured by this dilemma: either to replace a lost, religious, conceptual core with a new, non-religious one, which was ultimately a fruitless quest, fraught with grief and horror, as Byron and Shelley found; or to initiate a new, non-conceptual, or richer conceptual poetry, as Keats did, and Austen, and perhaps the Blake of the *Songs*. But Wordsworth's was the most conflicted and, for a century and a half at least, the most influential voice (at least, is not Heaney's, for example, a type of Wordsworthian voice?). Thus he has most to show us about the sense of loss, which in some respects is still a sense for us, as well as the misguided attempt at recovery, which is also in part still ours. We post-Romantics are still not whole or healed in some of the same ways as those in which he was already not whole or healed.

Wordsworth
Pleading for Conversion

Wordsworth's poetry encroaches with singular boldness on the domain of philosophy, and hesitates with an equally singular diffidence at the borders of metaphor. According to A. D. Nuttall it "pleads continually for something resembling epistemological conversion in the reader."[5] This is profoundly true. The poetry does constantly cross over into philosophy, and into moral philosophy as much as epistemology (indeed that latter boundary too is blurred in it, or by it); but more importantly, and still less conventionally for either poetry or philosophy, it *pleads*, and it pleads *for conversion*. Its interest is in how we know things and what kinds of things we know, and even more in how it feels to know them, in the kind of person who has this kind of feeling about knowing. But its style is that of urgent, desperate appeal to an indifferent, skeptical or hostile judgment ("in dreams I pleaded / Before unjust Tribunals," *Prelude* 10.376–77[6]): and what it wants is not just to persuade or convince such a mind, but to change such a heart; to induce, even in such a heart, a redirection that becomes a transformation (*convertere* has both senses).

So when Wordsworth claims that his poetry is "not unimportant in the multiplicity, and in the quality of its moral relations,"[7] the *show* of modesty is characteristic (a "proud humility," said Hazlitt[8]); but what he really thinks is that this poetry is as important as poetry can be, and that poetry is of the greatest moral importance, and that the greatest importance of poetry is moral. The claim is Johnsonian in its seriousness, but Wordsworth had 1789 to accommodate, not 1688. This is why the later Milton, setting out to justify the ways of Milton to himself with all the weight of 1640–1660 on his shoulders, is his true forebear. This is a matter of life and death: no, a matter of salvation and redemption, both religious and secular (once impossible antitheses but now essential contraries).

> Now, I know no book or system of moral philosophy written with sufficient power to melt into our affections, to incorporate itself with the blood & vital juices of our minds, & thence to have any influence worth our notice in forming those habits [i.e., of "affection" and "benevolence"] of which I am speaking.[9]

In this fragmentary *Essay on Morals* Wordsworth is thinking of poetry as a kind of writing so powerful that it melts into our hearts and minds, converts itself into the substance of our bodies—indeed into their very life. A stronger, more rousing claim could hardly be made for thinking in language, and I suspect that this is the kind of claim, explicit in passages such as this, implicit in the poems themselves, for which his readers have most revered him. For is this not the strongest remaining reason for reading poetry at all: reading poetry being otherwise an activity that is now not so much under threat as beneath notice, in a moral world frustratingly oblivious to the true scope of the metaphorical, rhetorical, and richly conceptual language-thought it everywhere lives with? And yet, after all, as Wordsworth puts the matter, is this poetry not to be only a kind of *re*-writing, rather than a true searching? Isn't the implication here that (Godwinian) moral philosophy has the same (Aristotelian) goals as poetry: namely, to form, or influence the formation of, virtuous habits—only it just is not as powerful? What "power" is this, then? Is it not the metabolizing, metaphorizing power posited earlier as peculiar to poetry?

Well, no: just the reverse. Wordsworth is *starting out* here, as he did in fact start out as a thinking man, with an Enlightened, in-principle enthusiasm for virtues such as "benevolence" or "affection." He has been called an Epicurean, a Stoic, a hedonist, a Hartleyan, a Shaftesburyan, an anti-Paleyan, an anti-Godwinian; but he is not really so interested in Socratic questions such as "What is virtue?" or even Aristotelian ones such as "How does virtue arise?" as in stoutly empirical ones such as "How does virtue *feel?*" But still, first you have the concept, then you find out what it feels like. He is only discontented with these philosophers' failure to enact virtues or cause others to enact them. Poetry, "the most philosophic of all writing,"[10] is to carry these concepts more powerfully than philosophy can into our bloodstreams and synapses—not rethink in its own metaphorical terms the very activity of rendering moral life. Its figurativeness is, so to speak, palliative, not restorative; its metaphors are ornaments, not fundaments, of thought.

This may seem a tendentious reading of the passage. After all, its own style is significantly metaphorical: melting systems, books (words) in our blood. A version of this metaphor is at the center of "Tintern Abbey," and it is hard to overstate or overpraise Wordsworth's ambition and achievement in coining it, for the reasons just given. But as we shall see in a moment when considering the thought of the poetry itself, this may be finally an instrumental and not a radical use of metaphor. The governing metaphors in the passage itself are of an infusing *system*, of *conceptual* habits. Wordsworth wanted to convert us all (starting with himself) by poetry—or *to* poetry; and this was indeed a literary revolution of the first importance. But by that very token he still, despite his own organic metaphors, saw us as convertible creatures, rather than metabolic ones: as principally ideal, not organic. What people generally get converted by, from, or into, after all, is a faith, which is a transforming set of ideas. It seemed to Wordsworth, even despite himself, and for reasons we shall have to seek out, that the trick modern poetry had to perform, its unique and sacred enterprise, was to convert ideas into organs, and so convert us to the ideas, convert us *into* the ideas. As we shall see in a moment, even the poetry's haunting signature, its astounding conversion of natural objects into "forms of beauty," and those in turn into moral forms, forms of good, is used to underwrite this tragic enterprise.

Such an ambivalence toward poetry's kind of language-thinking, and therefore toward life-thinking, was ultimately what so disturbed Hazlitt and Keats, the first and truest of Wordsworth's critics (Coleridge was much too implicated in the project). Their deep respect for the great moralist thinking into his own heart was offset by their dislike of the trite moralizer unable to think into anyone else's ("he sees nothing but himself and the universe,"[11] "egotistical sublime"[12]). What was it about his unique capacity for the first kind of thought that was at the same time an incapacity for the second? Arnold and Leavis, speaking for Victorians and Moderns, distinguished between the poet who thinks profoundly about life and the dogmatist who offers a creed "not felt into from within."[13] Does a kind of poetry that sets out to convert one's body work only for the poet himself? Post-structuralists after Hartman read him as a failed Milton, a would-be visionary whose apocalyptic imagination yearned for transcendence but was unable to confront it and retreated into the "merely ethical" or the conventionally Anglican (the Coleridge position, roughly). New historicists and cultural materialists after E. P. Thompson read him as a failed Shelley, a would-be revolutionary whose political imagination yearned for ideology but was unable to confront it and so repressed itself into the merely bourgeois or the conventionally Anglican (the Hazlitt position, roughly). Both groups sense the conceptual aspiration on the one hand, the metaphorical (but maybe not moral) shortfall on the other. It is the old caricature: in the red corner the "deep" poet of 1797–1807, the author of *The Ode, The Ballads,* and *The Prelude*; in the blue corner the "old half-witted sheep," the poet laureate, author of *The Excursion* and all those sonnets. "Never glad confident morning again," said the ever-confident Browning.[14] But behind any of the criticisms that take poetry seriously (as opposed to those which have claimed in the last fifty years or so that Wordsworth's poetry was essentially written by (a) literary history, (b) tropes of language, or (c) property—David Bromwich's sharp diagnosis[15]) lies Wordsworth's own serious and tragic hesitancy about a poetry that pleads so much for poetry and yet in the very pleading displays its own self-doubt, its own over-reach or under-achievement.

But again, what shortfall, what over-reach? Surely the moral ambition to convert, indeed to metabolize, ideas into organs, benevolence into blood, virtue into bodily *habitus* (how one "holds oneself," *habere*), is a noble one for poetry? And again, no. It is just that this is what we are used to thinking—since Wordsworth and Blake. Perhaps this is a noble ambition for *philosophy*: turning that nuclear nugget "benevolence" into a kind of pill to be absorbed by the mind. (Noble, but probably unattainable: Wordsworth did not think Godwin, Shaftesbury, or Hutcheson did it very well; and even Aquinas did not really attempt *this*.) Poetry's function, by contrast, should surely be to treat "benevolence" as *Othello* and *Persuasion* treat "jealousy": to metaphorize it into the fuller lived experience and rhythms of relational passion, to subdue it verbally to the quality and shape of a character, to merge it at the margins into approximating concepts. *That* kind of metabolizing *is* possible in language.

An observation from Iris Murdoch may help to define the problem further, although she did not have Wordsworth in mind when she made it: an aesthetic situation may be not so much an "analogy of morals" as "a case of morals."[16] Wordsworth meant his own poems to be cases of morals, not just analogies; they were to melt into our being, or it into theirs. But what exactly was the relation between the moral and the aesthetic to be in these "cases"? Could it ever be more than just analogous? Could the analogical gap ever be closed, and if so, how? Were these situations *merely* "aesthetic," in other words? Or could "forms of beauty," shapes graspable by *aisthêsis* in the moment of critical judgment (the *krisis*), also be "cases of morals"? Alexander Baumgarten had reinvented classical aesthetics as a "science of sensuous cognition,"[17] but Wordsworth said poetry was "the impassioned expression which is in the face of all Science"[18]—a form of language in which knowing is already passional, already moral. Was it in the end *only* a matter of (aesthetic) "expression"? If aesthetic forms "contain" beauty as a matter of palpable cognition, do good acts (even little, nameless, unremembered ones) "contain" good in some naturalistic (not just analogous) way? Murdoch (after G. E. Moore et al.) says they do not, but Wordsworth seems to think, or hope, that they do. *Could* a sense of beauty (even science's sense of the beauty of the universe) produce a good act? If not, is our only alternative to this kind of aestheticism, our only moral recourse, to believe that there exists some sort of numinous being immanent in forms and acts alike whose attributes include what we call beauty and goodness? Questions such as these suggest the scale of Wordsworth's reach and the potential measure of his loss.

Besides, what if these poems are after all just "cases," hermetically *en*cased in their own inscrutable peculiarity? Here it is of the very greatest importance that the poetry is essentially, not just incidentally, autobiographical. Wordsworth (even more than Milton, and unlike Blake) is pleading *with* his own life as well as *for* it; he is offering it *as* his plea. It is the only introspectible, therefore the only certain, case of morals, and therefore not really a "case" at all, but an example, a microcosm. Only the poet can feel the metabolizing of the benevolence pill into his own bloodstream, but having done so he can assume that this can happen in everyone else's. This generic trait inevitably, but still only incidentally, appears as the coat-trailing claim to be part of "real history" (the French Revolution, Salisbury Plain, vagrant dwellers, freeholders of Westmorland: I, Wordsworth, was there), a claim that has nevertheless often induced critics into exclusively biographical or ideological, factual or conceptual, readings of it ("apostasy," bad faith to peasants, etc.). And it is true that Wordsworth does ask for this. The coat-trailing does happen; history and politics *are* there, sometimes occluded, sometimes not. They make the poems real cases, hard cases: hard for readers of progressive views, certainly, who are prone to take them less seriously as poems on this account.

Yet the poetry is both empirical and moral at a more fundamental level than the political or historical. Objects (rocks and stones and trees) and emotions (guilt and grief and joy) are of more importance in it than facts or events. And much more than this: whether that kind of outer object, fact or event *can* be converted, including in and by poetry, into an inner bodily quality and a moral habit, and thus protect us against, or resolve, moral chaos: this is what Wordsworth desperately wants to know, and to be able to show us. The real disaster for him in this enterprise would be for his readers' judgment of the poetry's failure or success to be limited merely to its historical (let alone historico-philosophical) aspects. Poetry is necessarily fictive, a metabolizing of life-with-language; history is necessarily not. The dilemma of autobiography is how far to surrender to history, how far to poetry. What Wordsworth is mainly pleading for is a kind of salvation in language, a quasi-religious certainty. Here he is firmly in the tradition of Augustine, Descartes, and above all, the Rousseau of the *Confessions*. Poetry for Augustine, Rousseau, and Wordsworth is a process of autobiographical and archaeological self-disclosure, culminating (the poet hopes) in self-conversion into a state of grace. The most important thing in reading it is to look at how it goes about this conversion-in-language: what fear of utter loss or disintegration, what hope of redemption or bliss, lies behind and drives the pleading. The autobiography is essential, but it is primarily spiritual, not factual. There is no doubt that it hides things; indeed this sense that a concealment is going on is absolutely intrinsic to "Tintern Abbey," as we shall see in a moment.[19] But it is just as intrinsic to our age to assume suspiciously that what is being concealed is primarily ideological, some issue of gender, class, or party; or that it is primarily psychological, some issue of repression or projection; or that if it is religious at all this must still be in some way a question of bad faith. (These are the positions of Marx, Freud, and Nietzsche respectively.) Yet such assumptions blind us to more serious concealments, genuine moral and religious ones, which are to be regarded not disapprovingly, as evidences mercilessly to be seized upon of weakness, subterfuge, or apostasy, but sympathetically, as pathologies of despair and strategies of recovery.

2

"TINTERN ABBEY"
Restoring the Soul

This chapter is an attempt to read "Tintern Abbey" by getting as close as possible to the limits of its own language and the reader's forbearance. It seems to me that its most interesting aspects by far are emotional, moral, and spiritual, and that its historical, political, and ideological tendencies have been tracked down and hunted to extinction. An older and deeper sense of the poem, a long-neglected kind of response to its ways of disturbing us, needs reviving.[1] But to do this we have to follow another kind of pathway through the labyrinth of the verse, paying close attention to kinds of details recently ignored, arguing with the poem in another way, non-theoretical, non-historicist. This is a level of close argumentative attention that philosophers routinely expect of themselves with "their" texts (see the next chapter's sections on Kant), but that much recent criticism dismisses and is in some danger of forgetting about altogether with literary texts. Readers may, therefore, find some of what follows somewhat labyrinthine, particularly in the second and third sections. I hope they will feel that their efforts are paid off, redeemed even, in the other sections.

The poem is a highly original and ambitious "natural ode" (see the following section): a public celebration of the private restoration of a self. Its first paragraph affirms the value of a familiar place in reconstituting that self, but offers glimpses of what has to be suppressed in order to achieve this reconstitution: the more difficult emotions of human relationship. In the second and third paragraphs the metaphors are wonderfully, uniquely triumphant as representations of restorative value, as "forms of beauty"; but they stumble as virtue-bearing "forms of good." The poem's thought falters palpably as it turns from "blessed mood" to "unintelligible world"—because that world of inter-human emotion is what it has little insight into. In the climactic fourth paragraph it seems that the poet has indeed been fleeing from the humanity he could not accommodate, and that God, or Being, is reduced to a necessary backdrop for what amounts to a suppression of moral life. The embarrassing final paragraph confirms the poem's lack of inter-human insight. What we remember about the poem, however, is how close it comes to achieving its most remarkable ambition: that of transforming poetry itself into a kind of therapy, a language whose power to heal or redeem may be a substitute for nature's own—or God's.[2]

Impassioned Music, Little Lines
Title and First Paragraph

"I have not ventured to call this Poem an Ode," Wordsworth wrote in a note to the 1800 edition of the *Lyrical Ballads*, "but it was written with a hope that in the transitions, and in the impassioned music of the versification would be found the principal requisites of that species of composition."[3] Here is a stiff, typically Wordsworthian show of modesty, or "proud humility," in Hazlitt's words. One might imagine the show: "A real Ode? No, no: I wouldn't presume. Maybe just an entirely new *kind* of ode."[4] The language of the poem itself often strikes this note, as we shall see. And the stakes really are as high as they can be. Pindar, Horace, and Milton are all at the table, but this subversive new player disclaims all pretensions to such status, even while planning (not just "hoping," as he says) to change the very terms of the game.

"Tintern Abbey"[5] is an ode in spirit but not style, whereas "Simon Lee" and others are ballads in style but not spirit. This "ode" is *both* Pindaric, public, ceremonious, invoking or addressing the gods, praising participation in the life of a community; *and* Horatian, private, meditative, tranquil, invoking friendship and withdrawal from community, addressing a familiar and congenial readership. The deep contradictions here are part of the poem's constitution, for better or worse: part of what makes it a new kind of ode. For "impassioned music" read urgent public plea *for* the versification, *for* Wordsworth's new kind of poetry, not just *in* it. For "transitions" read private or autobiographi-cal narrative structure: both temporal and emotional. The lineaments ("principal requisites") of a strophe, antistrophe, second strophe, and epode can be made out beneath the four-part chronology (first visit to scene in 1793, five-year absence, present moment in July 1798, imagined future). This conversion of a complex perception of a rigid form or space into discrete impressions of fluid time is a typical Romantic and Kantian, or post-Humean, game-changing maneuver. Experience is not of a whole cosmic order but of a series of subjective impressions. And form is also converted into feeling; changes of mood, or what is much the same here, changes in the meaning of the scene, occur in parallel with the time changes. This is not a conventional "Ode to Nature," but it is what we might call a "natural ode."

"Lines written a few miles above Tintern Abbey, on revisiting the banks of the Wye during a tour, July 13, 1798": the modestly unadven-turous title prefixed to these little lines of sportive verse nevertheless seems to aspire to a meticulous objectivity. An alternative title might almost be, "What was discovered when introducing 1 cc of percep-tion / feeling into a solution of woods and copses in rolling waters on July 13, 1798, near Tintern." Wordsworth is apparently bringing to the subjective, introspective, and philosophical tradition of Descartes and Rousseau some thoroughly objective, empirical, and historical habits. His subversion of the ballad in the other poems has the same radical strategy with, it seems, the opposite tactic: subjective feelings giving importance to objective actions. In one case he anchors a fluid, tempo-ral story about feelings in the fixed particularities of space; in the other he anchors fluid, dramatic stories about situations, events and behav-ior in the particularities of feeling (although sometimes the feeling is too fixed, over-conceptualized, as we shall see). But of course the two tactics are deeply consistent. It will be the feelings of "Tintern Abbey" that give importance to its situation, a natural ode in a volume of lyrical ballads, a tourist's epiphany ("the day is come": a domesticated *dies ille*).

These empirical details are not clues to some "real" but hidden, deconstructible poem. We have the poem we have. We may *want* to ask, suspiciously, such questions as: Why does the Abbey itself not appear in the poem? Is Wordsworth taking a position on religious politics? Did he really write these lines above the Abbey, as he claims, or below it? Is he ignoring the evidences of poverty and hardship in the land-scape before him? What might this tell us about his secular politics? Is what matters most about the date that it is the day before Bastille Day, or that it is the anniversary of Marat's death, or that it commemorates Wordsworth's first visits to France and to this place? And so on and on: similar questions arise with "Simon Lee," "The Old Cumberland Beg-gar" and the rest, and much more urgently with *The Prelude*. But these questions are obsessive-compulsive reactions from a modern politico-conceptual readership,[6] aggravated by Wordsworth's own tendency to leave his unmetabolized liberal principles lying around on the floor of his poetry in the form of historical traces (Shelley was far mess-ier). These reactions have probably discouraged an entire generation of readers from recognizing the true importance of this poetry, to our very great cultural loss. It is *about the feelings*, or perhaps, even, it *is* the feelings.[7] It raises the startling possibility (whether realized or tantaliz-ingly unrealized) of a thinking with language that is also a moral emo-tion, of a case of morals that is also a form of beauty, of a metaphorized plea for conversion, a redemptive strategy. The question I want to ask here is whether *those* clues, the passional and moral ones, are worth pursuing; whether the poem's elusiveness is significant not at an his-torical but at an ethical and religious level. Its redemptive aspirations and shortcomings are much more important than its political ones.

Here is the first paragraph—four sentences, each longer than the one before:

Five years have passed; five summers, with the length
Of five long winters! and again I hear
These waters, rolling from their mountain-springs
With a sweet inland murmur.—Once again
Do I behold these steep and lofty cliffs,
Which on a wild secluded scene impress
Thoughts of more deep seclusion; and connect
The landscape with the quiet of the sky.
The day is come when I again repose
Here, under this dark sycamore, and view
These plots of cottage-ground, these orchard-tufts,
Which, at this season, with their unripe fruits,
Among the woods and copses lose themselves,

Nor, with their green and simple hue, disturb
The wild green landscape. Once again I see
These hedge-rows, hardly hedge-rows, little lines
Of sportive wood run wild; these pastoral farms
Green to the very door; and wreathes of smoke
Sent up, in silence, from among the trees,
With some uncertain notice, as might seem,
Of vagrant dwellers in the houseless woods,
Or of some hermit's cave, where by his fire
The hermit sits alone.

Each sentence is built around a close alliance between the chanted words "again," "I," and "these." A second kind of repetition, equally incantatory, is of the word "five" at the beginning of the paragraph. Five years, five summers, five winters, again I, once again do I, I again, once again I: here is the completed, self-affirming cycle of identity, place and time. *Here* I am again, I hear, I see, I repose (*re-ponere*, "re-pose, put back again, restore"), I connect (with myself, with the scene), I am not alone, I am not a vagrant, I belong somewhere, maybe most of all here, that belonging is a part of who I am, maybe the most important part. "I am here"; "I *am* when I am here." The return to a place and time is a return to the self. *Contra* Hume, the self palpably endures through time. But also, *contra* Descartes, the exterior reality confirms the inner, six times in the four sentences: "*These* waters," "*these* cliffs," "*these* plots . . . tufts . . . hedge-rows . . . farms." These very same ones—despite their changes. This very same person, enduring through vicissitude, literally finds himself, once again, in this "spot which no vicissitude can find."

The archetypal Kantian affirmation, one might say. We recognize an object (here a landscape) as one object, and in that very act of recognition we are conscious of it as recognized by one consciousness— namely, ours. We actively bring these impressions (or "intuitions") "under" concepts, in Kantian terms, and so turn the inchoate swirling intuitions of a who-knows-what by a who-knows-who into the coherent perceptions of a self-conscious person. Wordsworth is not specifically invoking Kant, of course, but both were trying to bind the self and its world together again, after the sundering effected (or perceived by them as having been effected) by the schools of Descartes and Hume. But Kant's famous pronouncement, extending his terms, that "we ourselves bring into the appearances that order and regularity in them we call nature," that the understanding "is itself the legislation for nature,"[8] would have horrified the Wordsworth of these lines (book 14 of *The Prelude*, with its talk of imagination as "that glorious faculty / That higher minds bear with them as their own," may be another matter—but probably not, as we shall see in later chapters). He needs these appearances to bring order and regularity *to him*. For him the categories of connection, repose, and disturbance; the specters of vagrancy and aloneness, of not belonging or not being housed in the world; the futility or emptiness (the visionary dreariness) of ordinary things in themselves, not just their independent physical reality: these are the phenomena at stake, and they are constitutive, not just epistemological.

The philosophical issue for Kant, Descartes, or even Hume (who was much closer to this empirical Wordsworth in disposition) was conceptual ("what is causation?" "what is imagination?"). Even ethics is conceptual ("what is the will?"). For a poet, however, the issue was both moral and metaphorical: "what is the *value* of this landscape *for me?*" The very thought that a mere stretch of ground could have *value* of this kind is itself a species of metaphor, a species compacted into the single word "value," with its twin roots in exchange and esteem. Here is the again-ness of this copse before me, this very me again seeing this very copse. This has become a matter not of its mere reality, nor of mine, but of our *meaning*. Not a matter, as for Descartes, of a *moi*, a "me," a self, that may be mistaken in perceiving this wax; but of a self that is confirmed in perceiving it. Not as in Kant, a self that shapes the scene in perceiving it, but a self that has been shaped by the scene. Not as in Hume, a self that may not be the same self as the one that last saw it, but a self that is reconfirmed, a soul restored, in the very seeing it again ("again" being not a philosophical worry here but a religious confirmation). By virtue of their recurrence for him, and some other quality of their own, these objects seem to be full of a life, a force or a value that they can return to him. Repetition, restoration, association, even causation: Wordsworth is metaphorizing and moralizing these concepts. He is doing what he promised, starting the process of converting them into blood. This is what he thinks his poetry, all poetry, should do—and perhaps so do we (the very phrase "he restoreth my soul" is what re-stores my soul). And who would cavil at this? How we have needed it!

So far, though, we do not know much about the underlying trouble to which this impassioned music is the response, so we cannot fully share the sense of reaffirmation that it seems to be expressing. We already feel some of the restorative power of the verse and, through that, the value-endowing power of this landscape. We sense, more dimly, the nameless but pointed threat of those five long winters (note the "!"): that disturbance, that ache of loneliness now palliated or even cured. This is only the opening paragraph, so it would be unreasonable to expect full disclosure or resolution just yet, but as we shall see this sense of something withheld (*too* deeply interfused), which has prompted so many misguided accusations of bad faith, is indeed intrinsic to the poem. Wordsworth's "dread," if that is what we are to call the culprit emotion here, is not so much of specifically probable feelings along the passional continuum from purely moral (guilt) through moral-affective (grief) to purely affective (fear of being alone)—this is both to anticipate later paragraphs of the poem and to draw improperly on information from outside it—but of the depth and kind of disclosure, which untrammeled metaphorical thought about those feelings and his sense of himself might prompt in the mode of autobiography (the danger of a truly poetic autobiography). The solution for him might be to treat guilt and grief as palatable, beautifiable concepts, sugared capsules, rather than dangerous self-metabolizing states. A dangerous passion can be tidied away.

This first paragraph is already edging toward such a solution. There are two other essential qualities of the compound experience it represents, besides that of "again-I-this," which are of relevance here: beauty and seclusion. "Beauty," according to Burkean and classical aesthetics, is a name for those sensible qualities in objects that together cause love, such as smallness, sweetness, delicacy, color, and gradual variation. All these "forms of beauty" (24) are to be found in this paragraph, and sure enough Wordsworth later describes himself as "a lover of the meadows and the woods" (104). Concomitantly, and in accordance with the same aesthetic, the sublime of the "steep and lofty cliffs" and "wild secluded scene," potentially massive and awe-inspiring, is muted here by its proximity to "the quiet of the sky." These "waters, rolling" with their "sweet inland murmur" must likewise be a form of beauty, not like the "mighty waters rolling evermore" of the straightforwardly Pindaric and sublime Immortality Ode. This too will turn out to foreshadow another and more disconcerting suppression of the dangerous sublime, as well as the more famous invocation of it, in paragraph 4. For now it merely adds to our vague sense of there is a "something" that is being concealed or evaded (or too deeply interfused).

"To seclude," meanwhile, is "to remove or guard from public view, to withdraw from opportunities of social intercourse" (*OED*). *Se-claudere* is to close off or shut in, even imprison. The movement here is toward ever more deep shutting in, that still deeper interfusion of self and landscape which *is* the restoration of the mind or soul. The wreath of smoke floating across the outer scene is barely distinguishable from the next paragraph's sweet sensations passing through the poet's mind; indeed it gives a more certain notice of the state of his mind (*se*clusive) than it does of the very existence of vagrants or hermits (*re*clusive) in the woods, let alone of *their* all but inaccessible minds and feelings. The strange withdrawing syntax of these lines leaves us wondering how the cliffs themselves can impress thoughts on the very scene they constitute. Whose thoughts?—the very possibility of the question demonstrates the passage's interfusion of mind and scene. Seclusion and interfusion provoke or generate deeper seclusion and interfusion. This is precisely not a public view: neither a view of the public nor a view available to it (*se*clusive not *in*clusive). This is a view for one mind alone, a view that is also a picture of that one mind.

The underlying metaphor of self- or soul-restoring is one of immense power and universal appeal. "Here is the scene which is me. In its beauty is my peace. My love for it proves its beauty and confirms my own reality. I can always withdraw into (become) this one view and close off all other views (including of *me*)." This is a mode of self-fashioning, of self-affirmation, even of self-redemption (reclaiming the sinning self from a sinful world by leaving the world), with which Western secular modernity is deeply familiar, and on which it heavily relies. Yet as the suppressed reference to Dante a moment ago suggests, our very familiarity with it is also our blindness to its idiosyncrasy. How well we know this feeling: "this is *my* place, it locates and identifies *me*." Yet to find this security, love, and beauty *primarily* in a landscape, a place,[9] rather than in another person or other people, or as earlier ages would have said, in God, must always bring a consolatory or second-order reassurance in a Christian or post-Christian world: for where is the reciprocation? What can be given back to me when only I am here? In his *will* is *our* peace implies (a) that *my* will is in abeyance and (b) that I am *in*cluded *with others* in this space or place of will. A direct reciprocity only of mind and scene is precisely the refuge of the hermit, the dweller in the desert (*erêmia*) who hears the still small voice but knows it is only his own. This is Wordsworth's fear: that his impassioned music of self-restoration may be an inaudible plea, because it does not address the real causes of that underlying distress which the music is supposed to resolve. The forms of secluded beauty, those woods and copses, wreaths of smoke, plots of ground, cliffs and farms, all those beautifully metabolized or metaphorized concepts: might they not amount after all to no more than a private language, an unheard music? Do they not merely bolster his will instead of dissolving it? So far has he actually *not* allowed himself to look with or at any of those deep feelings that have to do with other people,[10] but instead just consoled himself with the surface markers of solitary identity, mere analogues of affiliation? (We might say: something in Wordsworth resists the onrushing Kantian world of full responsibility for self, clings desperately to something far older and more protective, even when knowing that this is a lost cause.)

Forms of Beauty, Acts of Love
Second Paragraph

These disturbing questions emerge more clearly out of the poem's celebrated second paragraph. The more successful the poetry, it seems, the profounder the misgivings it enacts. The oddly hesitant opening trope suggests a deeper imaginative uncertainty to come, as often in this poem; and then after that brief puzzled glance back over our shoulders we find ourselves compelled forward into two long sentences making up one of the most entrancing prospects in English meditative literature, a critical statement of the Wordsworthian arch-theme.

Though absent long,
These forms of beauty have not been to me,
As is a landscape to a blind man's eye:

But oft, in lonely rooms, and mid the din
Of towns and cities, I have owed to them,
In hours of weariness, sensations sweet,
Felt in the blood, and felt along the heart,
And passing even into my purer mind
With tranquil restoration:—feelings too
Of unremembered pleasure; such, perhaps,
As may have had no trivial influence
On that best portion of a good man's life;
His little, nameless, unremembered acts
Of kindness and of love. Nor less, I trust,
To them I may have owed another gift,
Of aspect more sublime; that blessed mood,
In which the burthen of the mystery,
In which the heavy and the weary weight
Of all this unintelligible world
Is lightened:—that serene and blessed mood,
In which the affections gently lead us on,
Until, the breath of this corporeal frame,
And even the motion of our human blood
Almost suspended, we are laid asleep
In body, and become a living soul:
While with an eye made quiet by the power
Of harmony, and the deep power of joy,
We see into the life of things.

So, first, the hesitancy: why the blind man's eye? That faintest shadow of a falter over "absent" (them from him or him from them? perhaps it makes no difference? perhaps that is the point?) prefigures a real stumble. *How* is a landscape to a blind man? Not just invisible, presumably, but meaningless, non-existent, entirely beyond his ken. But why bother to compare this kind of non-experience with a mere absence, however long, from what we have just encountered in the preceding paragraph? Well, one might respond, because to an *aesthetically* blind man these cliffs, woods, farms, and so on are not "forms of beauty," but just "a landscape." Such a man could no more have the experience of beauty than a physically blind one could have the experience of sight.

But still, the objection continues, is not the syntax such as to compare, not the *original* experience of beauty with the one such an aesthetically blind man might have had ("these forms of beauty *are* not and *were* not to me as . . ."), but the ensuing *absence* of beauty ("*have not been* to me") with a landscape's complete non-existence for a blind man? Yes, but surely what is meant here is that mere spatial and temporal absence would (for most people) be like a blind man's non-experience, whereas *this* absence was so enriched by the quality of the original experience that it itself became a new kind of experience: a presence. This response seems substantial; it seems to be just how the poem might defend itself. But then (we might still say, ungraciously)— *could* any spatio-temporal absence be so complete? Is this seriously not to underestimate or discommiserate the utter non-experience of true blindness: complacently to overrate the aesthetic experience? And a final quibble: why blind man's *eye*? What other part of a blind man might a landscape be saliently absent from? Well, his mind, surely. This is the deeper point the poem seems to want to make but doesn't, or can't. It seems almost blind itself here, blind to another kind of blindness, a moral kind.

These really are not *just* quibbles, are they? Do you not have to follow the language down as far as you can in order to see, or try to see, where it's coming from? Is that not what a poem has a right to expect of you? As the second paragraph makes quite clear, what our speaker is *not* blind to, what is known to *him* not just by some basic or (as Locke might have said) "simple" ocular impression but by an *aisthêsis*, a more complex form of sensuous perception that is also a cognition and a judgment, is "forms of beauty." This is *aisthêsis* as opposed to *noêsis*, which is an abstract concept-perception by the pure intelligence. Wordsworth's "forms" are neither meaningless visual shapes, intuitions not yet "brought under" concepts; nor Platonic Forms of Beauty, super-concepts perceptible only to the philosophical intelligence. They are not Value, Meaning, or Beauty, but they are objects that are perceived by someone only *in that they have* value and meaning *for him*. They are brought under those concepts—that *is* their beauty, their graspable form. We are about to hear an impassioned plea on behalf of these forms, their effects and the mind they *in*form. This is therefore not just an aesthetic but a moral plea, before the tribunal of value, meaning, and goodness.

And yet it is of the very greatest importance that an aesthetic situation, which *is* a case of morals in one rather limited, personal sense (and what an achievement *that* is), is also being *represented* here as a case of morals in a much broader or deeper, interpersonal sense. Much more is claimed than is shown about this transition. To put this another way: a values situation is being represented as a case or ground of virtue. This distinction within the moral realm matters a very great deal in this poem, and in Wordsworth's poetry in general. Regardless of whether he intended this, having gone some way toward establishing his value-claims in metaphor Wordsworth gets carried away, and instead only embellishes his virtue-claims by dressing them up in poetic costume, rather than metabolizing the whole business of moral claim-making into poetry, fusing values and virtues, so that a blind man's landscape might look, for example, like Gloucester's. This makes a symptom out of his uneasiness with the paragraph's opening simile or second-degree metaphor ("*as is* a landscape"), initiating as it does the complex synesthetic metaphor of vision and sensation fully realized only toward the end. Once it enters the truly moral, interpersonal realm, this mind seems more comfortable with beautified concepts than with metaphorical forms. Perhaps this fear of metaphor is connected to the fear of blindness and silence.

The plea for (or model of) conversion and redemption that follows in the rest of the paragraph is one of the most captivating and authentic in the language (*auto-entes* is "self-being"). It melts into our affections and incorporates itself with our blood. Yet it is also full of metaphorical stumbling blocks. Its ambition is to show, or to be, an aesthetic situation turning into a case of morals, or even of religion: to glide over the fathomless void between the language of beauty and the language of the good. Yet the model constantly risks vitiating the poetry (an *authentês* is also a murderer—and a suicide). This noble ambition to write the most moral, most redemptive poetry in the world (not just in the language: remember "sickly and stupid German Tragedies"[11]) is in fact fearful of its own presumptuousness, of the possibility that it may lead tragically either to the death of poetry or to a moral abyss.

The paragraph has two sentences. After the short disjunctive preamble just discussed, the first sentence reboots itself with "But oft" and then continues for ten and a half more lines, ending with "love."

The majestic second sentence is a near-sonnet, fourteen and a half lines of amplificatory, anaphoric blank verse from "Nor less" to "the life of things." The grammatical core of each sentence is an acknowledgement of *owing*: "I have owed to them"; "To them I may have owed." The forms of beauty are grasped as forms of obligation: the perceiving self as a shape of gratitude. This is a religious recognition. But in Wordsworth's time, and even since, especially in dialect, "owe" had not entirely completed its long journey from *habere* to *debere*; "own" still lies close behind it. The forms are also now in him—indeed are him. "Have not been *to* me" hints at "have *been* me." So this is the first point: the paragraph shows the self in an attitude of restorative praise and blessing toward a landscape that is wonderfully real yet nevertheless also ideal (a *land-schap* is a painter's land-shaping): an attitude almost of prayer, in those "lonely rooms" like hermit's cells in an urban desert full of human "din" ("thunder" is at the Germanic root of the word) as opposed to a natural "murmur."

Secondly, the two sentences distinguish between three affective responses to this memory: "sensations" (as "sweet" as the murmur of the Wye); "feelings" (of "pleasure"); and a "mood" ("blessed"). At what one might call the most primitive end of this affective spectrum, beautiful forms cause, or rather *give* (are "owed"), "sweet" sensations. This may at first appear to be only a matter of taste (in both senses); but the business of the figure here is to extend the range of what counts as sensation to something that is perceptible "in the blood," "along the heart," and "into the mind"; something that evolves therefore from the perceptible to the remedial. The metaphorical ambition is immense. A memory has made a set of natural and domestic objects, a land-shape, into contours of the mind, morphing from object to form to sensation to organ. The calm river flows all the way into (in-fluence) and becomes the bloodstream, its sweet inland murmur becoming a tranquil inner murmur. Blood, heart, mind: each term less bodily and sensory ("purer") than the one before, each affect more emotional and therapeutic.

So far so good: a natural-remedial metaphor so original and profound that we all take it for granted now (though familiar metaphorical reservations arise: how can blood "feel"? why "along"? "purer" than what? than before?). Forms of beauty tranquillize and restore a mind disturbed and wearied by forms of ugliness ("din")—the aesthetic and the sensory consorting together. But now the paragraph starts to work the metaphor rather harder, and the cavils again become more pressing. These are "feelings" now, significantly, not "sensations." One might have thought that Wordsworth was merely shifting slightly away from a more abstract and purely Latinate term for a sense-impression (*sentire* does after all mean "to feel") to a more concrete and pan-European term for touch (*folma, palma*). But instead of successfully enhancing and extending a thin empiricist terminology, he is now venturing onto much shiftier ground, drawing on an originally ambivalent term (for touch *and* emotion: "felt in the blood"; "feelings of pleasure") that had increasingly come during the century before to occupy much the same sensory-moral space as the French and English *sentiment*. The poem has become part of the Age of Sensibility, in which feeling is simultaneously moralized and aestheticized. The Lockean self of sense has become a Rousseauan self of sentiment. This ambivalence seeps into the fabric of the poem as it had (and has) into the fabric of society.

But perhaps we should ask some more of the superficial questions before returning to this main one. Why "unremembered," then, and twice at that? Presumably this is to imply "never remembered in the first place," as distinct from "forgotten." Yet this is not like the blind man's landscape, never seen at all. There *were* such feelings and acts, but they were below the level of awareness, too "trivial" to register individually, but cumulatively substantial, or influential, like grains of sand. Presumably, again, these unremembered motes are to be distinguished from *remembered* feelings and acts because they are collectively constitutive in a way in which distinct memories could not be. Rocks do not flow like sand or form sediment like silt. A feeling of pleasure, especially unremembered pleasure, is not quite the same as a pleasant feeling. The pleasure is the subject, not the texture, of the feeling; what the feeling gropes toward or touches (*palma*), not the quality of the feeling; what it is about, not what it is. So the pleasure becomes the sedimentary layer at the bottom of the river, not the thrilling rush of the water. And the same kind of point might be made about "little" and "nameless." Would grand, attested, celebrated acts, large and generous gestures, not seem too ostentatious, too calculated even—is this not how the metaphor runs? Would munificence not be out of place? Here is a tranquil tributary of benevolent feeling flowing into a secluded stream of beneficent behavior. Here is beauty, surely, not sublimity. Even the modest "perhaps" and "may have had" contribute to this impression—unless we sense that Wordsworth is having his cake and eating it too (proud humility again). As for "kindness" and "love," the two approximated concepts influence each other. "Love" here is not *philia*, nor *erôs*, nor *agapê*, nor *caritas*, but precisely "loving-kindness," love of kind, feelings of tenderness or affection for others: *that* kind of love.

The point is not that these questions have no answers; at each point the metaphor, or the concept-set, can be saved. It is more that we have to work quite hard to save it, with a faint sense that now Wordsworth owes *us* something ("gentle reader . . . should you think, Perhaps a tale you'll make it";[12] but how hard should we have to think? when does the thought become mostly ours?). The passage's aspiration somehow seems greater than its language, although what it aspires to is profound, and it does convey *that*. But "love" and "kindness," "little" and "nameless," "unremembered" and "trivial," "perhaps" and "may," and above all "feeling": all contribute to that air of diffidence or coyness, of hanging back from attempting a fully articulated discovery in case of finding *either* that it is inarticulable and therefore, as poetry, inadequate, *or* that it is too overwhelming to bear.

The underlying problem here, the real source or root of the unease, is the specific claim that a peculiar set of feelings, including value-feelings, can cause or partially cause certain kinds of good *action*. This is part of the poem's much broader claim about self-making, not yet fully elaborated, which can most compellingly be put in classical terms: that not just *eudaimonia*, "well-being" or "flourishing," but also *aretê*, "virtue" or "excellence," can be founded on a certain kind of *hêdonê*, or "pleasure." Now the strict hedonist claim is the contrary one: that the good life has pleasure as its goal, end, or measure, not its foundation. In this sense Wordsworth is no hedonist, no Epicurean. The Lockean or empiricist claim that "happiness in general is our greatest good," and that passional and sensory pleasure is its determining quantum, *is* on the other hand a distant descendant of Epicurus, hedonic if not hedonist. Wordsworth's metaphor might thus be seen as corrective, starting with Locke's sensationist quantifying terms but warping them back into a more experiential and qualitative shape (the Shaftesbury-Hutcheson project).

There is something fleetingly but hauntingly Aristotelian, even, in Wordsworth's corrective, late-Enlightenment picture of a mind restored to well-being and even, finally, habituated to virtuous acts by its own sedimentary, disposing layers of sensation—or perhaps Thomist, rather than Aristotelian, since what haunts the picture is the ghost not so much of *eudaimonia* as of *beatitudo*, "blessedness." We will return to this more powerful and broader claim in a moment. But the specific claim here is about feelings, *sentiments*, as opposed to sensations; and (to continue with Aquinas) about acts, *actus hominis*, the instinctive behaviors of the human animal, as opposed to actions, *actiones humanae*, the deliberative behaviors of the human being. If Wordsworth's hopes for poetry were to be realized here, the metaphor would have to spark across the gap between this kind of feeling and this kind of action; guide us across the rocky terrain between nature's forms and our own behaviors, not lead us down the primrose path from the picturesque to the sentimental ("and then my heart with pleasure fills . . ."). If the gap were the standard one between satisfaction and benefaction, a matter of animal appetite (Nero, having dined well, freed the slave), no great magic would be needed. But in an account of self-constitutive humanity, of true dispositional moral consequence, such an account as Wordsworth exceptionally, wonderfully aspires to, any spark leaping from private aesthetic pleasure to sustained public benefaction seems to need just such a rich ethical or religious atmosphere that his conceptual variety of metaphorical thought seems ill-suited to provide (indeed we are only too ready nowadays with the stock and equally thin counter-example: the nature-loving serial killer, the Mozart-playing Gestapo officer). If the conversation between Anne and Benwick about feeling and poetry in *Persuasion*, or the one between Tilney and Catherine in *Northanger Abbey* that ends in her rejecting "the whole city of Bath, as unworthy to make part of a landscape," or the awkward Wordsworthianisms in *Childe Harold III* ("Are not the mountains, waves, and skies, a part Of me?")—if these are anything to go by, Austen and Byron, novelist and satirist, a supplier of rich ethical atmospheres and a scorner of thin ones, would have smiled, or squirmed, at the very idea of such a spark. These acts may have to remain nameless and unremembered because any attempt to name or remember them might expose either their thin alterity or their religious emptiness.

Seeing into Life
Second and Third Paragraphs

This withdrawal from relationship becomes more salient as the poetry's music becomes more impassioned (its power is in inverse proportion to its relationality). The second sentence, that irresistible near-sonnet with its "blessed mood," forms the poem's climax and *sanctum sanctorum*, with the short third paragraph following as a kind of coda or *dénouement*. The force of the sentence, significantly, is more rhetorical than metaphorical. Its cumulative invocation of power, mood, and weight ("that blessed mood . . . that serene and blessed mood"; "the power . . . the deep power"; "in which the burthen . . . in which the heavy . . . and the weary") is what its power, mood, and weight consist in. One might say that this is superlative concept-poetry; we are pressed to dwell on the concepts, absorb them into our blood. Its near-suspensions of meaning and motion, of its own "burthen," and its deferred enlightenments or hangings-back (*sus-pendere*), are similarly enacted in "suspended" and "lightened." The invocation ("O sylvan Wye"), the suspension ("how oft . . . How oft . . . How often," "in spirit have I turned . . . has my spirit turned") and the weight ("hung upon") are then carried over into the third paragraph, which is also linked to the opening lines of its predecessor (darkness/blindness, din/stir, beatings of my heart/felt along the heart):

> If this
> Be but a vain belief, yet, oh! how oft,
> In darkness, and amid the many shapes
> Of joyless day-light; when the fretful stir
> Unprofitable, and the fever of the world,
> Have hung upon the beatings of my heart,
> How oft, in spirit, have I turned to thee
> O sylvan Wye! Thou wanderer through the woods,
> How often has my spirit turned to thee!

The "blessed mood" has been a constant sanctuary from an urban limbo of hollow men ("many shapes") and affectless or spiritless enervation ("joyless," "fretful," "weary") making daylight into near-darkness (dark amid the blaze of noon). Eliot's *Waste Land* follows as hard on the heels of these lines as Keats's *Nightingale*; and these lines in their turn follow Milton and Dante as closely as they do Lady Macbeth's "life's fitful fever" or Hamlet's "weary, stale, flat and unprofitable." "Weary" and "wander" have the same root, *wor-*; the concepts of weight and burden are thus intertwined with those of loss and regaining of direction (blindness, leading on, turning to). The wanderer through the woods is also a spirit of the woods (sylvan/sylph), as the poet once more identifies with what he sees. He too is a wanderer and a spirit, as well as a hermit: "how often has my spirit turned (in)to thee." (Shelley's "Be thou, Spirit fierce, / My spirit," in the "West Wind" ode, typically turns Wordsworth's already risky leap from feeling to act into an impossible hyperspace jump.) The "mystery," the unspeakable or unseeable religious secret, is not just the world felt as a burden when one is in limbo, but the world experienced as an epiphany when one is in a sacred mood or place. The poet is both victim and priest. And if the intelligible is that which is perceived by *noêsis* (concept-knowledge), then the "unintelligible world" is the world seen not as unconceptualized but as unconceptualizable (just as "unremembered" isn't "forgotten" but "not rememberable"). This unintelligible world is knowable only by *aisthêsis*, such a kind of enlightening of vision that is also a lightening of the burden not only of the world but also of the body itself.

As for "mood," a more persistent or overarching psychic condition than the transient "feeling" or "sensation," though less so than disposition, temper, humor, or character: that is the trance-like contemplative state in which the seeing and unburdening happen. It is the state *in* which "the affections" lead us *on* (not *to* which the affections lead us): a diffused affective state. Enlightenment sentimentalism was inclined to distinguish domestic affection from wild passion precisely on the grounds that the former leads us gently (the beautiful) while the latter drives us violently (the sublime). *Ad-facere* is as much a making of the self toward experience as a being-made-by experience, and in these lines the affections have become parts of a mysterious process of self-generation, soul-becoming (Keats's "soul-making"). This third and final phase of the paragraph's sensation-feeling-affection sequence shows the affective self at its most active, leading on the soul until it attains life, joy, and vision, and the body and *its* "eye" until they attain quiet or rest. This has a profound appeal. It is a fleeting glimpse of a true change of state, a fundamental redisposition of the passions. But it is only a glimpse, and in the end a somewhat meretricious one; what is blessed is only a mood, not a life—for this is a renewal of dualism, a disjunctive personal withdrawal from body to soul, rather than a real realignment of the moral affections with respect to others. The passions no longer tranquilly restore the mind, no longer try (however vainly) to bridge the chasm between pleasure and act. Now they are dualistically both beautifully receptive and sublimely creative. The beautiful in the poem is what we love for its bestowing of what helps us bear things, the sublime what we dread for its disclosing of things we cannot bear. Now both together seem to have become the marker of a "blessed" state that can only be given unsought (unbought, Burke would say): a state of grace, just simply *given*.

Wordsworth is aspiring to an apotheosis of conceptual-aesthetic cognition. He is making a god in his *sanctum*, a being of aspect more sublime, out of forms of beauty and his own mood, a mood as much given to himself by blessing the forms as given to him by their blessing. "Blessing" is from *blóed-sian* (to mark with blood, to sacrifice) and here the moment of *sacrificium*, of making-sacred, is marked by the suspension of the blood, a kind of death. The paragraphs take concept-knowledge (of power, mood, weight, weariness/wandering, spirit, lightening/enlightenment, and finally life) as far as it can go toward making the world first intelligible and then, by aestheticizing concepts and world alike, bearable. It is a philosophical strategy more than a poetic one, a set of adjacent, linked, but distinct concepts rather than a fused metaphor, an asserted or claimed rather than a manifested or material sense of serenity, harmony, joy, quietness, stillness, and vision. The usual hesitations ("I trust," "I may have owed," "If this be but a vain belief") certainly seem in this light not so much like diffidence as like empirical prudence. "These are the phenomena; it seems like this to me; I can claim only belief, not knowledge." But in the end the claim is mystical. We see into not just the life of *things*, of objects and forms (the emphasis is necessary if the word is not to be throwaway), but the *life* of things, their meaning and value. And since we have become pure souls that seeing is an entering. We *are* the life of things.

Here's how Coleridge glossed these lines:

i.e by deep feeling we make our *Ideas dim*—& this is what we mean by our Life—ourselves. I think of the Wall—it is before me, a distinct Image—here. I necessarily think of the Idea & the Thinking I as two distinct & opposite Things. Now <let me> think of *myself*—of the thinking Being—the Idea becomes dim whatever it be—so dim that I know not what it is—but the Feeling is deep & steady—and this I call I—identifying the Percipient & the Perceived—.[13]

Wordsworth feels the identity of percipient and perceived, all right, and furthermore as an aesthetic and moral matter, not just an epistemological one. He knows at such times that he exists, and that things do, and that this co-existence is harmonious and meaningful. But the important "Ideas" for him are not only his "forms of beauty," his "things," but also his concepts: kindness, love, restoration, joy, power, life. It is the identity of concept and perceiver as much as world and self that matters here. And these life-giving concepts exist primarily in relation to *him* and to *things*: not to other people. There's the usual tell-tale stumble, too: why "*human* blood"? Do we have some blood that is not human? Is there something especially human about our *blood*, as opposed to our minds, or souls? If so, it is as if the human part of us must be suspended before we can be living souls or feel the power of joy.

What, after all, is so "unintelligible" about the world: what is the "mystery" that weighs so heavily? Not God or Nature. The world that the poem implicitly finds unintelligible is the human world, the din of cities and the people who live in them with their lonely rooms and their little acts of kindness and their dreadful acts of cruelty or betrayal. How is the restored and morally fortified soul, occasionally visited by blessed moods, by sublimity's "inconstant glance" and "unseen power," to deal with this world? (Shelley's phrases about "intellectual beauty" extract as so often a nugget of pure Platonism from the mixed Wordsworthian ore.) We know that this soul can survive humanity, chiefly by avoiding it; any ugliness can be made bearable if the sense of it can be sufficiently counteracted by a sense of landscaped beauty. But (harder question!) is this restored soul actually to go into the human world, let alone try to act in it? Or is the restoration a purely personal matter? Can that ever be so? Maybe it can be a matter between the soul and

God: but where is God here? On the other hand Wordsworth is principally engaged with psychic health, not moral behavior; and besides is not the poem itself his action, his way of doing good?

Maybe we have come here to the limits of aesthetics as a case of morals: to a point where good is more than a matter of the senses; where a sense of beauty will not necessarily produce good acts, or actions; where "moral relations" are unsatisfactorily represented; where the pleading is strained; where it turns out that Wordsworth cannot actually do what he set out to do. He is writing about *moral* unintelligibility without imagining relations *between people*: and then showing the unintelligibility being dispelled or lifted, but not clarified. He is seeking psychic health in solitude; but the individual who seeks it among other people may feel in the end at least as healthy, and this may be what Wordsworth cannot bear to think, or imagine how to think. The awful shadow of the unseen sublime only darkens the discourse further, taking moral effort even more out of the hands of the human agent. An invaluable foil for so spellbinding an account of joy in beauty would have been a parallel account of joy in goodness, and he does not attempt this, preferring to go straight from an account of beauty to a hint of the sublime. Austen, on the other hand, offers many such accounts of goodness, often in (but not only in) strikingly sensory terms: witness that famous episode from *Persuasion* in which the hitherto unseen Wentworth lifts the burdensome clinging child from Anne's back and the weight from her spirit. The Wordsworthian aesthetic looks by comparison with the Wentworthian one rather too like an *an*aesthetic, to be taken as required ("How often has my spirit turned to thee"). Forms of beauty are not, after all, forms of good.

Something That He Dreads
First Half of the Fourth Paragraph

Maybe all this is starting to seem harsh or unfair. But only in the way in which one must sometimes be harsh or unfair to oneself. That inner Wordsworthian voice has been so much the voice of our own souls that to doubt it is to doubt oneself. This is indeed to throw away the ladder we are standing on; as the most distinctive and original voice in English of a certain kind of post-Christian religious consolation, Wordsworth *is* the ladder. Yet somehow the throwing away must be attempted, or at least imagined. We have been able to see so much through this lens, but there is also a kind of vision it has come, cataract-like, to occlude: something that has to do with that connectedness, which is not mind-to-nature (or mind-to-God) but mind-to-mind. Both kinds of connectedness are ultimately religious in nature, aspects of re-binding (*re-ligare*); but while the poem purports to address both it really thinks about only one (and with the unevennesses we are now starting to see as radical)—while if anything it suppresses the other. To criticize a poem or poet like this is, after all, only to take him even more seriously than Browning did. He *is* a lost leader, but having followed him we are now in certain respects lost too, and the best way to find ourselves again is to see how he got lost, unravel his own awareness of the condition.

The fourth paragraph of the poem is the one in which all these questions come to a head. The paragraph falls into two halves almost equal in length but not at all so in tenor or situation. The second half is a *locus classicus* of the egotistical or Cartesian-Kantian present sublime (or sublime presence): "I have learned . . . I have felt . . . therefore I am." The first half is the poem's heart of darkness, a glimpse of a now-sublimed past, a suppressed horror:

> And now, with gleams of half-extinguish'd thought,
> With many recognitions dim and faint,
> And somewhat of a sad perplexity,
> The picture of the mind revives again:
> While here I stand, not only with the sense
> Of present pleasure, but with pleasing thoughts
> That in this moment there is life and food
> For future years. And so I dare to hope
> Though changed, no doubt, from what I was, when first
> I came among these hills; when like a roe
> I bounded o'er the mountains, by the sides
> Of the deep rivers, and the lonely streams,
> Wherever nature led; more like a man
> Flying from something that he dreads, than one
> Who sought the thing he loved. For nature then
> (The coarser pleasures of my boyish days,
> And their glad animal movements all gone by,)
> To me was all in all.—I cannot paint

What then I was. The sounding cataract
Haunted me like a passion: the tall rock,
The mountain, and the deep and gloomy wood,
Their colours and their forms, were then to me
An appetite: a feeling and a love,
That had no need of a remoter charm,
By thought supplied, or any interest
Unborrowed from the eye.—That time is past,
And all its aching joys are now no more,
And all its dizzy raptures.

The poem so far has had little explicitly to say about what we are to be saved, redeemed, or converted *from*. The world's ugliness, presumably: the "weight" of its loneliness, its "fever" and its "din"; its forms of ill, or ill-formed shapes, or disvaluing 'scapes (*land-schaap*). But the burden of the mystery is partly that the burden *is* a mystery. Wordsworth's "unintelligible world," as Byron sardonically observed, may indeed quite simply "prove unintelligible." Now we are at the core of the mystery, the scene of the original struggle in Wordsworth's life and mind between forms of natural beauty and forms of moral dread— and yet he still "cannot paint" that landscape of the self.

Since the appearance of *The Prelude* this struggle has attracted any amount of speculation on Wordsworth's condition in the summer of 1793. He was the father of an illegitimate child; he had abandoned both child and mother; he had no prospect of an income; his own sense of political identity had been transformed and split by revolution in France and repression in England; he was himself a near-vagrant, having just crossed on foot a Salisbury Plain filled with images ancient and modern of darkness, misery, and sacrifice. Perhaps worst of all, he was soon to embark (according to *The Prelude*) on a rationalist philosophical quest that was to lead him to "give up moral questions in despair": to the edge of an abyss only Dorothy, Coleridge and Racedown were to drag him back from. He was flying not just away from but *toward* something dreadful; from the vantage point of 1798 (let alone 1805) the two must have been hard to distinguish. This is the invisible binary companion affecting the movement of "Tintern Abbey," the one set of "recognitions" that could not possibly have been "dim and faint." Its hidden or subliminal existence in large part accounts for that sense of concealment variously felt by so many readers. The power of forms of beauty to provoke sweet sensations, restore the mind, solve moral questions, and dissolve despair has its dark partner, the power of forms of ugliness to bring painful sensations, distress the mind, devalue moral questions, and induce despair. And the natural sublime, too, has its dark side. These necessary but unimaginable complements are real presences in the poem.[14]

So what can we say about this frightful fiend treading so close behind the poet, or before him, on his lonesome road of fear and dread? It was not Coleridge or the "Ancient Mariner," surely, whatever one might make of Wordsworth's views on that most egregious of the *Lyrical Ballads*, inaugurating the volume, with "Tintern Abbey" as its matching bookend, in the 1798 edition; and then, demoted by Wordsworth himself, treading so close behind his poem in the 1800 edition. And yet his remarks about it are suggestive. "The Poem of my Friend has indeed great defects," he admitted.[15] We know Wordsworth openly claimed that most modern poetry, even his friend's, was hardly poetry at all, was indeed radically defective: but that his own was morally and affectively revolutionary. And yet "Tintern Abbey" also seems constantly to doubt itself. "The principal person has no distinct character . . . he does not act, but is continually acted upon": thus Wordsworth on the mariner.[16] But is this not also a version of his fear in—and for— his own poem, and others in the volume? The poem's recognitions of humanity are themselves dim, faint, indistinct, infused with "somewhat of a sad perplexity" (*plexus*: "entangled," "intricate"; *per-plexus*, "confused"); and this disturbing and confused thought is itself only half-extinguished. The poem does of course revive itself here as a picture or landscape of a revived mind, standing on that founding sense of present, and now rememberable, pleasure, which partly consists in the thought of its future value for a weary or fretful mind. This time the wanderer anticipates the meaning of his experience even as he has it— and naturally this makes it less vivid. No aching joys or dizzy raptures this time. Thoughts of future pleasure diffuse but dilute the sense of the present one. The pale cast of thought signifies an irresolute character, perplexed in the extreme, who does not act but is continually acted upon: "changed, no doubt," into a mere poet. The diffidence and enervation that this poet needs this landscape to help him overcome are just what he feels in the presence of real character. In the apprehension of mountains, rivers, and woods he feels like a god, not a human being. In the absence of such a direct and present apprehension of nature, poetry seems to recommend itself as the kind of substitutive thought that can redeem us from humanity, not the kind that tangles us up in its metaphorical complexities and perplexities. Or so he dares, in proud humility, to hope.

It is hard, in other words, to avoid the thought that the roe bounding over the mountains and along the lonely streams was not so much led by nature as fleeing the complexity, the intricate entanglements, of dreadful man. Not so much a man flying from something as something flying from man. The lonely stream now leads away from or out of the lonely room, healing by effluence not influence. But "alone" is "all-one" or "wholly one," complete oneness; Coleridge registers the point in the "Mariner": "alone, alone, all, all alone, alone on. . . ." So to say, probatively, *"For* nature then to me was all in all" and then, in apposition, that "I cannot paint what then *I* was," is to say that the fugitive was literally "all one" with nature, that the cataract looked like "a" (not even his) passion; he "haunts" or habituates or inhabits it as much as it does him. Rock and wood, or just (in Lockean vein) their colors and forms, *were* appetites and feelings. One might say, as if a magic lantern threw his nerves in patterns on a screen. Prufrock in his own lonely crowded room also found it impossible to say just what he meant, to paint what then he was, without resorting to scuttling claws all alone in silent seas—and thus metaphorizing experience. Picturing or painting one's mind and feelings as all one with the landscape is to see oneself as haunted, hunted, by the singular alien figure within the landscape that is oneself. This is the consequence of avoiding any discovery of one's real self, one's own dreadful humanity, passions, appetites, feelings. The colors and the forms of beauty can replace or crowd out human affections. "Remoter charm" etymologically means "more removed music" (*carmen, removere*). The appeal of these forms is that they do *not* need the far-off music of humanity. No half-extinguished or even pleasing thought is required to apprehend them. Their only distinctiveness or stake in experience ("interest," from *interesse*, to lie between or be among, means "it makes a difference to," and hence "it concerns") is borrowed as a pledge or security from the sense of sight: a landscape of form and color only, mere unconceptualized intuitions, to be repaid in equal denominations of pure visual impression when the blind man needs them.

This almost primitivist (or pre-postimpressionist) version of land-scape's restorative effect nevertheless discloses a more developed self-awareness than "the coarser pleasures of my boyish days" to be articulated in the "Fair seed-time had my soul" passage and else-where in book 1 of *The Prelude*: even though there too "I was alone and seemed to be a trouble to the peace." The bounding roe belatedly re-experiences a version of that glad animal movement, but now the natural forms of beauty and fear have become more projections or dis-placements than constitutive foundations of the self. The aching joys and dizzy raptures lie partly in sloughing off the outer layers of the self, its recently acquired human carapace (its sinful embodiment), by tak-ing it back to and immersing it in its oldest constituting sources. The intensity of feeling partly arises, as it did not when he was a boy, from his sense of escape from something else. As a boy and "fell destroyer," admittedly, he did feel *fear*: on his night-time woodcock-snaring excur-sions at the "sounds of undistinguishable motion . . . coming after" him; and again in the "elfin pinnace" episode, when the "huge Cliff . . . like a living thing, Strode after him," being transformed later into the "huge and mighty Forms" of "unknown modes of being" that "do not live like living men." But this boyhood fear was part of his constitu-tion in and as "nature," a non-human world of life. His *dread* in 1793 was precisely of his self-recognition in and as "living man." The mighty forms of nature held no fears any more, but his own form was a thing of more extreme dread, not as the reflex of a star or a mountain, but as a reflection of alien man.

So now we know what he dreads. It is humanity: brutalized and overwhelming, but humanity all the same. The poem's glimpses of the awful natural sublime, to be massively elaborated in *Prelude* 1, 2, 6, and 13, have a dreadful counterpart in these hints of a human sub-lime that is simply terrifying, a moral abysm or egotistical *abîme*, made up of Wordsworth's horror at human "atrocities," including his own "treachery and desertion," and of despair at his inability, with "a voice labouring and a brain confounded," to fathom, modify, or resolve its complexities, especially in poetry. Human nature had not long before seemed born again into a state of bliss, its earth a very heaven; now this same human sublime was bringing forth abysmal monsters who found joy in massacre: "never heads enough for those that bade them fall." The Terror had already begun as he crossed Salisbury Plain and arrived at Tintern, and in retrospect its dreadful shadow was cast backwards onto those July days. Wordsworth in 1793 and 1798 could manage the beautiful center of the moral spectrum, from dear friends to tranquil landscapes, with its ugly complement, the din of towns and cities, and even one of its sublime poles, the one we are about to be shown in the paragraph's second half; but not the other pole, not the blood-thirsty revolutionary mob, nor that "conflict of sensations without name" when patriotism and liberty collide (see figure 3.2). *That* picture of the mind is still unpaintable, its sensations still nameless. Could any poetry, any landscape, possibly redeem this condition?

Something Far More Deeply Interfused
Second Half of the Fourth Paragraph

What about the natural sublime in the poem, then: that aspect of the awful, even the fearful, which the poem *does* finally invoke, does stop withholding or concealing from us? Here is the second half of the paragraph:

> Not for this
> Faint I, nor mourn nor murmur: other gifts
> Have followed, for such loss, I would believe,
> Abundant recompence. For I have learned
> To look on nature, not as in the hour
> Of thoughtless youth, but hearing oftentimes
> The still, sad music of humanity,
> Nor harsh nor grating, though of ample power
> To chasten and subdue. And I have felt
> A presence that disturbs me with the joy
> Of elevated thoughts; a sense sublime
> Of something far more deeply interfused,
> Whose dwelling is the light of setting suns,
> And the round ocean, and the living air,
> And the blue sky, and in the mind of man,
> A motion and a spirit, that impels

All thinking things, all objects of all thought,
And rolls through all things. Therefore am I still
A lover of the meadows and the woods,
And mountains; and of all that we behold
From this green earth; of all the mighty world
Of eye and ear, both what they half-create,
And what perceive; well pleased to recognize
In nature and the language of the sense,
The anchor of my purest thoughts, the nurse,
The guide, the guardian of my heart, and soul
Of all my moral being.

The gift of 1793 was the "once again I," the reaffirmation and resto-ration of the self. A "faint I," dim and faint, became sharply defined again, as well as vigorous. But the "faint I" or "feigned I" (*feindre* lies behind both "faint" and "feint")—that assumed and enervated public self—has had to be restored many times since. These "other" gifts are the modes of the self we already know, memory, mood, sensation, and feeling: not its very fabric. But they all keep raising two questions: why are these called *gifts*, given things; and where are they given *from*, which is to say, by what or by whom are they given? Gifts imply givers, not just lucky receivers; gratitude implies grace. If natural objects can be seen as forms of beauty and then as moral forms, forms of good, should we be grateful, and to whom? Is the prophet grateful to the wilderness or for it?

Besides, what are the gifts, exactly? The first one appears to be "nature": or perhaps, on closer inspection, nature seen under an unfa-miliar aspect, where what is "seen" is in fact a sound, a music, and what makes the sound is not really "nature," the poem's forms of beauty, at all. Yet the gift is not even this. Instead, the syntax tells us, it is to have *learned* to see nature in this way. And the second gift, similarly, is not simply the "some thing" that dwells in and impels "all things," nor even just its presence, motion, and breath (spirit), the primary qualities or emanations of some mysterious thing-in-itself. The gift is to have *felt* all this, to have felt first the presence (pre-essence) and then the sense (essence). It is the sense that is sublime, not what it is a sense of. It is the learning, the modifying of sense, that is given, not what it is a sense of. The "presence" is one of joyous thought more than of some numinous being. Wordsworth is disturbed by joy, the deep power of joy, not by a divine or quasi-divine presence, and even the joy itself is caused by his own elevated thoughts, rather than by such a presence.

"I have learned . . . I have felt . . . Therefore am I still": this "I" is anything but faint now. "Who coverest thyself with light as with a garment: who stretchest out the heavens like a curtain: who layeth the beams of his chambers in the waters: who maketh the clouds his chariot: who walketh upon the wings of the wind": according to Psalm 104 (1-3) the answer is, straightforwardly, God. So it is in book 7 of *Paradise Lost*, Raphael's long answer to Adam's questions as to "'how first began this heaven . . . with moving fires adorned innumerable . . . and this . . . ambient air wide interfus'd'" (lines 86-89). But Wordsworth's "something," his "presence," though likewise inhabiting light, heavens, waters and wind, moving fires and ambient air, is at the same time always concealed, always retreating, always disappearing into what it impels and rolls through. It is *too* deeply interfused. This is a "something, we know not what," in Berkeley's dismissive phrase about the empty concept of some underlying "matter" that also supposedly rolls through or underpins all things. And yet the poem comes dangerously close at this point to representing the something as the ultimate ground not so much of matter as of value: "therefore am I still a lover," "soul of all my moral being." Do the forms of beauty, after all, derive their being, their meaning, from something like Being itself? Are they forms, so to speak, of Life? Can beauty and good be fully understood only by reference to this numinous-yet-immanent Sublime? Wouldn't that vitiate the poem's humanist ambition, to save our souls by converting beauty into virtue through poetry? Or, as the poem's own constructions seem to suggest, is this Presence merely the emanated feelings and thoughts of a projected and rather Cartesian "I"? To have the *sense* of a Presence is all that matters, it seems. Or maybe to have this lingering ghostly sense of One Presence in nature is more the inescapable fate of post-Christian humanity than the general inheritance of all human beings confronted with the sublime.

The other gift, after all, was to have *learned to look on* nature. And what the observer learned was to look on nature *as if hearing* the sound of humanity. This is not an aesthetic (in fact oddly synesthetic) situation presented as a case of morals, but the converse. Humanity is now a distant symphony whose tragic contours are discernible, and bearable, only from a great distance: a still small voice, heard after earthquake, wind, and fire. These are strange and remarkable accommodations to the human sublime. The forms of beauty can make humanity bearable not by crowding it out but by partially muting it, screening out its harshness, translating its ugly din into the power of harmony. Where once Wordsworth had been deafened by people and seen nature only as a distant picture, he is now dazzled by nature and hears people only as a distant music (all that is left of the voice of God): a solemn music, furthermore, chastening and tempering his aching joys and dizzy raptures, not so much impassioned as impassive. Ugliness is made beautiful by the haze of distance, and selfish pleasure is reproved by the consciousness of suffering. The poet's condition now is unlike what it was either in his "boyish days," when he knew no suffering, or in 1793, when he was escaping it. Both were times of "thoughtless youth." But the poem skirts unthinkingly round the edges of two uncomfortable propositions: that one deals best with other people's suffering as well as one's own by flying from them, by withdrawing from relationship; and that the main function of other people's suffering is to restrain or rarefy one's own aesthetic joy. Here is an even more refined variety of aesthetic hedonism, anticipating not so much Keats as Arnold or Pater—Arnold's ignorant armies and eternal notes of sadness are certainly not more gaze-avertingly pious. This, again, seems harsh, but it is where the poem has been taking us. It is one thing, and a valuable thing, to say, "This is me, this landscape is where I find myself"; it is another to say, "Looking at this landscape in this way makes me more virtuous / a better person." To represent an aesthetic situation as a case of morals, without its actually being one, is the shortest of steps from representing a moral situation, even a religious one, as merely an aesthetic case.[17] And the deeper the poem goes the more tangled it gets in this mesh. The more it seeks a moral law within, the more it makes gods not metaphors out of its concepts, projecting like Prufrock's magic lantern the poet's own crooked shadow onto the starry sky.

The paragraph's finale—resounding, confident, even rather smug ("well pleased")—reiterates both the ambition and the evasion in this Cartesian-Kantian undertaking: "for I have . . . and I have . . . therefore I am." What started out as an utterly radical and courageous plea for moral conversion, an empirical eduction of the good life from forms of beauty perceived in a familiar landscape, an intuitively plausible claim that an occasional immersion in the non-human world of life is a powerful antidote to the spiritual diseases caused by prolonged exposure to the human one, has become something like a rationalist epistemological creed. The mighty world is *only* "all that we behold"; it belongs after all to eye and ear, a mere *perceptibilium*. In so far as it is creation it is seen as *our* creation, intuitions partly brought under concepts. There is a double presumptuousness here. First, what we principally recognize nature as is *our* moral anchor ("purest thoughts"), rather than all the other things it is. Here Nature exists *for us*: yet is it not profoundly more consoling to think that it *does not*? Secondly, what we recognize ourselves as, a moral being or a soul, is derived from the non-human world, not the human one. The very recognition that dehumanizes humanity also denatures nature. As a corollary of both these attitudes, morality turns out to be a matter of being, not doing, and being requires no relationship, no living in the very world which was the world of all of us in *Prelude* book 10, but that in the end filled Wordsworth with such despair and dread.

For Thou Art with Me
Fifth Paragraph

And thy rod and thy staff they comfort me. He is walking "upon the banks of this fair river," not through the valley of the shadow of death, but the shadow of dread, or solitude, or fear, or pain, or grief, still treads close behind him. Yet the metaphorical and moral pressure of this last paragraph, more than a quarter of the poem's length, is so low that after the impassioned music of what has gone before, let alone of the great Psalm just invoked, it seems like an after-dinner stroll:

> Nor, perchance,
> If I were not thus taught, should I the more
> Suffer my genial spirits to decay:
> For thou art with me, here, upon the banks
> Of this fair river; thou, my dearest Friend,
> My dear, dear Friend, and in thy voice I catch
> The language of my former heart, and read
> My former pleasures in the shooting lights

Of thy wild eyes. Oh! yet a little while
May I behold in thee what I was once,
My dear, dear Sister! And this prayer I make,
Knowing that Nature never did betray
The heart that loved her; 'tis her privilege,
Through all the years of this our life, to lead
From joy to joy: for she can so inform
The mind that is within us, so impress
With quietness and beauty, and so feed
With lofty thoughts, that neither evil tongues,
Rash judgments, nor the sneers of selfish men,
Nor greetings where no kindness is, nor all
The dreary intercourse of daily life,
Shall e'er prevail against us, or disturb
Our chearful faith that all which we behold
Is full of blessings. Therefore let the moon
Shine on thee in thy solitary walk;
And let the misty mountain winds be free
To blow against thee: and in after years,
When these wild ecstasies shall be matured
Into a sober pleasure, when thy mind
Shall be a mansion for all lovely forms,
Thy memory be as a dwelling-place
For all sweet sounds and harmonies; Oh! then,
If solitude, or fear, or pain, or grief,
Should be thy portion, with what healing thoughts
Of tender joy wilt thou remember me,
And these my exhortations! Nor, perchance,
If I should be, where I no more can hear
Thy voice, nor catch from thy wild eyes these gleams
Of past existence, wilt thou then forget
That on the banks of this delightful stream
We stood together; and that I, so long
A worshipper of Nature, hither came,
Unwearied in that service: rather say
With warmer love, oh! with far deeper zeal
Of holier love. Nor wilt thou then forget,

That after many wanderings, many years
Of absence, these steep woods and lofty cliffs,
And this green pastoral landscape, were to me
More dear, both for themselves, and for thy sake.

If the poem is an ode, this is its cata-strophe, a culminating down-ward turn from the sublime to the bathetic. The suggestions that Wordsworth's "dear, dear Sister" or "dear, dear Friend" might be sub-stitutable for Nature as the soul of his moral being, and that he loves Nature even more for her sake, are afterthoughts, diffident to the point of insincerity.[18] In her "wild eyes" Dorothy shows him (twice) not her own "former pleasures," her earlier self—but his. In her "soli-tary walk" she is his *Doppelgänger*. His prayer that the winds "be free to blow against thee" approaches incoherence. Nature is seen all over again in her restorative aspect, "informing the mind," shielding it from calumny, insincerity, quotidian banality—as if "daily life" were everywhere, not just in cities, intrinsically "dreary" without her influ-ence, and as if this run-of-the-mill restoration were all that life's evils required. In *Beowulf* "dreary" meant "gory" or "bloody," and even much later it still implied extreme cruelty or grief. Wordsworth's later notion of "visionary dreariness" (*Prelude* 11), as opposed to "divine radiance," or perhaps to "blessed time," with its own senses of blood sacrifice and blood relationship, retains some lingering traces of this older and more sinister meaning (see above, and also the passage on "The Ancient Mariner" in chapter 3, for the relation between "blessing" and "blood"). He had, after all, just seen the remains of a murderer still hanging on a gibbet. Beneath the surface of existential despair lurks the shadow, or perhaps the memory, of some original crime or sin. Even here in "Tin-tern Abbey" this "dreary intercourse" is just what daily life is when it is *not* "full of blessings." Without redemptive sacrifice there must be cru-elty and grief, crime, and sin. These are the paragraph's strongest lines, but they fall short of what, coming here, they could be; and they add little to paragraphs 2 and 3. Indeed they weaken them, since Nature has become first a named entity, in paragraph 4, and now a capitalized one, replacing the "sylvan Wye." A dogmatic creed or "chearful faith" has taken root, displacing the fresh or raw experience, including of real dread, from earlier in the poem. Wordsworth's grand ambition to write a poetry of conversion has degenerated into the fervent hope that his sister will remember his exhortations with "healing thoughts of tender joy": that she will not forget having given witness to his "deeper zeal of holier love" for a Nature yet "more dear" on his return after long absence to those cliffs, woods, and green landscape with which the poem so impressively began, and to which we now also return—though changed, no doubt, from what we were when first we came among these Lines.

This turning back to human relationship is almost a back turned on it. The paragraph succeeds only in laying bare Wordsworth's severest shortcomings and confirming his deepest misgivings. The diminishing of Dorothy's status from that of his "dear, dear Sister" to that of an onlooker or talisman in his own autobiographical drama, indeed the mere appearance in the drama of another person, seems to devalue and sentimentalize them both. Instead of being the culminating embodiment of the claim that good acts arise from forms of beauty ("*this* is what a worshipper of Nature is like, what acts of loving-kindness are like . . ."), Wordsworth suddenly shows himself as a patronizing zealot. The feelings so discriminatingly analyzed elsewhere are exposed now as enactively impoverished, rather like J. S. Mill's embarrassing effusions about Harriet in his own *Autobiography* (and Mill was among Wordsworth's greatest disciples and converts).[19]

This matters because having claimed so much for poetry and nature in this poem Wordsworth seems to present us unwittingly with a counter-demonstration to his claims. Nor, one suspects, is this a merely contingent lapse. If poetry is a plea for conversion, a crossover form of restorative thought in which sensory impressions are turned into foundational and undeniable moral concepts, forms of good that change our behavior by flowing into our bloodstream—which is also to say, if poetry itself is the primary form of beauty-into-good, such that to absorb it is to be virtuous toward others and redeemed from or absolved of one's former wicked behavior—then how can we make sense of these claims if not with explicit reference to those others and that behavior, in all their fearful asymmetry? Yet not just this paragraph but the whole poem has repeatedly evaded such reference, in terms which even suggest that it cannot make it, which suggest that the corollary of making the claim is *not* making the reference. The reveries of solitary walkers *cannot* be unselfish because unselfishness, other-directedness, is not to be found in reveries but in behavior. This suggests a poetry whose force lies in promising redemption, not delivering it: in an *appearance* of redemptiveness. In fact delivery must be forever postponed, because the gap between beauty and good is actually the source of the poetry. If it were closed there would not be a poem, only a good man: a political actor, a brother, a father. This has to be a *form* of good, a hollow form: what it might feel like to become good, benevolent, saved, and so on, by contemplating beauty in nature and art—a kind of forlorn wish. Our attitudes to art were driven by this wish even into the modernist era; our attitudes to Nature still are.[20] The anxious impulse to write the impossible fifth paragraph gives the game away. Again: a form of beauty is not a form of good. To think it is, is one of the prime sins of modern art, and its admirers. Art won't deliver us from evil.

On the other hand if poetry can be a mode of thought in which the emphasis lies as it were in the fifth paragraph, in which the point lies in the satisfactory representation of human relationship, or of a God conceived as in the Psalm, as personal but protectively all-powerful, as our defense against death, including spiritual death, not just diurnal *ennui*, then for reasons explained in the introduction this has to be done metaphorically, not conceptually, and redemptiveness will become an entirely different kind of thing, lying in often-painful showing, not in being or doing. Again, this evasion of the metaphorical representation of relationship is a sign of Wordsworth's deep anxiety about poetry itself. Could it really be redemptive, convertive, and yet be poetry? Or was it philosophy he was writing—finding a new way of introducing concepts of virtue into the blood, replacing a lost religious conceptual core with a non-religious one? If metaphorical activity is pressed into this kind of transformative service, doesn't it just lose its solvent force *as* metaphorical activity? Is this not the death of poetry? The two most remarkable things about "Tintern Abbey" are how close it comes to achieving its aim, and how clearly it shows that the aim never can be achieved. It is the asymptote of redemptive poetry.

This poem, and therefore, if the poem is as central to Wordsworth's project as it seems, all his poetry, has two goals: to argue that (only) poetry can redeem us; and to redeem us. But it fails, on both counts. And the awareness of that failure, of the necessity of that failure, is intrinsic to it too. It also succeeds: if we just read it as "a failure" then we miss its achievement completely. Its achievement is to approach as close to success in its two goals as poetry ever has. Only that asymptotic success can enable us to measure its failure. Only such a wonderful near-realization of that ambition can truly, authentically, and plausibly show us that such an ambition must always arise in a post-Christian or post-faith world (for it is precisely *our* ambition)— and yet always be doomed; and that redemption can never be poetry's function even if there will always be those who think it could, maybe, one day. The trouble is, *our* trouble is (this *is* our trouble), that so many poets and non-poets have been influenced and encouraged to try again, and again. Wordsworth's greatness, and his legacy, for good or ill, was to have seen or enabled us to see both the vision and its inevitable unrealizability all at once, and to do so right at the start of the Romantic project, which is to say the modern project. Indeed the failure is intrinsic to the ambition: the disappointment to the dream. Romantic modernity is the belated condition of having both: of always failing and always trying again, knowing that we will fail. Realist modernity has to let go of the dream, in all its pervasive disguises and avatars. The fact that poetry cannot redeem us does not mean it cannot do *anything* for us.

3

SPONTANEITY IN KANT
AND WORDSWORTH

The search for conceptual redemption took another form in the most enduringly influential philosophical work of the era, indeed of modernity itself: Kant's first *Critique*. "Tintern Abbey" is a story about a hollow core; about empty forms of good; about something far too deeply interfused; about a soul somehow given back only to itself; about flying from some dreadful but indescribable inner space; about the need to find concepts to fill this space; about recoiling from the human. But philosophical conceptualism often found itself looking into that core or inner space with hope, not dread: seeing it as a source, not a threat. This hope could be more powerful in philosophical thought than in poetic, because Western philosophy's tendency since Plato has been to reify concepts, and what is reified can easily be deified. This tendency and this hope were more pronounced in the rationalist than in the empiricist tradition.

In the first half of this chapter we will follow the thread of Kant's argument about knowledge, judgment, freedom and will from its origins in earlier philosophers, through the coiled labyrinth of the first *Critique*, and into its apotheosis as "spontaneity" at the heart of that book, the "Transcendental Deduction." As with chapter 2, I have to hope specialist and non-specialist readers alike will bear with the somewhat tortuous reading processes of the second through fourth sections, in order to reach the more perspicuous material of the fifth and sixth: the portrayal in the "Third Antinomy" and the *Groundwork* of the spontaneous Kantian self: autogenous, autonomous and auto-redemptive. One half of one chapter may not seem much to devote to an account of the philosopher who shares this book's title. Kant's version of this originally Rousseauan model of the self, given enormous plausibility and influence by the sheer power of his intellectual apparatus, became definitive for much of philosophical modernity, especially in its continental European forms. One might say that any book about the modern self, whether in its redemptive or any other aspect, ought to mention his name in its title. The few pages on him here—and his name in the title—are meant only to intimate, mainly for the benefit of other non-philosophers, the presence of this vast parallel universe of thought, impinging only indirectly on the Wordsworthian tradition, but chiming strangely with one of its key motifs. This book is mainly about an English poet, and it assumes that poetry's modeling of the self is entirely as authoritative as philosophy's, and much more lifelike. But when our two principal forms of thought-in-language concur in their modeling, we would surely do well to pay at least some attention to each.

The second half of the chapter returns us to the *Lyrical Ballads*. In several of the volume's key poems, it turns out, as well as in *The Prelude* (to be examined in much more detail in chapters 4 and 5), the poets have recourse, without explicit reference to Kant, to a "spontaneous" model of the self suggestively similar to his in its reliance, ultimately, on a secret and impenetrable core from which moral imperatives mysteriously emerge. Redemption (to return to our touchstone) has become our responsibility; but because as a Christian mystery it was always ineffable, we still cannot explain it to ourselves now, even though it has supposedly become "ours." The same is true of all those other redemptive or quasi-redemptive impulses felt by such figures as the "Simon Lee" narrator or the Mariner. We have become opaque, inexplicable, to ourselves; and this opacity or inexplicability, this model of the self as both needing and lacking some kind of exposition or exposure, has become as essential to our sense of our humanity as the redemptive impulse itself. The feeling of not knowing where that impulse will come from, or when it will come, or if, makes the burden of moral responsibility very much heavier.

Self and Good
Descartes, Rousseau, Hume

Descartes set out to establish the meaning of the concept "I" (*"moi"*), first as self-certainty (the *cogito*), and secondly as the presence of will or free choice. "It is free will alone or liberty of choice which I find to be so great in me that I can conceive no other idea to be more great."[1] But this self-knowing and self-enacting "I" also contains within itself the concept of a perfect and therefore necessarily existent God, and the very existence of such a God-concept serves to confirm, in turn, the necessary reality and underlying goodness of the world. Kant's rebuttal of this final step, this last of the great ontological proofs of God's existence, was itself one of the decisive conceptual moments of modernity; but it was Descartes who had exposed "God" to this mortal blow in the very act of "proving" his existence, by resting the whole weight of belief on an ancient proof never previously so tested, never expected to function in this way, least of all on its own. A God who had become *only* an inner concept (Leibniz in the same spirit was to call him "the greatest geometer," the final reason, the perfect substance; while on the other hand the *philosophes* and Hume busily chipped away all the accidental attributes of this essential concept) was at the same time claimed as the *only* authenticator of the outer world (Spinoza simply thought he *was* the outer world, a view closer to Wordsworth's). When this prop collapsed, its partner, the concept of the self-authenticating and self-making "I," would then have to bear, again all alone, the entire weight of human experience, of freedom, of choice, of existence itself. Kant thought he could make this central Cartesian concept strong enough to do all that.

Still, while Descartes and Leibniz set the stage, the presiding genius of Romantic conceptualism was Rousseau. Here was the chief inspiration for Kant's moral philosophy. Not only was Rousseau the author of those seminal, unequivocally ethico-political treatises, the *Discourses* and the *Social Contract*; but also, in *Émile*, the first and most ruthless of all the *Bildungsromane*, he was the paramount engineer of human souls. In *Julie* he was the chronicler of the soul's search for *la source du sentiment et de l'être*,[2] of the inner eye or *œil perçant*, and of the general will to equality; while in the *Confessions* he was the initiator of an extraordinary secular Augustinianism, a doctrine of self-absolution and, ultimately, of self-redemption. Only Rousseau can forgive the sins of Jean-Jacques. Hardly a rationalist philosopher in the Cartesian mold: and yet Rousseau's achievement was to sentimentalize and moralize Descartes' *moi*—or Leibniz's "monad," his primary, autonomous world-particle. In Rousseau's hands the elaboration of the self-making "I," the crucial concept of modernity, became a task not for ontology but for deontology. In Rousseau the unfallen and eventually, perhaps, the redeemed self, the être that is *en dedans* or *intérieur,* is a chain of feelings, is *sentiment* itself—and this feeling, he is intuitively or introspectively certain, is *good,* composed in equal parts of compassion and self-esteem. The *moi,* or *being* itself, is essentially good feeling. Even the fallen self, brought down by agriculture, industry, and social chains, may be raised into a redeemed version of its unfallen state, may be forced to be free, or forcibly saved, by the grace of great lawgivers and teachers, who can actually change human nature, can help us to recover as "justice" and "virtue" that equality and goodness we once enjoyed experientially or unconceptually ("bliss was it in that dawn"). We were self-corrupted almost in a moment, in a strange moral singularity; but we can be self-redeemed (the *Confessions* are those of a self-justified sinner). The God, the faith, of the *Savoyard Vicar* is only a strong sentiment about the starry heavens above and the moral law within.[3]

But if Kant's ethical thought arose out of a deep assent to Rousseau, his metaphysics, at least at its creative core, arose out of his equally deep dissent from David Hume. The Humean self has no core; it is dispersed through its affections, its perceptions, and its all-important cementing associations, which together constitute the mind, rather than belonging to it: so dispersed, in fact, that famously it seems entirely to lack agency and even identity. Here there is no central source, no self-making or self-justifying *moi.* Many of Hume's analyses are not so far removed from Rousseau's. In the case of sympathetic benevolence I see you acting as a person in pain, and am led by my association of such actions with certain passions to feel the pain myself, and therefore act toward you as I would act for myself, or can imagine someone else acting toward me, in order to avert the pain (though Rousseau thought he could feel your pain more acutely than you can). Justice combines naturalness with artifice. It is partly derived from sympathy, but on reflection we see the benefit conferred on society by protection of life and property (though Rousseau thought this benefit was more like a shackle). Morals are ultimately a matter of sentiment: reason is ultimately a matter of sense (for Rousseau être is *sentiment*).

Hume differs from Rousseau, however, in two definitive respects: feeling for Hume is foundational but not "good"; and his ruthless elimination of all inners, essences, and noumena (including especially any kind of basic Leibnizian or Spinozan "substance") was entirely contrary to Rousseau's equally ruthless quest for the ethico-historical core of the self. Kant too dismissed monadic "substance." But despite his later contempt for the traditional religious practices and beliefs of his community, Kant's early upbringing made him dispositionally Pietist, which is to say neo-Lutheran. For him, as for the neo-Calvinist Rousseau, the self had to have a core, and a moral core at that. And yet for Kant and Rousseau this could not be a core of faith, a central point of will entirely subjected to the grace of God. For all his antagonism to "pure" reason, Kant was enough of a Leibnizian to see the self as a kind of monad, though not a "substantial" kind. He was never going to attempt some sort of constructive criticism of Humean association and imagination as the binding principles of a non-essential, extended self. But he was also enough of a Rousseauan to think of the rival monadic self as radically unsubjected, except to internal compulsions of its own. Kant's conceptual "good will" replaced Rousseau's sentimental "good feeling." God is the starry heaven analogous to but entirely outside and remote from this autonomous core. Kant re-thought the Cartesian inner or source as spontaneously self-making and self-enacting, autogenous and autonomous, but also, after Rousseau, as *good*.

The Punctual "Deduction" and the First *Critique*

An effective way to orient oneself in what may seem to non-specialists like a vast wilderness of technical obscurity and impenetrable intellect is to trace Kant's philosophical path in the *Critique of Pure Reason* from an anti-Humean metaphysics to a pro-Rousseauan morals, from an Enlightenment argument about the nature of the connection between the knowing self and the known world to a Romantic conclusion about the nature of the self in itself. This path takes us unerringly to and through the key junction-point in Kant's defining and foundational book: the elusive Northwest Passage of all his thinking. The fifty-page "Transcendental Deduction" or "Deduction of the Pure Concepts of the Understanding," usually referred to by specialists simply as "the Deduction," was that section of the *Critique* which cost him the most labor, as Kant tells us in the preface to the first edition of 1781 (Axvi); but even so he entirely rewrote it for the book's equally authoritative second edition of 1787. The composite, two-version Deduction has been called "one of the most impressive and exciting passages of argument in the whole of philosophy"; "the most important and central section of the whole Critique." While many non-Kantian philosophers may disagree with the first judgment, and some specialists may dispute the second, it does seem that we are here in the control room or nerve center of all Kant's thought about the self.[4]

Indeed its central position is clear enough from the structure of the *Critique*. In its very architecture the book represents precisely that punctual model of the self which it also discursively expounds. This labyrinthine arrangement takes the form of a series of nested or layered unequal pairs; figure 3.1 is intended to show how the vertical layers are also a kind of spiral in toward the Deduction, which is at the center of the model despite being only a third of the way through the book. At the top level or outer layer, following the introduction, are the two main segments or "Transcendental Doctrines" of the *Critique*. In Kant's forbidding terminology "transcendental philosophy" concerns itself not with objects, with how or how far we can be said empirically to "know" or experience them, as in Hume and his British predecessors: but with the very conditions under which experience itself is possible, with the way things *must* be, or rather the way the mind must be, for it to have experience, or for experience to be had, at all ("experience is cognition through connected perceptions," B161). The first segment, the "Transcendental Doctrine of Elements," is by far the larger: about 450 pages of the 600 or so in the Cambridge English-language text. Here Kant develops his own theory of knowledge, his own entirely new and enormously influential way of representing the knowing self or subject in its relation to the world or objects such that the very distinction we reflexively make between subject and object is the key to all philosophy. In the second segment, the "Transcendental

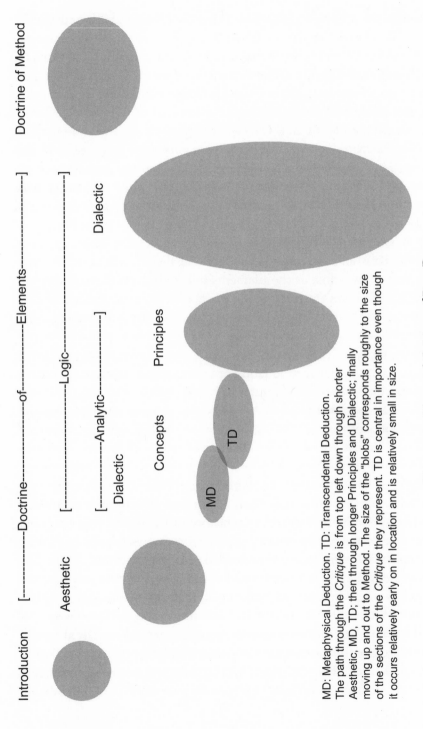

MD: Metaphysical Deduction. TD: Transcendental Deduction. The path through the *Critique* is from top left down through shorter Aesthetic, MD, TD; then through longer Principles and Dialectic; finally moving up and out to Method. The size of the "blobs" corresponds roughly to the size of the sections of the *Critique* they represent. TD is central in importance even though it occurs relatively early on in location and is relatively small in size.

Figure 3.1: Chart of *Critique of Pure Reason*

Doctrine of Method," less than a quarter of this length and far less important, he contrasts this new "critical" philosophy of "pure reason" with other kinds of philosophical thought or attitudes to thought, including, importantly, ethical kinds, or "practical reason." He also contrasts philosophy in general with mathematics, history, and other non-philosophical kinds of thought.

Leaving aside, then, this lesser second Doctrine, we can now subdivide the main Doctrine itself, the Elements—again into two unequal parts. This time the smaller one comes first; but this time it is not so unimportant. This is the "Transcendental Aesthetic," concerned with the mind in its passive or receptive aspect (*aesthesis* means sensation in Greek): its "sensibility" (*Sinnlichkeit*), its in-principle or *a priori* capacity to receive an "intuition" (*Anschauung*), or a "sense-impression" as an empiricist would say. "In principle": the Aesthetic amounts to less than a tenth of the whole of the Elements in length, and yet this short section is already revolutionary in its claim that the main determinant of our experience of the world, of our intuitions, is the *form* of our sensibility. In particular, the claim is that space and time are not external to us in some way, are not even concepts we impose on the outer world, but are actually part of the fabric of our sensibility itself, the forms of "outer" and "inner" sense respectively.

For all its novelty, and its vast subsequent influence on all subjectivist theories of time, including those of William James, Bergson, Husserl, and Proust, this has always been at best a controversial claim, even more so since the advent of quantum physics (it might also be said that John Locke anticipated Kant in thinking of time as an idea, not a thing). What is most enduringly important, and controversial, about the Aesthetic is its preliminary rehearsal of the fundamental Kantian maneuver—namely, to show experience as "transcendentally ideal," which is to say conditioned or enabled principally by how the mind is, how "ideas" are, not by how the real world is: and yet "empirically real," which is to say that it is still very much real experience for us, both of ourselves and of the world. This is not Hume, because there is an "us," and we ourselves are not merely constituted by but do really shape the world we experience (indeed the world *is* what we shape it as; Wordsworth also felt this, and surely would have even without Coleridge's post-Kantianism in his ear). And yet it is not Descartes, because the world is no more and no less real to us than we are to ourselves. At the same time the doctrine of transcendental idealism must involve the view that we can experience only appearances and not "things in themselves." We cannot ever know those. They do necessarily exist, and are indeed the "transcendental ground" of the appearances (A696/B724), which means something like their necessary basis in thought: but they are beyond our knowledge. We can know only our mediated or conditioned experience of them.

The archetypal enacting of this Kantian maneuver is to be found in the much longer (four-hundred-page) second Part of the Elements, the "Transcendental Logic," concerned with the mind in its active, concept-forming aspect. (It might be observed here that the very propensity to make such a fundamental division of the mind into active and passive, conceptual and sensible, is itself a marker not just of a philosophical as distinct from a poetic modeling of the self, but of a *dualist* model.) The Logic, as we might by now expect, is in two divisions. The second and slightly the longer of these is the "Transcendental Dialectic," and this is chiefly significant precisely for its "critique of pure reason." This is in an everyday sense the "critical" or destructive half of the Logic, the principal anti-Leibnizian or anti-rationalist section of the *Critique*, intended to expose the limitations and vanities of reason (*Vernunft*) when it spins out its own illusory metaphysical ideas or sophistical inferences without grounding them in intuition-experience (like a revving engine unconnected to the wheels, as Wittgenstein might have said). The soul is a real, simple, and unchanging substance; God must exist because the concept "God" contains the concept "existence"; there must be, or alternatively there cannot be, a first uncaused cause of the universe: in all these cases the reason is driven by its inherent need to find "unconditioned" or foundational principles, limiting terms, absolute beginnings or ends.

But Kant also wants to say that reason cannot help doing these things, and that its propensity to do them is instructive and even useful, as well as a basic human characteristic. The ideas of an immortal soul, or free will, or God, between them the triple core of what Kant calls "moral theology" (A632/B660), in particular, seem to be essential parts of the fabric of our minds, even the "cornerstones of morality and religion" (A466/B494). We seem to *need* them. Transcendental idealism tells us that we cannot know anything about the reality of these or any other "things in themselves," only about their appearances to us; and yet things in themselves not only do but also must "exist," in some sense, and some of them, a few, may be directly knowable, which is to say intelligible, not sensible. The self in its exercise of free will is one of these; the necessity of God is another. The purpose of the Dialectic, said Kant, was "to deny knowledge in order to make room for faith" (Bxxx): to deny reason its goal of filling the trans-sensory world with its own figments, crowding out any possible transcendent ground for our moral and aesthetic feelings.

We shall have to come back to this odd resiling from the strict application of transcendental idealism, this exceptional status Kant seems rather arbitrarily to afford to free will and faith such that metaphysics is allowed back into his system as a ground for morality. For now we must stay with that which those maverick parts of the Dialectic retreat *from*—namely, the positive or constructive first half of the Logic: the "Transcendental Analytic." The Analytic concerns itself with the ways in which the active, judging, concept-forming aspect of the mind, the understanding (*Verstand*), makes and imposes the *a priori* or conceptual framework of experience, something *prior* to experience, which is then filled out by the sensibility, the passive or intuition-receiving aspect dealt with in the Aesthetic. This is the central task of the *Critique*: to show how our concept-forming or concept-imposing faculty *also* allows us to get outside the magic circle of *purely* conceptual, analytic, or *a priori* certainty, in which enhancement of knowledge is essentially a quasi-definitional process of understanding concepts better (the Leibniz model), anso as to "synthetically" accommodate sense impressions, without being entirely constituted by or subservient to them as in Hume. "Synthetic" is from the Greek verb *sun-tithenai*, meaning "put together" or "place beside"; synthesis agglomerates knowledge whereas analysis, from *ana-luein*, loosens it up, disamalgamates it, untangles the conceptual knot so as to show the component threads. In Kant's model, sense provides the content; concepts provide the form; and synthetic *a priori* judgments (in which "two cognitions are bound together by their connection with a third in which they are both to be found," G95) alone link the two, making it possible for a *pure* concept also to *apply* to experience.

Naturally the Analytic is divided into two books. Book 2, twice as long as its companion at 120 pages or so, is the "Analytic of Principles." The Principles works through the specific detailed problems arising from the applications to experience of those twelve "categories" or basic concepts that according to Kant we employ in all judgments: concepts such as substance, causality, necessity, and negation. This exercise is no mere supplement. The relation between concepts and intuitions is complex enough that exemplification is essential to explanation. But still, the shorter "Analytic of Concepts," book 1 of the Analytic, is where Kant gets to the heart of that relation. His exposition of the twelve *a priori* categories necessary to all possible experience, basic to all synthetic *a priori* cognition, is, of course, in two chapters. In the first and shorter one, which he later calls the "metaphysical deduction" (B159), he lists his twelve categories, somewhat artificially (indeed quite arbitrarily) aligned with the twelve Aristotelian logical forms of judgment, and groups them under the headings of quantity, quality, relation, and modality (A70/B95). But this still does not *show* how the categories form our knowledge, or connect with intuitions. The crucial second chapter, heavily revised in 1787, is where this is done. The chapter is entitled "On the Deduction of the Pure Concepts of the Understanding"; its major and all-new second section in the 1787 (B) edition is entitled "Transcendental Deduction of the Pure Concepts of the Understanding."

Self-Making in the "Transcendental Deduction"

Formally, indeed almost scholastically, the Deduction is the second chapter of the first division of the second part of the first Doctrine of the first *Critique*. But it is also the heart of the Kantian labyrinth, its *cor cordium*. It is a *deduction* because the existence of the categories or "pure concepts of the understanding" has to be shown as rightfully or justifiably derived from the fact that we seem to understand our experiences. In the eighteenth-century Continental or Roman Law tradition, as Kant explains at the start of the Deduction (A84/B117), legal claims were settled by valid establishment of an entitlement ultimately *traceable back to* a question of fact (*quid facti*) but, more importantly, correctly *deduced from* the fact as a question of law (*quid juris*). The *train* of deduction must be valid. Now, the "claim" of the *Critique* is that categories are "pure," or "ideal," and yet have objective application. They are *a priori* and yet synthetic. Showing how this must be so is a process not of induction from the facts of experience but of deduction from the fact that we can *have* facts of experience.

And it is a *transcendental* deduction: the existence and nature of the categories are not induced from and thus ultimately *reduced to* the facts of experience, as in Locke or Hume; they are not "acquired through experience and reflection on it" (A85/B117). Otherwise, as Hume famously argued, causation would be merely a matter of constant conjunction. No matter how often you looked at one billiard ball striking another, you would never actually *see* "the cause" of the second one's movement, like some ghostly presence—only the first ball hitting the second, closely followed by the second one moving. Instead, then, the categories must be shown to be intrinsic to our very capacity to perceive a sensible world of objects, a world *of* sense that also *makes* sense: "it is already a sufficient deduction of them and justification of their objective validity if we can prove that by means of them alone an object can be thought" (A96). We see the movement of the second ball *as* an effect of the action of the first. We can cognize an object *as* an object, to take the most basic example, only if we *already have* the concept of "an object." "The objective validity of the categories, as *a priori* concepts, rests on the fact that through them alone is experience possible" (A93/B126). "The fact that": this is the only question of fact, the only *quid facti*, back to which the validity of the categories is traceable by the *quid juris* of the Deduction.

What the Deduction actually deduces is that in order to have experiences, in order to be the experience-having beings that we evidently are, we must actively "bring intuitions under concepts," as Kant puts it earlier (A51/B75). This activity of bringing intuitions under concepts, of applying concepts to intuitions, is what Kant calls "judging." Indeed the very word *Kritik* is rooted in the Greek *krinein*, which means "decide," "choose" or "judge" (Kant is sometimes said to have found the term in Lord Kames's 1762 *Elements of Criticism*, a treatise on aesthetics; and he returned to aesthetics in his final "critical" work, the "Critique of Judgment," whose title is therefore in effect "Judgment of Judgment"). The moment of truth, the crisis of judgment, is when the intuition is brought under the concept. The whole of Kant's "critical philosophy" turns on this critical moment.

Now we must focus the lens yet more sharply for the last time: on the second and third sections of the 1781 edition (A), later revised into the second section of the 1787 edition (B)—that is, about twenty pages in each version.[5] What Kant tries to show in this crucial two-version passage is the key to everything he tries to show in his philosophy: that the moment of judgment, of bringing intuitions under concepts, that single most vital act of our understanding, is both the moment when objects are created for us *as* objects, and at the same time our single most vital act of *self*-creation. It is not just that the world is what we make it; it is that *we* are what we are *in* making it. In knowing objects as objects, we also and in the very same act know ourselves as ourselves. The *fact* is that we have experiences, connected perceptions, of a world of objects (not as they are "in themselves," of course, but as they appear to consciousness—yet still these are real experiences of real objects); the *deduction* is that our minds, our very selves, must be constituted in a certain way in order for this to happen. The Deduction, as Peter Strawson profoundly observed, is not only an argument but "also an explanation, a description, a story."[6] It is the story of the modern self: a self that is not just structural but *ethical*, indeed quasi-divine.

The second section of the first edition or A version (A95–130), entitled "On the *a priori* grounds for the possibility of experience," opens its account of the "pure concepts of the understanding," the twelve fundamental categories, the "ancestral . . . original and primitive concepts" (A82/B108) from which all others are "derivative," such as causation, negation, necessity, existence, and substance, by arguing that all "intuitions" or impressions of objects must be brought under these categories in order for experience to be possible at all. "By means of them alone can an object be thought" (A97). In other words, these concepts must be applicable to objects, or they would be just the empty forms of concepts. Thus they *need* objects, so to speak, in order to be what they are (the fact that they evidently *are* more than just empty forms shows that objects exist for us). Here is the Deduction's first formulation of how this interaction, the process of "understanding" (not just thinking), actually happens (A97):

> If therefore I ascribe a synopsis to sense, because it contains a manifold in its intuition, a synthesis must always correspond to this, and receptivity can make cognitions possible only if combined with spontaneity. This is now the ground of a threefold synthesis, which is necessarily found in all cognition: namely, that of the apprehension of the representations, as modifications of the mind in intuition; of the reproduction of them in the imagination; and of their recognition in the concept.

Even in an English translation this passage gives an accurate enough impression of the book's unfortunate style, clogged with idiosyncratic terms and usages. Kant's oeuvre is vast, and he can write clearly and inspiringly ("crooked timber of humanity," "starry heavens above, moral law within"), but, significantly, not here, not at the very center of his thought. This is a philosophy heavily reliant on "concepts," not so much in the ordinary non-Kantian sense of that term as in the sense of technical verbal instruments: a far cry from the concepts we actually live with, which would need to be dissolved and remade to fit into this neo-scholastic vocabulary.[7] A view of the self-expressible only in such terms will sooner or later run up against its own limitations, against conditions of the self it cannot express, as we shall shortly see. But still the passage is substantially of the greatest importance within Kant's model.

What it says, in plainer English, is that having experience or "cognition" of the world of objects, the physical world about us, is a threefold combining or "synthetic" process. First (as elaborated in A98–100), our receptive sensory "intuitions" of objects are "synoptic" and "manifold"; they give us a single overall picture or impression of a highly complex, multi-faceted piece of reality. But in order to achieve this overall manifold impression, these "representations" of reality as "appearances," we have to be aware first of the myriad component sub-impressions *as* components, which impinge on our senses in successive micro-moments but nevertheless seem to hang together as the components of one single thing: ultimately, of one spatial world. If we did not have this sense of smaller bits making up the larger object through a series of impressions in time, we would not have the impression we do have of complex objects or a complex reality, but just of solid unchanging homogeneous blocks, indeed of reality itself as one solid block. Time as the form of inner sense enables us to perceive space as the form of outer sense (the arguments of the Aesthetic lie behind this view). All these are "modifications of the mind in intuition"; this is the "synthesis of apprehension" or "sense." (This is indeed consciousness seen as a stream.)

Secondly, as elaborated in A100–102 and then in the third section (A120–21), these incoming, sequential mini-impressions have to be retained somehow in the mind. Just because they come to us in successive micro-moments of time, the earlier ones have to stay with us somehow while we are receiving the later ones, so that the whole can *seem* whole even though it comes to us in discrete bits. The earlier appearances thus have to be revived or "reproduced" when they are no longer actually present themselves, and the synthetic faculty that does this is called "the imagination." This reproducing is itself an activity; the imagination is not passive. But it has still more to do. Besides recalling earlier appearances, it also has to sort or combine them, with each other and with later ones, so as to make associated bundles of representations. This associating capacity makes the imagination not only reproductive but also "productive." Only it can grasp the bundles of representations as *in principle* associable, so as to bring those bundles under concepts; the imagination thus has a crucial and active intermediary role to play between sense and understanding (indeed self-understanding, as we shall see in a moment).

Thirdly, and most importantly, as elaborated in A103–110 and (third section) A121–128, we can recognize or re-cognize these agglomerated representations only "in the concept." Only in bringing them under the concept, our most significant mental activity, do we achieve cognition, understanding of the object *as* an object. But we cannot even bring them under a concept unless we are at some level aware of them as *our* sequence of micro-moments: a sequence belonging to a single consciousness. Otherwise (the Hume problem), how is it that we seem to know that the old representations now being reproduced were received by the same self now doing the reproducing? Or how would we know ourselves as something more unified than just a welter of impressions? (B134–35 raises this question more clearly.) Unification of the manifold can be done only by a unified self. There has to be some ground in which the unifying happens. The very existence of the unifying concepts of all cognition "transcendentally" presupposes such "apperception," such perception of perception, such self-awareness. Yet at the same time this self-awareness reciprocally derives from concepts. We think of ourselves as unified only because we are aware of our cognitive activity, which is to say our active applying of concepts to intuitions. "Thus the original and necessary consciousness of the identity of one-self is at the same time a consciousness of an equally necessary unity of the synthesis of all appearances in accordance with concepts" (A108); "the synthetic unity of consciousness is . . . something under which every intuition must stand in order to become an object for me" (B138); "only because I ascribe all perceptions to one consciousness can I say of all perceptions that I am conscious of them" (A122).

The imagination here plays its vital mediating role. Its capacity to seize all appearances as in principle associable, as synthesizable manifolds, is "the pure form of all possible cognition," enabling our idea of a unified self as the ground of all cognition (A118–23). If instead of "all appearances" we simply say "nature," which is only the sum of all appearances, and not a "thing in itself," then the unity we perceive in nature consists "solely in the radical faculty of all our cognition"—namely, "transcendental apperception" (A114). When we think we are aware of nature as a whole, of "all objects of all thought," what we are really aware of, what the imagination shadows forth to us, is the identity of ourselves. In these terms the "presence that disturbs" Wordsworth in "Tintern Abbey" is indeed his own. "We ourselves," Kant famously declares at this point, "bring into the appearances that order and regularity in them that we call nature" (A125); "without understanding there would not be any nature at all" (A126); "the understanding is itself the source of the laws of nature . . . is itself the legislation for nature" (A126–27).

The Problem of Spontaneity

Now we come to the point of this long account. In this subtle, highly if idiosyncratically articulated, and (at least in intention) transparently comprehensive account of experience, it is easy to overlook one very important discontinuity. We now know that our experience of the world, of nature, of objects, is a matter of (i) passively receiving incoming intuitions or representations through the senses, (ii) retaining and actively bundling or associating them through the imagination, and (iii) bringing them under concepts so as to recognize them as objects, nature, etc. The third of these functions and, in one of its aspects, the second, are both active and *constitutive*. In these actions we come not only to recognize the world as itself but also to recognize ourselves as ourselves: indeed to *be* ourselves. The second recognition is determinative of the first. Bundling intuitions and bringing them under concepts turn out to be not just the most important things we do but in a vital sense the things that make us what we are, even as we make nature what it is. Yet the microscope Kant so systematically, not to say schematically, turns on "us" seems to be put aside when it comes to examining these all-important self-constitutive actions. Where do *they* come from?

According to the initiating passage in the A account, quoted earlier, "receptivity can make cognitions possible only if combined with spontaneity." And toward the end of the account (A126) we read Kant's summary: that he has

> explained the understanding in various ways—through a spontaneity of cognition (in contrast to the receptivity of the sensibility), through a faculty for thinking, or a faculty of concepts, or also of judgments—which explanations, if one looks at them properly, come down to the same thing.

On the one hand there is "receptivity," on the other, activity of various kinds, or under various names for the same thing. Judgment, thought, concept-making: these are all aspects of the active, imaginative-and-cognitive functions the passage has been concerned to articulate. And again that word: "spontaneity." Cognition, apparently, happens out of nowhere. The actual business of collecting and ordering impressions and then conceptualizing them is mysterious: just *spontaneous*. We just *do* it.

This striking lacuna in an otherwise exhaustive exposition is even more apparent in the B account, Kant's second edition, in which he tries to tell the Deduction's story of the self with less "obscurity" (Bxxxviii). Right at the start he tells us that the "combination of a manifold . . . is an act of the spontaneity of the power of representation" that "can be executed only by the subject itself, since it is an act of its self-activity" (*Selbsttätigkeit*) (B129–30). Only a few lines later he is explaining, much earlier in this account than in the A version, since "apperception" or self-consciousness plays a far more central role in cognition in this edition of the Deduction, the necessity for self-consciousness as the basis of all perception, prior to all thought. "I call it the pure apperception," he says of this self-consciousness. Such apperception is "an act of spontaneity" in that "it cannot be regarded as belonging to sensibility" (B132). Being able to think "I think" is the purest foundation of selfhood, and the thought comes to us "spontaneously," without any apparent source. A later passage from B (150–52) further emphasizes this critical linkage between spontaneity and the active powers of imagination and understanding. The "receptivity" of sensibility is first contrasted with the "spontaneity" of understanding; and the synthesizing work of the productive or "figurative" imagination is then called "an exercise of spontaneity, which is determining and not, like sense, merely determinable." "Insofar as the imagination is spontaneity," he adds, "I also call it the productive imagination." The imagination thus finds itself elevated in Kant's model of experience to a status second only to and essentially precursive of full conceptual understanding (and in post-Kantian accounts, such as Coleridge's, to even dizzier and mistier heights). Meanwhile an important conclusion of the B version is that we cannot know ourselves as we "really are" in ourselves, any more than we can know things as *they* are "in themselves." All I can know, or cognize, of my real self is that I spontaneously combine appearances (B158–59). "I do not have yet another self-intuition . . . of the spontaneity of which alone I am conscious" (B157–58n). "I am conscious of myself not as I appear to myself, nor as I am in myself, but only *that* I am" (B157). All we know of our real selves, in other words, is spontaneity.

To sum up: at the heart of Kant's philosophy is the *Critique of Pure Reason*; at the heart of the *Critique* is the Transcendental Deduction; at the heart of the Deduction is an account of the experiencing self as a conscious, legislating agent, using both figures and concepts to determine both nature and itself; and at the heart of this account, this self, is the single, unexplained, opaque concept of "spontaneity."[8]

Spontaneity and Freedom
The *"Third Antinomy,"* and the **Aeneid**

Before briefly considering the enormous implications of this epistemological hiatus for Kant's moral philosophy, we should perhaps pause for a moment to recall, as Kant does not (nor do any of his principal

English-language commentators, so far as I am aware), that the German and English terms *Spontaneität* and *spontaneity* derive alike from the Latin *sponte*. Etymology and philology are provinces visited more frequently by literary scholars than by philosophers. Kant's silence on his reasons for using this key term possibly indicates among other things a kind of blindness to the ways in which concepts live in us and, indeed, make us. It would be easy to say that this blindness to the diachronic historical life of concepts, as opposed to their synchronic definitional content, which is in effect a serious *loss* of concepts, is a modern or post-Enlightenment phenomenon, but it is already there in Socrates. It is a loss incurred as the price of clarity, or precision, when one shifts from poetry to philosophy, from metaphorized concepts deployed in "working" lives to unmetaphorized concepts deployed in schematic models of life. Nevertheless some philosophers, such as Aristotle, or Wittgenstein, or Gadamer, are more aware than others of this price, and therefore of the nature of philosophy as distinct from one of its neighboring modes of thought. Kant was not one of the more aware.

In any case, *sponte* is the ablative form of the "defective" noun *spons*, which exists only in the genitive and ablative cases. *Sponte* means "of free will," "of one's own accord," "of one's self," "voluntarily," "willingly." Perhaps the term's most notorious occurrence is in *Aeneid* IV, when the hero tells his furious and incredulous lover that "*Italiam non sponte sequor*": "I do not seek Italy of my own free will" (line 361). Aeneas justifies himself to Dido, most unsuccessfully, on the grounds that his own will has become merely a vessel for, indeed identical with, that of Jupiter. He has no choice but to abandon her; he has already abandoned the very capacity to choose. This submerging of the human will in the divine Will uncannily resembles Augustine's account of the process, or condition, in *Confessions*—and Augustine tells us in that book that Dido was in his adolescence a figure for the ardent, burning self he later saw he had to transcend, whereas Aeneas, presumably, though Augustine does not say this, was a model for him of the resolute, self-abnegating, and potentially fanatic man of faith he sought to become, and indeed finally did become. *Sponte deum* was a traditional Latin expression meaning "by the will of the gods"; both Virgil and Augustine concern themselves at the heart of their thought with how we inject God into an emptied-out space at the core of the self; post-Christians, conversely, concern themselves with what to inject into the space when God is taken back out. The verb *spondere* means "to bind, engage," or "solemnly and sacredly promise or pledge oneself," and is circuitously derived from the Greek *spendo*, "pour out," as in a sacred libation; the sense of "libation" crops up frequently in Latin usages of *spondeo*. Here is a holy commitment, then, a pledging or pouring or emptying out of the self in recognition of God: or alternatively, analogously, and in the end contrarily, a model of the self as having at its core a mysterious and inscrutable sacred fountain or source. From this holy and mysterious chasm, this mighty fountain momently forced, this *will* that may be divine, human, or an inscrutable combination of the two, flows the sacred river of the self.

This is therefore an extraordinary term for Kant to put, spontaneously, at the core of *his* model of the self. Was an adolescent Pietism still exerting its metaphorical power over him? So far this chapter has concerned itself with the first *Critique*, not the second; with pure not practical reason; with epistemology not ethics. But in the end the two cannot be separated, nor did Kant think that they should be. The free will "must be viewed as also giving the law to itself," he wrote, famously, in the *Groundwork of the Metaphysic of Morals* (1785);[9] "giving the law to *the* self," one might say. The two editions of the first *Critique* (1781 and 1787) straddle the writing and publication of the *Groundwork*. We will therefore follow for a while some of the clues offered in the Deduction as they lead out beyond it, into Kant's preliminary discussion of free will and the self in the Dialectic, and then into the *Groundwork* and the second and third *Critiques* (1788, 1790).

One of the chief and longest tasks of the Dialectic is to expose the contradictions or "natural antithetic" that reason spins out of itself on certain key subjects, when its "glittering pretensions" exceed "all the bounds of experience" (A463/B49). These four "antinomies of pure reason" are analyzed in a one-hundred-page chapter. The point of each Antinomy is to show that its two theses, or properly its thesis and antithesis (for example, there must be a first beginning of the world; there cannot be a first beginning of the world), are not contradictories, as pure reason supposes, one of which must be false and one true. Instead *both* may be false—or true. The Third Antinomy[10] is about one of these subjects—namely, causality. Either there must be an uncaused cause or there cannot be an uncaused cause, says reason. Either everything in the world happens solely in accordance with the laws of nature, in an infinitely long string of empirical cause and effect in which, suggestively, there is "no freedom" (antithesis), or there must have been some other kind of initiating or "intelligible" (not empirical) cause, outside the laws of nature, to start the string off (thesis). This would be "another [kind of] causality through freedom," "an absolute causal *spontaneity* beginning from itself" (A446/B474, emphasis added). In this latter case "reason creates the idea of a spontaneity, which could start to act from itself" (A533/B651).

The central Kantian notion of freedom (*Freiheit*) is thus momentously introduced as a "thesis" into his accounts of causality and of experience: *and associated at once with the notion of spontaneity*. A key ethical and political term starts its life in the major sequence of Kant's opus as a strange and inexplicable kind of causality, a generative absolute. But if he wants to validate this strange force Kant has to resolve the Antinomy's apparent contradiction. This freedom exists only if the purely empirical, laws-of-nature account of causality can be shown to be incomplete. The resolution follows (though questionably, as many have pointed out) from the very doctrine of "transcendental idealism," from Kant's model of the experiencing self.

Our experience consists of "appearances," intuitions of objects, bundled together by the imagination and then brought under concepts by the understanding. We do not have experience of "things in themselves," of what Kant calls the "noumenal" as opposed to the "phenomenal" world (*phainomena* are "appearances" in Greek, things perceived by the fallible senses, whereas *noein* means "to perceive by the intelligence"). We have experience just in the way we have experience and not in some other way. A "thing in itself," a noumenon, is something like a hypothetical construction of how an object *might* be when *not* experienced by sense as appearances in space and time, and then conceptualized in the way we do this: an object as it might be independently of all human experience, or just of all experience of any kind. Put another way, a noumenon is a "boundary concept" (A255/B311): not exactly a "thing," but our idea of a thing as abstracted from all our actual cognitions of things (A252–53). This makes the noumenon a kind of "correlate of the unity of apperception" (A250/B306–9), that unity of the self so necessary for experience, known of from the fact that we *have* experience, but still known only from appearance, still only *corresponding* to some posited "real" self we cannot ever know *in* itself. Still, "it follows naturally from the concept of an appearance that something must correspond to it which is not in itself appearance" (A251). This "something," though not actually a *thing*, and maybe not even real, is nevertheless intelligible *and necessary* to the understanding—for "the world is a sum of appearances, *and so there has to be* some transcendental ground for it, i.e., a ground thinkable merely by the pure understanding" (A696/B724, emphasis added). Kant's account of things in themselves, including of the self in itself, is notoriously unsatisfactory. Quite often in the *Critique* noumena seem to be real things lying behind but always inaccessible to the ordinary world of appearances and to our knowledge; at other times they seem to be no more than necessary conceptual constructs enabling us to make sense of experience. And yet the necessity that they "exist," in some sense, is entirely crucial to his resolution of the Antinomy.

For if appearances were just the same as things in themselves, if phenomena and noumena were identical, there would be no Third Antinomy, because the contradiction would be resolved in favor of its antithesis. Nature would simply determine everything. Causality would be fully natural and would go "all the way down." And Kant simply cannot allow this. He has to leave room for the thesis: "for if appearances are things in themselves, then freedom cannot be saved" (A536/B564). And he clearly wants to save freedom, which is, so far, no more than the idea of spontaneous causality. So in order to show once again that appearances are *not* the same as things in themselves, he embarks on a long, repetitive argument, dangerously close to circularity (A534/B562–A558/B586), to show that without "transcendental freedom," the very *idea* of a self-caused cause, of a spontaneity that can start to act from itself, we would have no *concept* of "practical freedom," of free choice or *arbitrium liberum*, of a "faculty of determining oneself from oneself" independently of physical necessity (A533–54/B561–62). ("Ideas" are what reason produces; "concepts" are produced by the understanding.) We do after all seem to have "inner determinations which cannot be accounted at all among impressions of sense" (A546/B575). Most importantly, we have the sense of an "ought," which seems to rest on the idea that we can produce something new entirely out of itself (an ought is what did not happen but should have and so in principle still could). Our sense of an "ought" is strong evidence of intelligible or transcendental as opposed to natural causality: causality resting on "grounds of the understanding" (A545/B573). "The ought expresses a species of necessity" and "a connection with grounds which does not occur anywhere else in the whole of nature" (you cannot say "the volcano ought not to have erupted"). It "expresses a possible action, the ground of which is nothing other than a mere concept" (A547/B575). The "ought," free choice, practical freedom: these refer us to an idea, and in doing so show us that appearances are not the same as things in themselves.

This does not prove that freedom can be saved: only that it is not contradictory to say that it can. Reason "with complete spontaneity . . . makes its own order according to ideas"; "it even declares actions to be necessary that yet have not occurred" (A548/B576). Its "faculty of beginning a series of occurrences from itself" (A554/B582) exists outside the empirical world, although the occurrences themselves do not. We have a notion of human agency outside empirical "character" ("there were many factors influencing him, including his own nature, but still, he *should not* have lied"). If we did not have this, if we could not conceive of an "ought," then freedom would disappear. All this seems to Kant to show that appearances are not things in themselves, that there is a transcendental idea of freedom, and that therefore causality through freedom could co-exist with causality through nature.

Freedom, Faith, and the Self in the *Groundwork*

Kant said the Dialectic was meant to deny reason in order to make room for faith. Its true function is to deny natural causality in order to make room for freedom. Through the tiny conceptual gap created by the mere possibility of such a denial Kant drove an entire system of ethics. Faith itself, indeed, is rarely mentioned in the *Critique*. The standard proofs of God's existence are refuted, though not without sympathy. What is left of an attitude to God is as to an intellectual requirement, a necessary belief, without which the really important ideas, which are those of morality and freedom, would be ineffective. It is the moral law that leads us to propose the idea of God, not the other way around. "We will not hold actions to be obligatory because they are God's commands, but will rather regard them as divine commands because we are internally obligated to them" (A819/B847). We have "the concept of God as the highest good," according to the *Ground-work*, "solely from the *idea* of moral perfection that reason frames a priori and connects inseparably with the concept of a free will."[11] A "moral theology" is Kant's goal; "the thesis of the existence of God belongs to doctrinal belief" (A826/B854).

Kantian ethics exemplifies and anticipates a modern secularism that still feels the subconscious obligation to acknowledge a God it no longer believes in, partly to avoid recognizing its real belief, which is in its own quasi-divinity. Kant himself moves closer to this position at the end of the third *Critique* (*Of Judgement*: in German, *Kritik der Urteils-kraft*; 1790, 1793), combining his account of aesthetic judgment, of our feelings of beauty and sublimity, with his account of the moral law, in the claim that aesthetic and moral judgments alike "have something similar to a religious feeling about them," some sort of "veneration."[12] *Urteil* is cognate with "ordeal," and translates as "means of adjudicating, reaching a verdict, apportioning a share." *Kraft* is "power" or "capacity." So how do we judge—from what deep inner place do our judgments of the outer world come? Sublimity, for example, is "only in our mind," and only by extension from this idea do we conceive the sublimity of a being who has given us such a capacity for judging nature and for feeling our own sublimity in comparison to nature.[13] We have the very concept of God from the *idea* of our superiority to nature (and natural causality). "Nature is here called sublime merely because it raises the imagination to the point of presenting those cases in which the mind can make palpable to itself the sublimity of its own vocation even over nature."[14] Reverence for what exactly, then? *Heiligachtung* is a reinforced concept, combining the idea of the holy with that of an attentiveness to the moral law that is already reverent. What we revere as holy, in the end, is ourselves. We displace the object of a religious feeling emanating from our own minds into those very minds themselves. As for beauty, Kant is careful, where Wordsworth is not, to distinguish between forms of beauty and forms of good. One pleases the senses; the other is a matter of concepts[15]—never of habituated virtues, as Wordsworth almost says. And yet even Kant cannot help associating them at a deeper level. "The beautiful is a symbol of the morally good," he argues: the paradigm case in which a deeply interfused concept is linked intuitively to a "sensible sign."[16] Nature and art are systems of signposts pointing to something beyond or beneath what even the reason can say. So their value ultimately lies outside them, in what they refer us to, not in what they are themselves (this is an ancient and deep philosophical attitude to art). But what do they refer us to?

The faith Kant was trying to make room for had little to do with God and everything to do with an exalted sense of the free self. As he also says toward the end of the third *Critique*,[17] two of the three "pure ideas of reason," God and the immortal soul, are *also* two of the three great "matters of faith" (as opposed to mere *articles* of faith, which are the stuff of doctrine); while the third pure idea of reason, freedom, is the only idea that is also a fact, though its ends, the goods to be achieved through it, are the third great matter of faith. In the case of the second of these matters of faith his task in the *Dialectic* is again a negative one: to show that the self of apperception cannot be the substantial "soul" of Descartes or Christian theology. But in the third and most important case the task is both positive and compensatory. In making room for freedom-as-a-matter-of-faith Kant is also offering alternatives to those conceptions of God and the soul that he rejects in the *Dialectic*. His sustained attempt to do all this begins, as we have already seen, in the Third Antinomy; it culminates in the *Groundwork*.

There is only one unconditionally, limitlessly *good* thing, only one really *holy* (*heilige*) thing, whether in the world or beyond it, and that is a good will (*ein guter Wille*) (49–50, 77, 88).[18] Courage, intelligence, power, wealth, happiness, all the goods of endowment, temperament, and luck are only as good as their effects on our minds and actions. But the very activity of willing (*das Wollen*) in itself (*an sich*), as opposed to its effects, to its natural or worldly consequences: *that* has "absolute worth," that *is* character (*Charakter*), that is the magnetic field of the self which determines the orientation of all its other goods, straightens out or "makes right" (*berichtige mache*) their "influence" (*Einfluß*) on our basic disposition (*Gemüt*). Nothing quite straight (*nichts ganz Gerades*) can ever be made of this crooked timber (*krummen Holz*), as Kant famously wrote elsewhere;[19] but the will is, so to speak, the metal frame or jointer, the *beau ideal*, to which the timber is accommodated, and so made more *gemütlich*. The timber feels that it is crooked; it seems to remember a Carpenter who died to make it straight; now like the wooden puppet in the story it must *make itself* straight, become a real child, redeem itself. (But what are real children like? Well, we all know that, because we were children. They also lie, sometimes.) The metaphor changes its tenor as the activity of willing becomes a *thing*, called The Will; but from these first paragraphs (49–50) the *Ground-work* is organized dualistically around its basic singularity: a sacred, quasi-divine goodness at its core or informing all its thought.

Still, perhaps this time the activity at its source, in the secret inner cave where the divinity dwells, is not just spontaneous. The will itself, crucially, is said to be "determined" (*bestimmen*) by "respect" or "esteem" (*Achtung*) for "law" (*Gesetz*). And what *this* means is that willing is just necessitated, impelled by a force as irresistible as gravity—namely, a certain *feeling* we have toward a certain *idea* of reason. "Duty is the necessity of an action from respect for law" (55). *Gesetz* means something like "statute" or "principle"; and in this case the "principle of volition," our esteem for which so irresistibly impels our will, is the linchpin of the book: "act as if the maxim of your action were to become by your will a universal law of nature" (73). Whatever you will must be such that you could will it for and on behalf of all beings at all times, as if it were a law of nature and you were the divine legislator. We can leave aside here the rather important question as to whether this actually *is* a sound moral principle (although it probably is not: many trivial or repugnant maxims could be universalized). Our interest is in Kant's model of moral impulsion. We are not being forced to be free, exactly, but the idea of a universalized will is seen as instantly determinative. It metamorphoses at once from a concept *via* a feeling into an "ought," a felt duty to act. The action itself may for some natural or contingent reason not happen, as Kant rather breezily concedes (ought implies can, as he was to argue in an important passage from the second *Critique*,[20] but it cannot impel action). But otherwise it will—he is confident of this—and then causality has magically crossed the freedom-barrier between intellect and nature. Goodness is just the propensity to grasp the categorical or unconditional nature of the driving imperative, not the resultant action. If I *will* the good I *am* good.

But what about that certain feeling? In a revealing footnote (56), Kant defends himself against the charge that *Achtung* is merely an escape-hatch feeling-term, saving him from having to provide a properly conceptual account of the good will filling all the space between reason and action. *Achtung*, he says, is just the name for my "consciousness" (*Bewußtsein*) of "immediate determination of the will by means of the law," of "the *subordination* of my will to a law without the mediation of other influences." But now there is nothing filling the space at all. *Achtung* (*reverentia* in Latin, as for example in Aquinas) is a concept with far more dynamic potential than, given his preconceptions about the self, Kant could ever find in it. His explanation is entirely reductive or dismissive of the important feeling he cites. A rich concept becomes no more than a thin smear (not even a lubricant) on the steel surface of an irresistible idea. And the idea is of a universal will to good (Rousseau's general will is not so far behind this). Our own wills are entirely subordinated to this idea of reason, as Aeneas' and Augustine's were to the idea of God. Kant is half-aware of the threat to his system posed by feeling, of how much moral life he is brushing under the carpet in his account of moral impulsion, but the very nature of his model prevents him from exploring this.

The third of the key ideas in the *Groundwork*, after the good will and the universalizability maxim, is the idea of a *person*. This is Kant's term (it is the same word in German) for the rational moral being, abstracted from all his other human and animal qualities, who is capable of feeling this "respect" for reason's law. This very same capability for seeing the categorical or end-in-itself nature of the moral imperative is what makes the person an end in *him*self, or herself. Beings who think like this are said to have "dignity" or "worth" (*Würde*) (84) and must be treated with the same respect as that accorded to the law by other beings who think like this. The collectivity of all beings who think like this and who in subordinating their wills like this to the moral law also at the same time legislate for all other beings like themselves is called by Kant the "kingdom of ends" (83). The will of such self-legislating beings is said to be *autonomous*. Such a will is the "supreme lawgiver" (82), bound only by itself, although since the laws it gives are universal it is really bound by them in being bound by itself. A complete fusion of law and will has taken place in this "supreme principle of morality" (89).

The *Groundwork*'s account of good will, universalizability, and the autonomous person has now come full circle, and we are back to freedom. Autonomy *is* freedom of the will; "a free will and a will under moral laws are one and the same" (94–95); autonomy is the will under moral law. The free will is the will that is constrained by reason: its unfreedom under reason's law is at the same time its freedom to make its own universal law. But then freedom, as the Third Antinomy intimated, is also causality. Ought implies can. To feel reason's imperative is to act on it—again, material nature permitting—and that means that from the perspective of nature the will is an uncaused causer. Practical reason, moral reason, "has causality with respect to its objects" (96), just as the person, the *"homo noumenon,"* is "the subject of morally practical reason" (these last two quotations are from the 1797 work *Metaphysics of Morals*[21]). Practical reason is pure reason in action.

This brings us to the greatest crux in Kant's ethics, even in the formation of the modern concept of the self. The first *Critique* told us repeatedly that we cannot know the *noumena*, things in themselves. Likewise at the very core of Kant's ethics is the idea of a noumenal self that cannot know itself—except in acting. It *does* act—somehow. In these final pages of the *Groundwork* Kant reworks the material of the first *Critique*. Just because we cannot know things in themselves, but only appearances, we "assume," we "feel," some distinction between the world of sense and the world of understanding. Indeed this feeling or assumption "perhaps" (*allenfalls*) originates in our sense that there is a difference between those representations that are given to us from outside in which we are passive, and those that we "produce from ourselves" in which we are active (the analysis is far less conceptually fine-grained, more reliant on "feelings" and "perhapses," than in the first *Critique*: because, one cannot help thinking, Kant is so intent on establishing his concept of the self).

As with the outer world, so with the inner: we likewise assume "something else" (*etwas anderes*)—namely, the *Ich* (the *moi*, the inner self, the *ego*)—lying beneath the appearances of our nature as their "ground." This *Ich* belongs to the intellectual world, the world of things in themselves, so we cannot know it. Although its actions happen in the world of sense, it is itself "independent of the determining causes" of that world, deriving its actions only from reason and the moral law. This derivation *is* freedom, which therefore we also cannot understand except in its effects in the world. Freedom is "only an idea of reason" (102), whereas nature is "a concept of the understanding," proving its reality only in experience. The two causal systems co-exist, as the Third Antinomy had suggested, but the actions of the free will are reason's "pure self-activity." They cannot be explained. How the idea of freedom is possible "can never be seen"; "how pure reason can be practical" can never be explained (105-7). We just know there is "more" (*mehr*), that there is "a 'something'" (*ein Etwas*). In the end reason, the intellect, operates out of—here's that word again!—"a spontaneity so pure" (*eine so reine Spontaneität*, 99) that neither sense nor understanding can fathom it, even though (or precisely in that) it marks us off from all the rest of nature. It is so refined as to be invisible (like the emperor's clothes?).

Remarkably, and suggestively, Kant's punctual conception of a spontaneously redemptive self, a member of an entire kingdom of dignified self-straightening persons who only recognize themselves in that, in the moments when, they respect reason and thus will the good, closely resembles Wordsworth's in certain critical respects—notwithstanding the vast differences between a systematizing, rationalist German philosopher, writing before the Revolution, who wants to save the self (the soul, even) from a mechanical nature, and a sentimentalizing, aestheticist English poet, writing after the Revolution, who wants to save the self (or soul) from a monstrous humanity. One such respect is the degree of influence both conceptions have exercised on English-speaking and wider post-European modernity, though here Wordsworth's influence is heavily mediated through Byron. Another is the debt both owe to a tradition much older than Protestantism but certainly reinvigorated by Luther: one shaped originally by Augustine, St. Paul, and Virgil. We will return to Wordsworth, and that tradition, in just a moment. As far as Kant is concerned we can conclude that the deep intimate connection in his thought between the spontaneously autogenous or self-creating self and the spontaneously autonomous or self-legislating will is the point of origin of both his epistemology and his ethics. The *connection* is the point: the fact that autogeny and autonomy arise together, as one, in his mind. An entity or an energy that makes the good, or makes freedom, in spontaneously *willing* them, and another that makes itself, and thus makes nature, in spontaneously *knowing* them, are performing the same quintessentially Kantian operation: a kind of human *ex nihilo* creation. When the God of *Genesis* said, "Let there be light," he was legislating for, knowing and creating the universe; but Kantian humanity legislates for, knows, and creates *itself.* More: in so doing, it redeems itself, straightens out its own crookedness. Even God could not do all that.

Is this what a deconstructionist would call an *aporia?* Not really. We have not come up against a deep contradiction in the text such that it dissolves or unravels itself. This is not a non-porous (*a-poretic*) layer of unreflective thought, an intellectual or imaginative impasse inherent in the text itself (autonomy is not antinomy). Kant is actually proposing the dualist model he says he is proposing. He is not unconsciously tripping himself up; he is genuinely and consistently (if a trifle ingenuously) presenting us with a dynamic something that he *knows* cannot be explained: *ein Etwas.* The Kantian model is just *like* this. It needs reason to create the idea of a spontaneity that can initiate action by itself. If *this* is an *aporia* then so is the modern liberal self. Indeed creation *ex nihilo* is precisely Kant's concern, the underlying metaphor being just what a modern cosmologist would recognize: this is in effect a *singularity.* In physics and mathematics a singularity is a zero point at which a rate of change, for example, in the density of matter, becomes infinite. An asymptote always approaches infinity; a singularity is what you would find if you got there. Division by zero is a singularity: so is the point or moment at which the universe appeared out of nothing. Science has nothing to say about this point. It is or was the beginning beyond the word, a place where the theory cannot penetrate. It is a white hole, not a black hole. The universe emerges from it, rather than collapsing into it.

At the heart of the Kantian universe of the self is just such an originary point, an event horizon over which we cannot see, and yet from the far side of which issue imperatives we cannot disobey, and knowledge that actually constitutes us. This is an ultimately mysterious, creative, self-generating, pouring-out, fountain-like sacred core: a holy, quasi-divine, unknowable energy source, an inner noumenon, a matter of faith. This is the space where God was, and Kant knows that if he wants to save freedom from nature he has to put something else in the space instead. Wordsworth wanted poetry to redeem us from evil but to his sad perplexity could only approach, never reach, that asymptote (a lost leader). Kant wanted philosophy to redeem us from mechanism, snatch the good by an act of will out of the closing jaws of natural causality; and he found himself able to claim, gladly and confidently, that it could reach and use that singularity even if it could never penetrate it (a leader not lost).

Ultimately, however, in both philosophy and literature, this spontaneous Kantian self, breathtakingly and even brazenly hypothetical (the hypothetical made categorical), adapted and exalted by Kant's successors, was to place an enormous burden on the twin human ambitions to know the world and be the good, since in the end the spontaneous self has to appear as the source of both the world and the good. Herder, Hamann, Fichte, Schelling, Hegel, Schleiermacher, Schopenhauer, Nietzsche, and Kierkegaard, to say nothing of their innumerable literary and philosophical heirs, all articulated or objected to or thought they had solved this existential problem in its various aspects, this burden of anxiety at the levels of responsibility and of uncertainty incurred by a self that has to do everything for itself, including justify and purge itself, and yet that does not really know, *cannot* know, what the sources or hiding-places of its power are: just because it has created a certain dichotomous model of itself in which "power" (energy, will, motivation, freedom- or knowledge-creation) looks *like this*, like a punctual or closed central engine, a black box, a nuclear core, a human singularity in a mechanical universe. Pinocchio wants to be a real boy, a *good* boy; the dangerous Kantian promise is that he can redeem himself, shed the burden of his crooked timber, just by an effort of will.

Spontaneous Overflow
The "Preface"

Wordsworth was notoriously anxious, of course, about the hiding-places of *his* power, those renovating points or spots of time that spontaneously reveal the mastery of the mind over nature. They show some minds as "higher," raised entirely above sense. They even seem to reveal nature itself *as* a singular mind (an emanation of his own), a Presence brooding over the abyss and feeding on infinity, but one that, after he was about thirty-five years old, always closed or receded, asymptotically, as he approached those places. His greatest poetry is almost always about them. Picture it as arranged on a graph, with beauty and the sublime along one axis, and nature and the human along the other (see figure 3.2). This produces four quadrants: natural beauty (exemplified in the Wye Valley, say); natural sublime (setting suns, Snowdon, Alps, etc.); human beauty ("small" relationships: Dorothy, Coleridge, . Simon Lee, Matthew, Old Cumberland Beggar, etc.); and human sublime (the bliss of revolutionary dawn, the terror of 1794–1795). We saw

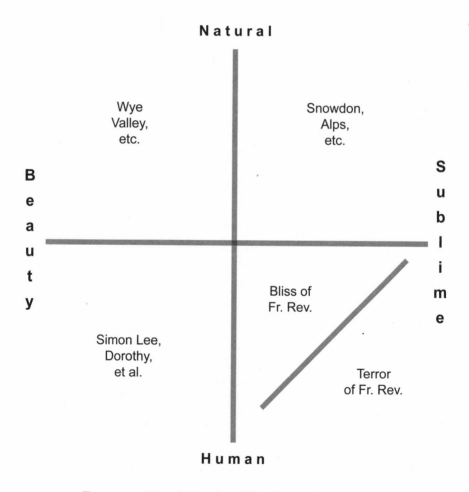

Figure 3.2: Moral Graph of Wordsworth's Poetry

that in "Tintern Abbey" some of these sources inexplicably elicited a correspondingly spontaneous creative response, while others either intimidated response or found it wanting. The most striking characteristic of the response is that it either quails or falls short only when facing the human sublime and human beauty (the lower half of the graph; the bliss after all was short-lived). Other people are what this poetry cannot accommodate; it lives or dies in its dualist relationship with an inanimate world in which or of which it is the only soul. How far is this true of other shorter poems, especially other *Lyrical Ballads*, besides "Tintern Abbey"?

Wordsworth's most celebrated use of the word "spontaneous" is in prose, not poetry, but he is talking *about* poetry. This is in the "Preface" to *Lyrical Ballads*:

> For all good poetry is the spontaneous overflow of powerful feelings: but though this be true, poems to which any value can be attached, were never produced on any variety of subjects but by a man, who being possessed of more than usual organic sensibility, had also thought long and deeply.[22]

Yet Wordsworth's own poetry "has little even of the appearance of spontaneousness," as John Stuart Mill shrewdly pointed out during his lifetime,[23] and as Wordsworth himself more or less concedes in both this passage and a later one. Here he continues:

> For our continued influxes of feeling are modified and directed by our thoughts, which are indeed the representatives of all our past feelings; and, as by contemplating the relation of these general representatives to each other we discover what is really important to men, so, by the repetition and continuance of this act, our feelings will be connected with important subjects, till at length, if we be originally possessed of much sensibility, such habits of mind will be produced, that, by obeying blindly and mechanically the impulses of those habits, we shall describe objects, and utter sentiments, of such a nature and in such connection with each other, that the understanding of the being to whom we address ourselves, if he be in a healthful state of association, must necessarily be in some degree enlightened, and his affections ameliorated.[24]

The long sentence meanders, its direction changing more than once, but its general tendency in the overall context of this part of the

"Preface" is apparently to argue that the poems have "a *purpose*": or at least "carry [one] along with them," as Wordsworth says a few lines earlier in a characteristic formulation, half metaphor and half concept, having his cake and eating it too. A purpose, a *pro-positum*: they propose first, they are propositions before they are constructions. This is Mill's point too; these are poems even a philosopher can understand!

The purpose, as the next paragraph reminds us, is "to illustrate the manner in which our feelings and ideas are associated in a state of excitement." But in the foregoing lines the purpose appears to be what it is in "Tintern Abbey": not illustrative but remedial. Sensibility and thought, understanding and affection, description and sentiment, feelings and thoughts, feelings and ideas: the matched pairs all revolve around the same incomplete epistemological claim, that emotion and intellect are best seen as associated, not separate. The very form of the claim seems to sunder them even more completely, to overlook poetry's significance as "vitally metaphorical,"[25] as life-thought. But besides that, this association is chiefly important in these poems, the sentence argues, because it brings *health* and *value*, to the reader but presumably also to the poet. As with Kant the epistemological theory is ultimately subservient to a moral end. Wordsworth returns to his famous claim later in the "Preface":

> I have said that Poetry is the spontaneous overflow of powerful feelings: it takes its origin from emotion recollected in tranquillity: the emotion is contemplated till by a species of reaction the tranquillity disappears, and an emotion, kindred to that which was before the subject of contemplation, is gradually produced, and does itself actually exist in the mind.[26]

One might say that the spontaneity is contemplated until *it* disappears; poetry on this account seems to consist precisely of non-spontaneity, of a calculated re-evocation of emotion.

So Wordsworth's celebrated and somewhat Kantian claim that "all good poetry" is a "spontaneous overflow" is contradicted almost before he has made it, or in the very terms in which he elaborates it. Indeed, as we saw earlier, the word "spontaneity" carries its own negation in itself, "of one's own free will" imperceptibly shading into "from an inner source beyond the scope of the will." The claim seems intended to apply to everyone else's poetry, revealing his *own* spontaneity as uniquely redemptive by virtue of its associated deep (and therefore unspontaneous) thoughtfulness. It is as if his poetry is seen by the "Preface" as a kind of extension of the "Preface" itself: as being really about something other than itself, rather than just being itself. And analogously, when we do turn to the poetry, it is often *about* moments of spontaneity, rather than *being*, or appearing to be, a spontaneous overflow: rather as it is as much *about* metaphor as it is metaphorical. Mill may have noticed here, without realizing it, an absence not so much of spontaneity as of that profound astonishing creativity which is inherent in great metaphorical thought.

The Tangled Root of "Simon Lee"

Wordsworth rarely uses "spontaneous" in the poems themselves. "Spontaneous wisdom breathed by health, Truth breathed by cheerfulness," from "The Tables Turned,"[27] is a rare though telling usage in which spontaneity itself is the subject of a half-formed semi-metaphorical thought about concepts, in which wisdom and truth become the mysterious exhalations of either Nature or a human psyche. The categorical confusions inherent in "Tintern Abbey" stand starkly revealed, both here and in the even more unfortunate following stanza about that notorious "impulse from a vernal wood," which teaches us more "of man, / Of moral evil and of good / Than all the sages can." Maybe, then, another poem can teach us more of man by showing us such an impulse, such a moment of "spontaneous wisdom," rather than talking about it; and of course the impulse is not from a wood, either vernal or sportive.

Here, then, is "Simon Lee, the Old Huntsman, with an incident in which he was concerned."[28] The poem has another of Wordsworth's enigmatic titles; "in which *we* were concerned" would have been more accurate, since the incident concerns the narrator at least as much as it does the old huntsman. As with "Tintern Abbey," we need to see the poem in front of us, indeed read it aloud, with emphasis on or even a pause before the rhymes, in order to grasp its effect properly. These are the first eight and a half stanzas (or seventeen, if read in the conventional ballad quatrains lying just beneath their surface):

> In the sweet shire of Cardigan,
> Not far from pleasant Ivor-hall,

An old man dwells, a little man,
I've heard he once was tall.
Of years he has upon his back,
No doubt, a burthen weighty;
He says he is three score and ten,
But others say he's eighty.

A long blue livery-coat has he,
That's fair behind, and fair before;
Yet, meet him where you will, you see
At once that he is poor.
Full five and twenty years he lived
A running huntsman merry;
And, though he has but one eye left,
His cheek is like a cherry.

No man like him the horn could sound,
And no man was so full of glee;
To say the least, four counties round
Had heard of Simon Lee;
His master's dead, and no one now
Dwells in the halls of Ivor;
Men, dogs, and horses, all are dead;
He is the sole survivor.

His hunting feats have him bereft
Of his right eye, as you may see:
And then, what limbs those feats have left
To poor old Simon Lee!
He has no son, he has no child,
His wife, an aged woman,
Lives with him, near the waterfall,
Upon the village common.

And he is lean and he is sick,
His little body's half awry;
His ancles they are swoln and thick;

His legs are thin and dry.
When he was young he little knew
Of husbandry or tillage;
And now he's forced to work, though weak,
—The weakest in the village.

He all the country could outrun,
Could leave both man and horse behind;
And often, ere the race was done,
He reeled and was stone-blind.
And still there's something in the world
At which his heart rejoices;
For when the chiming hounds are out,
He dearly loves their voices!

Old Ruth works out of doors with him,
And does what Simon cannot do;
For she, not over stout of limb,
Is stouter of the two.
And though you with your utmost skill
From labour could not wean them.
Alas! 'tis very little, all
Which they can do between them.

Beside their moss-grown hut of clay,
Not twenty paces from the door,
A scrap of land they have, but they
Are poorest of the poor.
This scrap of land he from the heath
Enclosed when he was stronger;
But what avails the land to them,
Which they can till no longer?

Few months of life has he in store,
As he to you will tell,
For still, the more he works, the more
His poor old ancles swell.

The reason for quoting all sixty-eight of these lines, or two-thirds of the poem, is to illustrate their combined effect. There is no combined effect. Something very close to nothing at all happens for a very long time. Wordsworth and Coleridge had in their sights the flourishing magazine tradition that had arisen after the publication of Bishop Percy's *Reliques* in 1765: the vogue for "ballads" owing less to "Sir Patrick Spens" or "Chevy Chase" than to "Margaret's Ghost" or "Lucy and Colin"; to Southeyan he-before-his-cottage-door doggerel whose vacuity it was Wordsworth's polemical purpose to expose.[29] So he wrote a parody, a pseudo-poem, with all the clunking rhythms and rhymes, the shell of verse, but neither the story (incident) nor the haunting emotion to be found inside a true ballad.

So, this old fellow: is he seventy or eighty? Little, but tall once. A fine blue coat. One eye, as we can hardly help seeing since we are told twice, once for each of the two eyes we have but he, of course, does not. Poor old ankles. Poor old Simon. Poorest of the poor. Once happy and strong, now old and weak. What else that rhymes with "merry" could his cheek possibly be like? What word denoting a species of agricultural activity rhymes with "village"? And so on—and on. The poem advertises and even flaunts its own redundancy. Even the studiedly understated pathos (gleeful and merry life of vigorous activity and local celebrity ends in loneliness and disability—or not quite, since the subject still experiences joy, is not alone, and, for those who find a story of exploitation here, may have had the satisfaction of outliving his master); even the ambivalent social and ethical sympathy (how can this be, that such a life should end, should be *allowed* to end, in this way? is it that such people as we, as this oddly disengaged narrator, allow it to be so? *was* he exploited and in the end disabled, or was he rather enabled, his life given meaning, by his master, by this community or "social system"?); even these tones are so muted as to be nigh-inaudible, or else so obvious that they too collapse into cliché.

If this seventeen-stanza withholding of meaning and value is intended to annoy, then the reader's accumulated frustration and boredom is just what the eighteenth stanza is intended to precipitate:

My gentle reader, I perceive
How patiently you've waited,

And I'm afraid that you expect
Some tale will be related.

The condescension is infuriating. Whether "gentle" means "well-born," "of my kind" (*gens*), or "mild and calm," the reader will bridle at this familiarity.[30] Yes, we have been *very* patient, one might say, and yet you, Master Poet, now seem to be hinting as much at our limitations, our ungentle expectations, as at your inadequacies. Instead of the tale we were expecting, what exactly *are* we to be offered, after all this? But it gets worse; here is stanza 10, or ballad stanzas 19 and 20:

O reader! had you in your mind
Such stores as silent thought can bring,
O gentle reader! you would find
A tale in every thing.
What more I have to say is short,
I hope you'll kindly take it;
It is no tale; but should you think,
Perhaps a tale you'll make it.

How we have disappointed him! How imperceptive we are! How lacking in the stores of silent thought! It turns out to be *our* responsibility to make the tale, not the teller's. "Kindly" cuts like "gentle": Are we worthy to be his kin—to understand this incident, this poor old man, as well as he does? Do we think long and deeply enough? Fortunately for the poet we can see by now that there are only three (or six) stanzas left. Maybe we should hold on to our brickbats a little longer:

One summer-day I chanced to see
This old man doing all he could
About the root of an old tree,
A stump of rotten wood.
The mattock tottered in his hand;
So vain was his endeavour
That at the root of the old tree
He might have worked for ever.

"You're overtasked, good Simon Lee,
Give me your tool" to him I said;

And at the word right gladly he
Received my proffered aid.
I struck, and with a single blow
The tangled root I severed,
At which the poor old man so long
And vainly had endeavoured.

The tears into his eyes were brought,
And thanks and praises seemed to run
So fast out of his heart, I thought
They never would have done.

The real poem begins with "One summer-day" ("It was a summer's evening," begins Southey's contemporary poem about Old Kaspar and another incident, in which he was *not* concerned)—except of course that the effect of what follows is in large part a function of the frustration that went before. In any case, there is nothing muted now about the pathos and sympathy. Simon Lee does all he can *about*, not *to*, the root; he *works at* it, endlessly; all is fumbling, ineffectual, inconclusive, as the poem itself has been, a tangled root at which the poet might have worked for ever. The old huntsman *is* the stump of rotten wood; he totters as much as his mattock does (in his hands this tool becomes just another stump). The tableau is of "vain endeavour," a duty or self-imposed value (*en-devoir*) made empty or futile, rotten-tottered, root become rotten. Again, the poem itself is implicated.

In calling this state of futile decay "overtasked," the narrator immediately returns to his condescension of two stanzas earlier, though now it is expressed toward the old man, as it was before to the reader, making it easier for us to identify with him: "good Simon," "your tool"—a "gentle" man's polite or patronizing vocabulary. Wordsworth does not spare himself or us our twinge of self-recognizing dislike as he pompously "proffers his aid" and complacently assures us of its glad reception. His own situation, admittedly, is almost impossible to carry off gracefully, especially for someone who takes pride in his humility, someone who perhaps *is not* quite a gentleman (Byron and Shelley certainly did not think he was). But here at last is the "incident" he has to describe (this is *his* endeavor): literally something that be*falls* (*incadere*), that happens to; indeed it is the only thing that happens in the poem, according both to our usual notion of what counts as "happening" (though Wordsworth wants to enrich this notion) and to the underlying sense of "hap." The action is the narrator's, but the incident *concerns* the old man. In this befalling we are, it seems, to perceive or sift him (*cum-cernere*), to make certain of him (*certus* is the past participle of *cernere*).

So, "I struck." With that single blow the long vanity, the true pathos, of his endeavor is exposed; the long vanity, the true sympathy, of the poem is revealed; the feeling gives importance to the action and situation, as promised in the "Preface." What is severed is an ancient knot: of exhaustion; of frustration with the stump that one has become, or with the indifference of a community once so richly constitutive of oneself but to which one is now a mere stump; perhaps, yes, of condescension and humiliation long forgotten, as well as grief for comradeship and youth long lost. What gushes out of the old huntsman's heart and eyes comes from a deep well and is under a great deal of pressure. And so the poem's proposal seems clear. It is *about* this incident, about the root of an old tree, about the old man's feelings: a spontaneous overflow of powerful feelings, expressed in thanks and praises, with no sufficient external cause (the torrent out of all proportion to the single blow) and therefore entirely determined by inner causes that are not themselves willed. This seems a genuinely redemptive moment, too. Here is a real sense of what regaining one's soul, one's life, might look like, grasped in a moment of connection with another self, a kind of redeemer.[31]

But Wordsworth asked us to think, and when we do we may find more in his tale than he intended, or find ourselves thinking about the tale we make of him rather than the one he makes of the old man. Here is the last half-stanza, omitted earlier:

> —I've heard of hearts unkind, kind deeds
> With coldness still returning.
> Alas! the gratitude of men
> Has oftner left me mourning.

Even now the poem's purpose is partly sustained. Gratitude is the name given by the narrator to Simon's complex feeling, and in a sense gratitude is a movement of "spontaneous wisdom." Milton's Satan confesses that he "understood not that a grateful mind / By owing owes not, but still pays, at once / Indebted and discharged," regarding "endless gratitude" instead as a still-owed burden of "debt immense." In fact in this passage from book 4 of *Paradise Lost* (lines 49–57) Satan's inability to "do gratitude," so to speak, is the main part of what makes him Satan. He *feels* it passively as a burden, as "subjection," instead of *being* it as an act, a discharge or acquittal; and this burdened condition is despair. Simon Lee on the other hand shows himself a proper Christian and almost a redeemed soul in his endless gratitude, his transcending of despair and pride. From the narrator's perspective he is a Pinocchio, a stump of wood or crooked timber suddenly crying real tears.

But in this tale the part of the Redeemer, maybe even God, is played by the poet/narrator himself, his grace being the reflex of Simon's gratitude (Latin *gratus* and *gratia*, Sanskrit *gurta* or "welcome," and Greek *geras* or "reward" lie behind both words). And so it turns out that we only now see his true proposal. We are left with it at the very end, as he is left with it: his own "mourning." The poem turns out, finally, to be about *his* feeling, not Simon's, and as with "Tintern Abbey" the delicate suggestiveness and restraint of the whole construction are cast in an entirely new light by this final twist, almost a palinode or retraction of the earlier insight. *Why* mourn this gratitude, or all gratitude ("of men")? A wasting and pining from the loss of what one is fated to remember, with an enduring sense of its absence: this is the root of mourning. In older societies mourning had its observances and practices precisely to avoid this pathology. But here only the poem has such a function, and the poem worsens the problem, instead of solving it, just by drawing attention to it ("here, see how often I mourn"); "oftner left me" suggests a more chronic condition unalleviated by observances.

Yet surely, one might object, excessive gratitude may very well be seen as poignant evidence of lifelong deprivation or immediate decrepitude, and *that* is what is being mourned. But the half-stanza undercuts this. "I've heard of hearts unkind," it begins, and we recall the poet's hope for his tale, that we will "kindly take it." His second "kind deed" is to write the poem, and he hopes we will be kindred spirits, gentle readers, in our responses and returns: not cold (is there a suggestion of "cold and still" in "coldness still"?), but grateful. The contrary emotions to gratitude here are unkindness and coldness. There is none of

Milton's probing of the psychology of gratitude: only a sentimental connection of gratitude not to grace but to kindness, of ingratitude not to despair but to coldness. And mourning is correspondingly cheapened and vulgarized: not a profound pining or grieving, nor an active acquittal of those emotions, but just a "mournful" shake of the head.

What has happened is that the poem has become about the narrator's undemonstrated mourning (an incident in which *he* was concerned), rather than the old man's demonstrated gratitude. The latter in all its complexity is reduced merely to a trigger for the former (the "still sad music of humanity" problem). The old man's vital spirits are stronger than the poet's, although the poet's grief and suffering supersede and frame the old man's (this is no "unremembered act"). Why couldn't he acquit the mourning just as Simon acquits the gratitude (and suffering)? And if the poem *is* the acquittal then it is so for him, not us (thank you, Master Poet). Do we all respond to poverty or even age (an urban slum, a senile grandmother) just by musing on how sad they make us feel? In its unwitting (as distinct from its intended) condescensions the poem avoids these thoughts. It kindly allows its gentle readers to do the same. The spontaneous emergence of mourning from gratitude is unexplored. Redemption, including of the ballad form, is glimpsed, almost achieved, but then falters because in the end the poet's framing moral thought, about the human sinner, about himself as a kind of redeemer, about the gentle reader as fellow-redeemer and, even, as the collective secular "God" called "Humanity" who will judge this redemptive act—because his moral thought about all this just is not deep or persistent enough. That, surely, rather than some political apostasy, is why he is the lost leader.

Surely, however (one might object), we have simply reached the conclusion about the narrator that the poet meant us to reach: that he always means us to, about all his narrators? Is it not an elementary critical mistake as well as a misunderstanding of his purposes in these poems to confuse the two figures? Does his personal redemption not lie partly in realizing, in poetry, that he, that we, can all be guilty of just these radical insensitivities? I don't think so. In the next two poems in the volume, for example, "Anecdote for Fathers" and "We are Seven," he certainly exposes the complacency inherent in an adult's reasonableness when confronted with a child's vivid imagining, just as "Simon

Lee" exposes the prime-of-life, well-to-do gentleman's complacency in the face of the lambent emotions of the proud poor man almost in his second childhood. But in none of the three cases is the poet standing right outside his narrative self. He is saying, as if to a friend, "here, look how pompous I was being." *I* was being: still the same "I." There is no sharp poet/narrator distinction: just one man sheepishly aware of his limitations. The real trouble in "Simon Lee" comes at the very end, with that weighty, sententious half-stanza following the significant em-dash pause, its tone so much profounder than anything that has gone before. It simply has too much of the summative judgment about it *not* to sound like the poet's own voice. What might have been just another low-key admission of his own complacent condescension has become, not a devastating criticism of it in a dramatically distanced "narrator" (Wordsworth was no dramatist), but an equally devastating, because unintended, elevation of it to a new level in the poet himself: as with the final paragraph of "Tintern Abbey."[32]

This particular "Incident," said Wordsworth in the "Preface," was meant to illustrate the association of feelings and ideas in a state of excitement, to carry out the "purpose" of these poems, "by placing my Reader in the way of receiving from ordinary moral sensations another and more salutary impression than we are accustomed to receive from them."[33] This is a corrective purpose, as Wordsworth immediately makes clear. Urban life, corrupted partly by "frantic novels, sickly and stupid German tragedies, and deluges of idle and extravagant stories in verse," produces "a craving" or a "degrading thirst" for "extraordinary incident" and "outrageous stimulation," and reduces the mind "to a state of almost savage torpor."[34] Leaving aside the word "German" and replacing tragedies with movies or computer games, the purpose retains all its appeal today. Ordinary incidents and sensations may excite the mind to real action whereas extravagant deluges of fantasy will over-stimulate it into exhaustion (studies have repeatedly shown that this is exactly what happens with computer games vis-à-vis reading). Moral health is still despaired of today in similar terms. Maybe one reason many undergraduates do not like Wordsworth is that they do not want to hear all this. They especially do not want to be told to read him as if he were some kind of health food and they were torpid savages. But this is what he asks for. The trouble is in those last stanzas, those framing prefaces. He is right about the idle stories, but will we read his just for the salutary impression? Just to be advised that mourning is the proper response to gratitude? Similarly, is it the function of the old Cumberland beggar (1800 *Lyrical Ballads*) to provide "that first mild touch of sympathy and thought" through which "lofty minds" begin to "find their kindred" with a world of "want and sorrow"? To give even poor people the chance to "be kind to such / As needed kindness"? To be an occasion for virtue, a "silent monitor" against which everyone else can measure his own good fortune, a living record of village charities "else unremembered" (nameless unremembered acts)?[35] The account is movingly persuasive as we read, and yet on reflection we know nothing of the beggar beyond these public functions. Is Wordsworth exposing only a narrator to these criticisms?

Singularities and Spots of Time
"The Two April Mornings," and The Prelude

As with the account of "Tintern Abbey" in chapter 1, these criticisms may seem almost willfully to ignore some of what is most beautiful and profound in Wordsworth. And yet it is often its last-ditch retreat from an achieved beauty and profundity, its failure of human grasp after the breathtaking ambition of its reach, which most characterizes this poetry. Take another ballad, also about spontaneity, first published, like "The Old Cumberland Beggar," in the second or 1800 edition of *Lyrical Ballads*: "The Two April Mornings."[36]

> We walked along, while bright and red
> Uprose the morning sun,
> And Matthew stopped, he looked, and said,
> "The will of God be done!"

> A village Schoolmaster was he,
> With hair of glittering grey;
> As blithe a man as you could see
> On a spring holiday.

> And on that morning, through the grass,
> And by the steaming rills,

We travelled merrily to pass
A day among the hills.

"'Our work," said I, "was well begun;
Then, from thy breast what thought,
Beneath so beautiful a sun,
So sad a sigh has brought?"

A second time did Matthew stop,
And fixing still his eye
Upon the eastern mountain-top
To me he made reply.

"Yon cloud with that long purple cleft
Brings fresh into my mind
A day like this which I have left
Full thirty years behind.

And on that slope of springing corn
The self-same crimson hue
Fell from the sky that April morn,
The same which now I view!

With rod and line my silent sport
I plied by Derwent's wave,
And, coming to the church, stopped short
Beside my Daughter's grave.

Nine summers had she scarcely seen
The pride of all the vale;
And then she sang!—she would have been
A very nightingale.

Six feet in earth my Emma lay,
And yet I loved her more,
For so it seemed, than till that day
I e'er had loved before.

And, turning from her grave, I met
Beside the church-yard Yew
A blooming girl, whose hair was wet
With points of morning dew.

A basket on her head she bare,
Her brow was smooth and white,
To see a Child so very fair,
It was a pure delight!

No fountain from its rocky cave
E'er tripped with foot so free,
She seemed as happy as a wave
That dances on the sea.

There came from me a sigh of pain
Which I could ill confine;
I looked at her and looked again;
—And did not wish her mine."

Matthew is in his grave, yet now
Methinks I see him stand,
As at that moment, with his bough
Of wilding in his hand.

The resemblances to "Simon Lee" are evident: the inconsequential details, the banal forms, an incident involving the narrator and a single interlocutor, the circuitous, tediously preambular approach to the moral center, as if the poem were stalking its own purposes, and then the sudden change of complexion or aspect, the spring, as it were. The poem stops short just after its halfway point, in the eighth stanza, just as Matthew does, beside his daughter's grave—we were not expecting this. His words are laconic, undemonstrative; but his feelings are compelling. She was his daughter; she was only nine; she sang so beautifully that everyone was proud of her (like Simon Lee she belonged to the whole village); now she lies stifled under six feet of earth (rolled round in earth's diurnal course). For some reason—the second stopping-point—he suddenly loved her more than he had ever loved anyone, including her. And at this strange moment of feeling there appears to him without warning, not just as ghostly apparition but still bound up with that same feeling, like an emanation of his sudden profound love, another girl, a dancer not a singer, but otherwise almost a replica, a fountain-like sprite or dryad. His feeling of love becomes pain at the immeasurable gap between the two similar girls, that most unfathomable of all chasms: one blooming, one dead. And yet, in the third turning-point, "I . . . did not wish her mine." Did *not*, we should hear, denying what might have seemed natural; other girls before this one he *had* wished were his. The spontaneous moment of deeper love for his dead daughter enables him to see her analogue afresh, and unpossessively; sight is cleansed as spirit is liberated. He can "let go," as we say nowadays, of *both* girls, one in the other.[37] It is a spontaneous ineffable moment of unsought and unbought grace, a redemption, loving his daughter and seeing this child. He "cannot chuse but feel" what has been sent to him (*Prelude* 13.84). Only by trying to imagine how that moment of deeper love and then of renunciation must have felt can we make sense of this poem in its turns and returns.

This is perfect in its kind. Despite the resemblances, there is none of the moralism of "Simon Lee." The final stanza finds Matthew in his own grave and yet also still standing, just as he was when he told this tale, or when he recollected his original emotions. We too see him standing there as at that moment, with his bough of wilding in his hand. No further comment is necessary. This is "Simon Lee" without the narrator's sententious mourning, "Tintern Abbey" without the last paragraph. This helps, because criticism cannot be taken here as fault-finding; the poem's touch is faultless. So what has criticism to say?

The moment of sudden love followed by renunciation is a religious moment, a singularity, just in that there is no accounting for it. There can be no argument about spontaneity. Either we grasp it or we do not; either it happens or it does not. And in a sense that is all Matthew is: a lost daughter, a moment of love and of grace. And so the poem also trembles on the edge of incomprehensibility. Why this moment of love? Why did he not wish her his? There cannot be any *answer*, any full account, because this is all we know of blithe Matthew, just as his thanks and praises are all we know of grateful Simon. On a larger scale something like this is true of "Michael,"[38] in which the old shepherd is trapped between his love for his land and his love for the (eventually) dissolute son in whom "the Old Man's heart" had "seemed born again" and who could have ensured the future ownership of the land, the union of the two loves. His grief manifests itself in a specific, locally remarked inactivity: his difficulty in continuing the building of a sheepfold begun with Luke before the boy went away. "Many and many a day he thither went, / And never lifted up a single stone" (compare "And did not wish her mine"). The feeling is to be communicated, the shepherd is to be perceived, in this *incidental* detail. And it is utterly telling. But the considerable rest of what we see of Michael, in 482 blank verse lines, is often emotive, lachrymose, almost maudlin: excessive, perhaps, rather in the way in which the first two-thirds of "Simon Lee" are excessive. It is as if the laconic, lapidary strength of the key lines must be framed and compensated by the sentimental elaborations of the rest: as if their very strength comes partly from that contrast.[39]

Wordsworth's own daughter Catherine was born ten years later, and he lost *her* at the age of three (though one might say that at the time of "The Two April Mornings" he had already in another sense lost Caroline, his daughter by Annette Vallon). How much more we know of him in the 1815 sonnet "Surprized by Joy,"[40] where a spontaneous moment of joy and love moves him to "share the transport" and turn to a daughter who is long gone and whom he has even briefly forgotten to think about: indeed "that thought's return" was the "worst pang that sorrow ever bore," except for the first true realization of her death. We still do not know about the originary moment of joy; but the rest of the feeling (joy—impatience—sharing—transport—love—loss—remorse—sorrow—unrestorability) is developed more completely, though in fewer lines, than it is with Matthew or Michael. The hiding places of his power opened one last time, as capriciously as ever.

It is not that such moments do not occur in the poems, or do not ring true; they do, and are often profoundly moving. It is that Wordsworth repeatedly presents them as *the* truth, as the experiences that give meaning to the rest of life: just as in Kant the singularity, spontaneity, produces experience as it were out of nothing. The "mourning" of the narrator in "Simon Lee" is merely one such moment that does not entirely convince. The old huntsman's gratitude is another, which does. Matthew's moment of sudden love does. Michael's unfinished sheepfold does. They convince us in themselves, that is—so well that they look like what meaning *is* in a life, while everything else in the poems (and so in lives) looks flat or banal by comparison.

The entire *Prelude* (to stray briefly outside the bounds of the *Lyrical Ballads*) orients itself around many such moments, distinct pre-eminent spots of time with their "renovating Virtue" that nourishes and repairs the mind (11.258–65), each spot a singularity, each one a mystery from whose depths proceed our "honours" (11.328–29). "I should need / Colours and words that are unknown to man / To paint" them, the poet avers (11.308–10). They speak with a "strange utterance" as if from another universe (11.348–50), these gentle visitations or severer interventions of Nature (11.368–70); these intimations of "unknown modes of being," of "huge and mighty forms" (11.420–24); these "presences of Nature" (11.490) shown only "when the light of sense / Goes out in flashes that have shewn to us / The invisible world" (6.534–36), utterable only in "the language of the heavens" (12.270) by those for whom "words are but under-agents in their souls" (12.272). The cumulative redemptive meaning of these moments shows itself at the end of the poem, when the Snowdon moon-landscape "appeared to me / The perfect image of a mighty mind . . . that feeds upon infinity" (13.69–70), the "counterpart / And brother of the glorious faculty / Which higher minds bear with them as their own" (13.88–90). Such minds, almost as far beyond gentle readers as they are beyond old huntsmen, live in "a world of life," not needing "extraordinary calls" (or incidents) to "rouze them" (13.101–2): "for they are powers," fully self-aware; they can "hold communion with the invisible world" and are "truly from the Deity" (13.105–10).[41]

The backbone of Wordsworth's greatest work, as with so many of his lesser ones, is made of these vertebral singularities, beyond the capacity of ordinary language to express, in which we, and the greatest among us most of all, the "higher minds," are constituted and activated as human by instantaneous and dimensionless lightning flashes of spontaneous connection with a deity, a corresponding Mind, or unknown modes of being. *The Prelude* is made of much more than this, of course; but its orientation is such as to proffer these inexplicable, ineffable moments, these epiphanies, these spots that no vicissitude can find, as the primary constituents of our humanity.

What is happening is that Wordsworth is retaining the religious cast of meaning-giving: treating meaning-giving as an essentially *quantized* religious matter, within an otherwise unintelligible, joyless, or fretful world of life, "the very world which is the world / Of all of us" (10.725–26)—while otherwise turning his back on that very life, except as a set of such quantum moments. Redemption is almost the type of this mode of meaning-giving: a singular, mysterious quasi-divine act absolving and renewing all of humanity. The only real (and rule-proving) exception to this understanding of meaning is just when Wordsworth uses the foregoing phrase; when he is part of the early Revolution, a political actor for the only time in his life. In the celebrated hymn to political participation at 10.689–727 he experiences politics as a "pleasant *exercise* of hope and joy," hope and joy experienced as untrammeled or realized activities, released, unleashed (*ex-arcere*). This is a state of salvation, of Love and Bliss, in which Paradise is suddenly real, in which laws and statutes become Romance. *Then* "Not favoured spots alone, but the whole earth, / The beauty wore of promise"; *then* all people alike worked together in the world of all of us. But he fled from that too soon, or it from him (into the hiding places of its power), and nothing was ever the same again. In a sense all the redemption that came later was second-best, a consolation prize. As we saw in "Tintern Abbey" and the other poems of 1798–1805 he was otherwise obsessed, thereafter, by Life, not really by lives. Ordinary lives no longer seemed sublime or even real. There was that odd sense of distance between himself and others: a distance not closed an inch by his criticisms of his complacent narrative self. This is not a world of life, but a world spontaneously visited or intervened in by Life. Simon, Matthew, and Dorothy are not real relationships for him, with him. They are seen (they see him) almost as if he were God, or the Redeemer—not one of them. One wants to say: Wordsworth never really interacted with another human being at all, after that brief experience of Heaven as an *exercise*, not a spontaneous epiphany, of hope and joy, and then after the unspeakable experiences not mentioned in "Tintern Abbey" except as the "something that he dreads," and referred to obliquely in *The Prelude* as "a conflict of sensations without name" (10.265). Single emotions—gratitude, mourning—can be embodied for a moment in an ordinary life, but its meaning is the same as the meaning of those single emotions. The lives themselves are not so much thin as one-dimensional, punctual. They are reduced to the concept to which they refer us.

Coleridgean Coda
Spontaneity in "The Ancient Mariner"

We will take up the matter of *The Prelude* at some length in the next two chapters. For now we must consider one final lyrical ballad about spontaneity. The only other poem in the collection of the same stature as "Tintern Abbey" was not written by Wordsworth at all. It was the first poem in the first edition.[42] Again there is a narrator or listener, a wedding guest who "cannot chuse but hear" (22), rather as men "cannot choose but feel" the hidden "power" Nature intimates to them in *Prelude* 10; and an old protagonist, a Simon- or Matthew-equivalent. This time, however, the incident is supernatural. The guest knows without being told that the mariner is haunted, plagued by fiends (79–80). The purpose of the poem, nevertheless, is the same: to engage *our* feelings, our "affections" or orientation toward experience ("affection" is ad-*facere*, "making toward"), by dramatizing or highlighting the association between an incident and someone *else's* feeling, in this case through forcing us to consider an impossible (supernatural, ideal) incident as real. Ideas and feelings are associated in a state of excitement. Even Wordsworth's poetry, said Coleridge, was after all meant "to excite a feeling analogous to the supernatural":[43] so a supernatural poem may even be better at the same job, which is essentially one of isolating and framing a feeling/incident cluster so as to intimate a Power behind the apparent world. The "film of familiarity"[44] Coleridge says this poetry is meant to remove is like the doggerel of "Simon Lee." It is the surface of life, or our perception of life's surface, like a cataract as much as a veil. Again, the purpose is remedial, not ingenuously illustrative. Our lives are only half-felt, seen through a fogged glass, or so runs the argument, and this poetry pierces through to reality. But is this removing the cataract, or just making pinholes in it?

While this poem is apparently full of "incident," in the conventional sense of "things happening," and is in this respect most unlike "Simon Lee" and its companions to the point where Wordsworth later felt inclined to disavow it ("many defects"; "extraordinary incident"; "extravagant stories in verse"), its many events nevertheless pour out like a stream, a sacred river, from a hidden, underground source. The relationship between all these events and their source is much the same, making allowances for the transposition into a supernatural or thrilling key, as that between the trivial details of "Simon Lee" and *its* key incident.

A bird of good omen, an albatross, appears to mariners of a ship-trapped in ice in the far southern ocean (61–64):

> At length did cross an Albatross,
> Thorough the Fog it came;
> And an it were a Christian Soul,
> We hail'd it in God's name.

They feed it; the bad weather breaks; the ice splits; "The Helmsman steer'd us thro'" (68). A "good south wind sprung up behind" (69); for nine days the bird follows and befriends them. But then, quite suddenly, *the* incident occurs (77–80):

> "God save thee, ancyent Marinere!
> From the fiends that plague thee thus—
> Why look'st thou so?"—with my cross bow
> I shot the Albatross.

Remarkably, there is no further comment on why the Mariner did this, on where the impulse came from. It is just a singularity. He does it spontaneously, in the now-familiar double sense of that term: out of his own free will but also out of some dark, inaccessible inner place, beneath or behind the will.

This is truer to the old ballad ethos than Wordsworth's poems are. Coleridge's poem was indeed a brilliantly original *real ballad*, not one of Wordsworth's (equally original) neo-ballads, which partly accounts for Wordsworth's discomfort with it. Coleridge's own comment on his poem was that it

> ought to have had no more moral than the Arabian Nights' tale of the merchant's sitting down to eat dates by the side of a well, and throwing the shells aside, and lo! a genie starts up, and says he *must* kill the aforesaid merchant, *because* one of the date shells had, it seems, put out the eye of the genie's son.[45]

"Sir Patrick Spens," for example, an important model for Coleridge's poem, is indeed in this sense without a moral: what happens happens, in all its stark inscrutable reality. The seafarers set sail with their sense of foreboding ("the new moon with the old moon in her arm"), the tempest comes, they all drown, and that's that. But Coleridge thought the problem with his own poem was exactly the opposite: the "obtrusion of the moral sentiment upon the reader." Not a recasting of the ballad but an unnecessary moralizing upon it: just what Wordsworth so often does. We need look no further than the final stanzas (643–50) to see how right he was:

> Farewel, farewell! but this I tell
> To thee, thou wedding-guest!
> He prayeth well who loveth well
> Both man and bird and beast.

> He prayeth best who loveth best
> All things both great and small:
> For the dear God, who loveth us,
> He made and loveth all.

The wedding guest is now a "sadder and a wiser man" because he has heard something deeper than what these complacent stanzas say. It is as if the pattern of "Simon Lee" is inverted: the banality is saved for the coda, "the moral," rather than the coda's being the real poem; while the rest, the preamble, is all too banal. The moral sentiment is what Wordsworth proposes: it is what Coleridge feels apologetic about. In Blake's hands this would have been the ending of a Song of Innocence ("Where Mercy, Love & Pity dwell, / There God is dwelling too"), and hence, even without its Experience foil, a thoroughly ambiguous replacement of the divinity in a "Divine Song," or a Christian children's prayer, of an Isaac Watts attitude to God, by a humanist, or even a Kantian, concept-formation ("So if all do their *duty* they need not fear harm").[46] A more naïve form of piety is both endorsed and superseded (sublated, a Hegelian might say). Here, though, after all that has happened, it is a crashingly facile parody of a child's prayer, just as the preamble of "Simon Lee" is a facile parody of a ballad. Coleridge's achievement here, much as he deprecated it, was to subvert childish religiosity by contrasting it with the deeper, inarticulable morality of the incident/feeling cluster.

Many evils, this time, rather than goods, spring from the mariner's singular or "incidental" shot (compare "I struck, and with a single blow . . ."). The ship is becalmed in the tropics; the crew one-by-one die of thirst, cursing him, having hung around his neck "instead of the Cross the Albatross." The etymology is itself uncanny: "albatross" is *al-qaduz*, in Arabic the bucket on a water-raising wheel, applied originally to pelicans because of the shape of their beaks, sometimes thought to be water carriers for their young; altered by the Portuguese to *alcatras*; and loosely transferred by seafarers to another large member of the same seabird family, possibly in association with *alba*, "white." Instead of being marked for redemption and eternal life the mariner, like Cain, whom Coleridge was writing about when he began this poem, is burdened by the murder he has committed: he has destroyed the fountain of life. The drying up of this source dries him up too, cuts his heart and words off from *the* Source, rather as if killing the bird was the self-realizing act of an arid soul (the Kantian soul that knows itself only in acting):

> I look'd to Heaven, and try'd to pray;
> But or ever a prayer had gusht,
> A wicked whisper came and made
> My heart as dry as dust.

The thirst is a spiritual pathology as much as a condign punishment; the mariner cannot drink just as he can neither sleep nor die, just as he murdered the water-bearer (236–39).

But then comes the poem's second incident or turning point: this time almost an exact replica of the one in "Simon Lee." The mariner catches sight of some nearby "water-snakes" (269–83):

> Within the shadow of the ship
> I watch'd their rich attire:
> Blue, glossy green, and velvet black
> They coil'd and swam; and every track
> Was a flash of golden fire.

O happy living things! no tongue
Their beauty might declare:
A spring of love gusht from my heart,
And I bless'd them unaware!
Sure my kind saint took pity on me,
And I bless'd them unaware.

The self-same moment I could pray;
And from my neck so free
The Albatross fell off, and sank
Like lead into the sea.

He drinks as if with his whole body; sleep "slides into his soul" like water; it is as if he has died, so "light" (unburdened) is he. It rains; the becalmed ship moves as if by magic. The dead men return as zombies to crew the ship again. Their souls, unlike his, are apparently saved, but they have no pity for him. He has been a Jonah as much as a Cain. A vengeful submarine ice-demon, a "spirit" that had "lov'd the bird that lov'd the man," has become the "frightful fiend" treading close behind him, and is now exacting retribution (408–10, 455). It controls the motion of the ship, and eventually returns it home, but only to condemn the mariner (condignly again) to an arid life of compulsive speech, telling his tale forever as an expiation and a warning, an empty reiteration or perpetual emptying-out of his inexplicable spontaneous act. Here is Coleridge's Arabian Nights tale of the genie who *must* kill the merchant for inadvertently blinding his son.

But the first singularity or spontaneity was no mere inadvertence, and neither is this second one; the spirit or fiend recognizes this in the terms of its vengeance. The mariner's two "incidents" both come from a place deeper and more essential to the self than the one the merchant's act comes from. The unutterability of his awareness of happiness, life, and beauty entirely outside himself finds expression as a "spring of love," a gushing fountain of thanks and praises not unlike the old huntsman's. "Aware" is related to "warden" and "guard"; the mariner lets his guard down, opens the flood barriers, and *blesses* them. Despite its long association with *benedicere*, "blessing" is etymologically not unlike sacrifice and libation, *spendo*. *Blóed-sian*, as mentioned in chapter 2, is to pour out as in a libation: specifically to pour out blood, or mark with blood, and thus consecrate, praise God, enter the sphere of the holy through the act of blessing. Earlier the parched mariner had seen another ship but had only been able to cry out "A sail! a sail!" by biting his own arm and sucking the blood (152–53). Once that quasi-redemptive sacrifice is made, once we pay in blood or are marked by blood, then we can enter through the barrier. Then prayer, which is an entreaty for an inflow of grace, can gush forth like an outflow or grateful giving from the heart (as Satan knew). Expiation is the outward (*ex-*) sign of an appeasing piety (*-piare*) shown to a god, the averting of evil by self-sacrifice. The expiation to which the mariner is finally condemned by the ice-demon is a self-sacrifice in which he has forever to suck the poison of guilt out of himself by telling his story to others and perhaps delivering them from the evil of killing other albatrosses: awakening their consciousness of the happiness and beauty in other living things that are not the self—or perhaps just passing on the poison to them. Expiation cannot be true redemption, any more than atonement or reparation can. The sinner is also the sacrificial victim, and he will never be truly saved; the god is essentially vengeful, not merciful or forgiving: an older, more bloodthirsty god.

So here, leaving aside the moralizing, is a ballad of spontaneity, rather than inadvertence, in which the protagonist's sudden and inexplicable acts, issuing from a quasi-divine, unutterable source within himself, *ein Etwas*, provoke corresponding consequences from a divine source outside himself, a Power behind the apparent world. Indeed the source and the divinity are necessarily connected. The moral of the poem appears to be "he prayeth best who loveth best," and so on: but really it is that love and evil alike spring fathomlessly out of a clear blue sea or sky; or out of the dark depths of the self. There's no predicting or accounting for them. They are mysterious, inscrutable, holy and free. They occupy that space in our selves where God used to be. Now he is not there any more, and an ancient, pre-Christian demon has moved back in. And that frightful fiend, who did after all love the bird, is much more like us (the point about God is that he is *not* like us). But if we are so unaccountable, and especially so unaccountably evil, then however are we to live with ourselves? What, indeed, is the point of trying to? Eternal expiation can only be some nightmare life-in-death simulacrum of redemptive salvation. No wonder the wedding guest arose sadder as well as wiser the next morning.

Redemption and Spontaneity

Much Romantic poetry is both redemptive and normative, both an attempt to deliver us from evil and a claim that this is what all poetry should do. At the same time it is the awful realization that both the evil it attempts to deliver us from and the heaven it attempts to deliver us to are within us. They are also capricious, emerging unpredictably or spontaneously from their deep source as feeling-concepts (gratitude, joy, sorrow, love, blessing) as much as or even more than metaphors (albatross, tree root, single stone, bough of wilding). The proposed redemption is highly conceptual in spirit. Kantian philosophy has the same thrust, but the concepts are intellectual not emotional, the metaphors are fewer, and the overall tone is more confident. The heaven of freedom and self-realization gushes forth spontaneously out of some mysterious inner place. These two movements of thought about the self, one in Continental philosophy and the other in English poetry, could be said to spring from a single master metaphor, partly locked up in the root sense of "spontaneity" itself. They depend on an image of pouring out or pledging the self: even more, of an inarticulable, sacred, mysterious, even dangerous *source*. A curious feature of Charles Taylor's magisterial *Sources of the Self* is its silence on this matter of sources.[47] Taylor's exposition of the origins of our modern conceptions of the self does not take into account the idea of the self *as* a source. Yet the notion of a solemn engagement or giving of the self to a sacred or sacrificial cause, or more radically and disturbingly, of the self *as* such a cause; the notion, therefore, that this is what the self essentially *is*, this pouring-out *of* itself *for* itself in a capricious, redemptive self-cleansing that can stop as suddenly as it starts, with no apparent cause or control: this, is, surely, the notion that Kant and Wordsworth alike bequeathed to us, however great the differences between them.

At the center of both the Kantian and the Wordsworthian (or indeed Coleridgean) self is a kind of black box that there's no looking into, different in kind from but determinative of the rest of the self. From it emerge real imperatives, indeed all moral life. Could we not in fact call this the definitive Romantic maneuver, the crucial step back from Enlightenment materialism, from rationalism and empiricism alike: the reserving, the non-negotiable withholding, of a special inner-most corner of the self from the new science and philosophy, from their determinist scrutiny? The keener the gaze of the Newtonian or Cartesian eye, the Galilean telescope or Benthamite panopticon, the *œil perçant*, the more dogmatic the resistance to its perceptions must be ("sorry, this is the reserved section, you can't come in, I can't explain why": and yet it just *is*, maybe for that very reason, the most impor-tant section), the more private, far-off, secret and inviolable the inner self must be, the more work it must do, the greater the moral burden it must bear—and of course bear alone, since of its nature it is out of reach of any other inner self. It is the solitary observer, knower and chooser. It bears the terrible burden of *knowing* that all that makes sense of the world and makes it non-contingent—is itself. If everything seems meaningless, is that not *its* fault, its sin? Must it not redeem this sin itself? And yet it is itself capricious, unfathomable, even unintelli-gible. *This* is "a heavy and a weary weight," all right. Other people are at best ends in themselves, therefore things in themselves, unknow-able things rather than the sources of all our knowing. In a sense this is a Lutheran, Augustinian and Pauline conception; in another sense it is Cartesian. It is dualistic. But the Romantic generations of 1780–1830, reacting against the science and philosophy of the seventeenth and eighteenth centuries, were the first in history to feel that ancient tendency to dualism quite like *this*, to experience life without God, the burden of self-redemption, like this: and in doing so they created modernity.

4

WORDSWORTH AND POLITICAL REDEMPTION I
Paradise

From Political to Postpolitical

The notion of spontaneity represents a perennial but forlorn hope. The hope is that redemption will gush out of some unfathomable depth of the self and deliver us from evil, make us new and better, like a pure fountain welling up from some volcanic fissure at the bottom of the ocean, its source both within us and beyond us. Such a thing is and yet is not a matter of our own will. This forlorn hope was really the first civilizational experience of the loss of faith: of living with that loss as a continuing presence, like a ghost limb. The loss itself was a complex matter. It was really a *sense* of loss, deriving from a seventeenth-century confusion about what kind of thing faith was, such that one might "lose" it. If faith is no longer a set of reflective practices and mutually supportive dynamic concepts, but just a few vestigial and hypostasized concept-objects "inside" a mind, then it has also become much easier to "lose."

Tracing the scale of that loss in those terms would take another book. Suffice it to say, for our purposes here, that this forlorn hope took a great many forms in Romantic and post-Romantic thought, and that some of the most important of these were political. Just as Romanticism in art is a belief in the redemptive power of art, Romanticism in politics is a belief in the redemptive power of politics.

Now Wordsworth's poetry certainly enacts and advocates a redemptive *art*.[1] The poetry can (at least in principle) be the agent not just the angel of redemption. This cannot be so with politics, however, since writing about it is not *doing* it (this is just as true for political philosophy as for political poetry). The point and origin of Wordsworth's life as a poet were that he turned out, after all, *not* to be a political agent. So poetry, with him, was in the end a substitute for the fulfillment that political action had promised but not delivered.[2] Poetry was an insulation from the murderous clamor of the *polis*. His very need for redemption, for a sense of being bought back from sin (that is, at a price), had its roots in an intoxicating experience of discovery, arguably *the* discovery of his life. What he discovered, as a kind of heaven, was active and collaborative political community. But this discovery was closely, and perhaps inevitably, succeeded by an experience of alienation, of isolation and despair, of a kind of hell, of that disintegration of both community and personality that might be called a secular damnation. Humanity, and especially Wordsworth himself, came to seem dreadful, even evil. Politics turned out to be a kind of sin. This was partly because his brief foray into politics as *action* was destined to failure through his more persistent sense of it as *vision* or *mission*. He could not help seeing it as redemptive even though he had seen that, at its best, its virtue was not of that kind.[3]

The suppressed Annette/Caroline episode, indeed the very suppression of it, was also, of course, an important part of this disintegration and damnation. Some might say it was all-important—that it was Wordsworth's grief at losing his family and his guilt at abandoning them that were the main causes of his breakdown. But there is nothing in Wordsworth's writing, not even "Vaudracour and Julia" (*especially* not "Vaudracour and Julia"), nor the *ersatz* emotions about Dorothy and Coleridge in "Tintern Abbey" and elsewhere, to suggest that this episode constituted in its intensity his primary experience of the period, or even came close.[4] There is nothing to suggest that Wordsworth's sensibility, in 1792 or later, was open to and creative of such erotic or familial affection in anything like the way it was open to and creative of the political affections. Indeed the absence of love in "Tintern Abbey," the inflated sentimentality of its fifth paragraph, feels less like suppression than incapacity. Only in comparatively rare daughter-loss poems like "Surprized by Joy" or "The Two April Mornings," or other loss poems of enigmatic provenance, such as the Lucy lyrics, do we sense some of the lingering traces of Wordsworth's own domestic affections in France. Otherwise his poetry is not deeply expressive of affection or need for other individuated people. It looks much more like the search for a quasi-divine cure: a cure, this chapter will argue, for a fundamentally political disease. The human unawareness or blankness manifested in the poems hampered not just the *representation* of his deepest feelings for Annette and Caroline but, surely, the original feelings themselves—whereas the whole of book 10, with its deep roots in the rest of the poem and its consequences infiltrating the rest of his life, shows us only too clearly how deeply he felt about England and France.

In chapter 1 we saw Wordsworth in "Tintern Abbey" expounding a philosophy of withdrawal as a cure for political disillusionment. The next two chapters are about why he needed this cure: what it was, in his mind, a cure *for*. A withdrawal of this kind was not in itself a new maneuver. Horace, Cicero, and Marcus Aurelius, for example, had all tried it. One might even say that Taoism is such a philosophy. But in the West the maneuver is recognizable mainly as Stoic. Stoicism has its religious dimension too, a conception of the immanence in us of a universal Primary Being not so far removed from Wordsworth's sense of "something far more deeply interfused." But Wordsworth is not a Stoic, just in that Stoicism is not redemptive. His delivery from evil is not just a matter of withdrawal from the human into a contemplation of Being, or a re-conception of the human as just a part of Being. He wants to make us all *better*: not just to improve or learn to endure everyday life, but to transform it.

This impulse took root in his early twenties, when for the first time in his life he found a cause—found *his* cause. This is common at that age, although it can happen at any age. Part of what it means is that people come to understand causation itself as a matter of human, not just inanimate, agency. Politics is the archetype of such causation. Wordsworth felt that cause as an almost religious recognition, as the true arrival of meaning in his life and everyone's life. This might have made him a political Romantic: one who, as suggested earlier, feels politics chiefly as redemption, as a path to somewhere else, in this case to a better or even a saved soul, *beyond* politics. But he also, at much the same time, against the grain of his own personality, almost incidentally, made the utterly un- or anti-Romantic discovery that politics is a supremely participative and worldly human activity: that the more it is conceived as a matter of higher ideas, as conceptual, rather than as a matter of agency or practice, the more destructive it will become of both self and community. Wordsworth witnessed this destruction at first hand, both within himself and in two societies. But having witnessed it his next response *was* Romantic. He reverted to type. He re-introduced redemptiveness at a higher or deeper level, by turning to Nature and Being not just as refuges from the horror of social humanity but as cures for it: almost as cures for society itself.

This attempt to turn the trajectory from political to post-political experience into redemptive poetry was, as he recognized himself, closely analogous to and perhaps as ambitious as Milton's precursor attempt to turn the Fall into poetry *tout court*: but not into *redemptive* poetry, because for Milton only God can redeem us. Wordsworth's question in books 9 and 10 of *The Prelude*, our principal texts in these two chapters, was whether, after the *political* Fall, poetry itself could become, at least for some special people, not just a social instrument, broadcasting their sense of the injustices suffered by old beggars, destitute mothers, starving children, and so on, but a real moral agent, a thinking with language about politics that could actually transcend, refigure or displace politics. Maybe this was nonsense; but if so, what *else* could poetry be?⁵

Rousseau and Redemption

The Romantic conception of politics as redemptive was essentially Rousseau's. His second and third *Discourses*, on inequality and political virtue (1754–1755), together with the *Social Contract* (1762), constitute between them the most profoundly redemptionist of all political treatises. Their subject is not the original condition so much as original sin. Equality is our original condition, and is just *good*, simply given, part of basic human nature; but it is no longer to be found among us. Inequality, though, is the interesting evil variant, and is all around us. *Amour-propre*, self-love, the fallen form of *amour de soi* or self-esteem, is what *amour de soi* mutates into without the balancing passion, the prime social virtue, of *com*passion. It is essentially the desire for inequality. Rousseau calls it *un sentiment relatif, factice, et né dans la société, qui porte* *chaque individu à faire plus de cas de soi que de tout autre, qui inspire aux hommes tous les maux qu'ils se font mutuellement* ("a relative, artificial element born in society, which leads each individual to place greater value on himself than on anyone else, which inspires all the evils that men do to one another").[6] This relative and artificial feeling is what makes society and its institutions so *méchant*, so wicked. The fallen, post-agricultural and post-industrial Tartarus in which we are politically and morally chained, the crippling burden of *le cas de soi* (*cas* is both "case" and "fall"), came into existence in an ineffable moment of singularity, of originality, like the one in which Satan suddenly felt his "disdain for subjection," his desire for pre-eminence, his relative sense, in *Paradise Lost*. Like him, we turned ourselves, at that moment, into a special "case." On Rousseau's account, this was not the moment when the idea of property was first conceived and imposed, nor when the first tools were invented, nor even when we first compared ourselves with others. It was "the moment any one man needed help from another" (*besoin de secours d'un autre*). *This* was the relative moment, the one when "equality disappeared, property was introduced, work became necessary," metallurgy and agriculture sprang up, and the resultant arrival of wealth caused the more wealthy, in self-defense, to propose social structures and laws. After that "all ran headlong into their chains"—the chains of society and law.[7]

Rousseau's great insight, his radical mutation of the language of the self from a Christian into a secular register, was that evil, or inequality, is a matter of human relativity and artificiality, whereas good, or equality, is absolute and natural. Needing help from each other is our original sin, the first crossing of the atomic boundary between selves. There could hardly be a clearer or more influential recommendation of the inviolable inner or punctual self, the "black box," mentioned at the end of the last chapter. Nor could there be a stronger repudiation of the Aristotelian "political animal," the interactive social self. According to Rousseau, "savage man lives within himself; social man knows only how to live beyond himself" (*le sauvage vit en lui-même; l'homme sociable, toujours hors de lui*).[8] Needing to live with others is what makes us wicked. Needing help is a kind of subjection, a prostration, a humiliation: a discovery of human bondage, not of human bonds. How are we ever to deliver ourselves from inequality, from being subjects, the *sub-iecti,* "those who are thrown under"? We are *méchant,* "fallen badly": from *mis-cadere* (our "mischance"). We are obsessed or burdened with *le cas de soi,* the case of self that is also the fall of the self, or fall *into* self. This is actually a fall *out of* the original, but good, savage self *into* an awareness of the wicked social self. The social self is wicked because in it we see ourselves as relative to others, not constituted by them. We are trapped in our self-consciousness by our oppressive awareness of others. A *subject,* one might say, is a wicked person, someone literally fallen into evil and inequality, someone encased in her relativity, rather than liberated by her relationships or, as formerly, living entirely in herself. She is someone who is aware of others as *better* or *worse* than she is, as richer or poorer, never as equals, certainly never as reciprocally self-constitutive. The original (and good) *sentiment relatif* was compassion, which now, in its hyperbolic form, exists only in the one good person left—namely, Rousseau himself. It amounts to a stronger sense of another person's feeling than that person has herself. The fallen or universal version of this relative feeling, its sinful shadow, is *amour-propre.*

If this is sin, then, this sudden sense of needing help, how shall we be redeemed? The answer is: by ourselves; and in politics. We must learn to feel the *amour de soi* of our *polis* as our own, just as Augustine learned to feel God's will as his own—except that this new God is made of other people's impinging will. We can regain at the level of political "grace" that moral identity and that equality we lost at the level of ethical "sin." This is how it is done, according to the *Social Contract:*[9]

> *Each of us puts his person and all his power in common under the supreme control of the general will, and, as a body, we receive each member as an indivisible part of the whole.* . . . In place of the private person of each contracting party, this act of association at once produces a collective and artificial body, composed of as many members as the assembly has votes, which receives from this same act its unity, its collective self, its life, and its will. (book 1, ch. 6; emphasis in original)

> In order, therefore, that the social pact may not be an empty formula, it tacitly includes the commitment, which alone can give force to the others, that anyone who refuses to obey the general will shall be compelled to do so by the entire body; this means nothing else than that he will be forced to be

free, for such is the condition which, by giving each citizen to the homeland, protects him against all personal dependence . . . (book 1, ch. 7)

At the moment the community is formed, each member gives himself to it, just as he is at the time, himself and all his forces . . . the fundamental pact . . . substitutes a moral and legitimate equality for whatever physical equality nature had been able to impose among men . . . (book 1, ch. 9)

Anyone who dares to undertake the founding of a people (*instituer un peuple*) should feel himself capable of changing human nature, so to speak, of transforming each individual, who by himself is a perfect and solitary whole, into part of a greater whole from which this individual receives, in a way, his life and his being; of altering the human constitution in order to strengthen it; and of substituting a partial and artificial existence for the physical and independent existence we have all received from nature. He must, in a word, take away man's own forces in order to give him new ones which are alien to him, and which he cannot use without the help of others. (book 2, ch. 7)

These extraordinary passages have indeed changed human nature, or at least many people's conception of it as it appears in the political realm. The way of thinking manifested here was certainly fundamental to the political ideas of many revolutionaries in France in the 1780s (and in Germany, Russia, China, and elsewhere in the nineteenth and twentieth centuries). *Instituer*, says Rousseau: this is not just the founding but the very creation of a people, the making of a new human reality, the transformation of the human condition. Human nature is redeemed from itself, bought back from the factitious sin of *amour-propre* at the price of a still greater artifact: the loss of nature itself. This is what "a people" *is*, from now on: a human society of this sort. Within it, individuals are aware of themselves as partial, artificial, and disempowered, alienated from themselves by the very mechanism that protects them against dependence on other individuals, protects them against thinking of themselves in relation to others. The psychic space formerly occupied by the offending *sentiment relatif* is now filled by something else. Each of us now depends on *everyone* else. Equality has returned in that willed act of association which creates the *amour de soi* of a *polis*, its *moi commun* or collective self, its *volonté générale*. That general will is what fills the space.

The deepest significance of the notorious "forced to be free" idea does not lie in its sinister and now obvious Orwellian undertones, so presciently detected by Tocqueville in his own treatise on equality, with its frequent warnings that equality, the master-force of the age, must never be confused with freedom ("none but attentive and clear-sighted men perceive the perils with which equality threatens us"[10]). The real importance of the idea lies in its conception of human nature, and our political nature especially, as henceforth divided into an inserted, artificial, "general" component, and an original, natural, "particular" component. Natural man must always be subordinated, now, to general man. Even the *Confessions*, Rousseau's master-work of self-absolution, essentially demonstrates that only one man has ever been or can ever again be truly natural. Politics is like a permanent and universal gene therapy, or perhaps a hormone therapy (*Brave New World*), or an electroconvulsive therapy (*Nineteen Eighty-Four*). It must forever change and diminish our natures in order to protect us from our own rogue instincts. But the model of the self on which that conception of politics is based is just the dualist, punctual one Rousseau inherited from Descartes. The real rogue, which is actually a concept, not an instinct, is the concept of *equality*. This concept has occupied the center of the Rousseauan self, making all other human characteristics secondary to it. Either sin has become secular or equality has become religious; in either case the two categories are now merged.

So a political engineering of the soul is ostensibly undertaken just to eliminate that inequality between individuals which is shown in any act of assistance toward one person by another person, and which, more importantly, is felt as dependence on that other person. Instead of the sense of inequality there is now a new kind of dependence, not personal but collective. I depend not on you specifically but on everyone, or some notion of everyone, equally. We are all re-equalized in our mutual dependence; when I am helped it can only be by the collective, acting through you. In fact this psychic engineering is a thought experiment, a conceptual invention. Rousseau subjects recalcitrant, oppressive, sinful individuality (the condescending other; the humiliated, inadequate self) to a quasi-divine controlling center, thought of as the avatar of a collective, homogenized humanity. The tutor in Émile and the legislator in the passage from the *Social Contract* above are just such avatars. And this is how politics will redeem us: in that singular, conceptual moment of spontaneous association a new kind of God is born and human nature is remade, its sins sloughed off, its history forgotten, its constituent members indistinguishable. Montesquieu's conception of a nation's *ésprit général*, made up of its climate, religion, laws, customs, and manners, with all the evidences of its past, was annihilated in Rousseau's conception of its *volonté général*. *L'Ésprit des Lois* had been published only fourteen years before the *Social Contract*, and yet it might as well have been from another age entirely.[11] Rousseau's social contract theory, a theory of spontaneous association, was the foundation of Romantic redemptiveness in politics. Wordsworth felt its spell as keenly as anyone else in the early years of the Revolution.

Locke and Milton
Divine Reason, Liberal Man

"I began / To think with fervour upon management / Of nations—what it is and ought to be," wrote Wordsworth of the early summer of 1792 (10.684–86).[12] He was in France. He and his friend Michel Arnaud de Beaupuy, thirty-seven years old to Wordsworth's twenty-two, aristocrat, officer (then captain, later general), and revolutionary "patriot," often spoke with this same fervor, Wordsworth writes, of

> Man and his noble nature, as it is
> The gift of God and lies in his own power,
> His blind desires and steady faculties
> Capable of clear truth, the one to break
> Bondage, the other to build liberty
> On firm foundations, making social life,
> Through knowledge spreading and imperishable,
> As just in regulation, and as pure,
> As individual in the wise and good. (9.363–71)

"Fervour" sounds Rousseauan enough, certainly; but in their references to the management of nations and to "social life" these lines appear much closer in spirit to Tocqueville and Montesquieu than they do to Rousseau. Liberty is something *built*. A just society, not an equal one, is its subject. Justice is its outcome, not its conceptual pre-condition. *Maneggio* (whence "management") is "handling," especially of horses;

natio is originally "race," "breed" or "stock." "'The horse is taught his manage,'" Wordsworth was to reflect, alone and fearful in Paris just after the September massacres (10.70). The metaphors suggest a governance of husbandry and chivalry consistent with Beaupuy's own class and upbringing, and suggestive of ésprit and freedom, not *volonté* and equality. They also evoke, perhaps despite themselves, a Burkean conception of politics as *handling a material*: more on this shortly. But in so far as they are consciously philosophical the lines are not Tocquevillean or Montesquieuan but, naturally enough for an Englishman of Wordsworth's background, Miltonic and Lockean, firmly within the tradition of English revolutionary, republican, liberal, and even conservative political writing since the Civil War.

This tradition certainly had as many egalitarian as libertarian strands. These are evident in the contractarian and communitarian tracts of Richard Overton or Gerrard Winstanley, for example, or even in James Harrington's *Oceana*, in which human reason finally regains only in a republic the original perfection of divinity itself. In Locke's own state of nature it is as important that all men are equal as that they are free, although he is far from making a fetish of inequality. But Locke's *Second Treatise* also owes much to "the judicious Hooker," the anti-Puritan theorist of Church government. Locke's post-contract "Civil Society" is chiefly a mechanism for resolving disputes over "property" (i.e., life, liberty and possessions), with no more "will" in it than the majority of its constituting persons have jointly and contingently resigned to it (Locke's "will" is an empty thing beside Rousseau's). Society has no other end but the preservation of this "property." Locke's liberal person is a rational being ("opposition to Reason . . . is really Madness") that also perceives itself as God's property. What this person renounces in forming the social contract is not a perverted natural self but a duty to preserve God's property. "Justice" in such a dispensation is indeed a kind of "colour'd" violence, as Locke says, a majority imposition; but it is neither an enforced freedom nor a foundational concept. Behind or underpinning Locke's model is a conception of God quite absent from Rousseau's thought: as a final court of appeal, or grounding for all rights, with a will that is just what we call Reason, but with few other attributes. Locke's desiring human will and indemnifying but inscrutable God are the (perilously thin) concepts grounding the constitutional rights legislated for themselves by the "persons" who form civil society. There are no legislators here seeking to iron out and remake human nature. Man's nature is the gift of God, but the management of nations is left to his own powers, as Wordsworth's lines acknowledge. Locke's preservation of a foundational role for God in his social contract sets it apart from Rousseau's. Only God could remake us.[13]

As for Milton, Abdiel's words to Satan in book 5 of *Paradise Lost*, on the blasphemy of debating either liberty or equality with God ("shalt thou dispute / With him?" lines 822–23), are consistent with Locke's conception of God, but might also be advice to Rousseau: presume not God to emulate. The Milton of *Areopagitica* or the pamphlets, especially the *Tenure of Kings and Magistrates* and the *Defensio Secunda*, such important models for Wordsworth's *Letter to the Bishop of Llandaff* (1793) and *The Convention of Cintra* (1809), stood above all for "that real and substantial liberty, which is rather to be sought from within than without."[14] This is a liberty that is "in [man's] own power," as Wordsworth puts it. The elimination of restraint on thought, enabling knowledge to spread, was what Milton meant by liberty. Milton's God was little "thicker" or richer, and even more nakedly arbitrary, than Locke's; and his Satan is an unmetaphorized concept-construction on which the entire machinery of *Paradise Lost* depends. But the foregoing *Prelude* passage speaks to us almost as a secular, humanist Raphael or Michael might have done to Adam. We have our natures from God; we are divided into blind desire on one hand and reason on the other; we seek liberty; and social life is to be lifted in its justice and purity to the level of the best *individual* lives, not remade such that those best lives are weakened or denatured into a collectivity. Neither Locke nor Milton, perhaps, offered the best of models for a poet to use in thinking about either politics or the self, but in his liberal instincts and Christian pieties Wordsworth still seems far closer to them and the seventeenth-century tradition they represent than he does to the French radical tradition of the eighteenth century.

And yet, as W. J. T. Mitchell pointed out twenty years ago,[15] how could *The Prelude not* be a kind of suppressed reiteration of the *Confessions* itself, as well as (in these political books) of the *Social Contract*? In so many of its detailed episodes, its overall trajectory and its *credo* regarding nature, man, feeling, and religion, Wordsworth's autobiography tracks Rousseau's. *Émile* and *The Social Contract* were the talk of intellectual Europe from the 1760s on, and had a profound influence on Kant. The *Confessions*, published in 1782 and 1789, sparked Burke's notorious "philosophy of vanity" attack on their author ("benevolence to the whole species, and want of feeling for every individual . . . a life he flings in the face of his Creator") in the 1791 *Letter to a Member of the National Assembly*.[16] Wordsworth says he "had read, and eagerly / Sometimes, the master-pamphlets of the day," surely including this one (9.96–97). The fervent Beaupuy and his equally "patriotic" but more inhibited English friend (9.124), no matter how much of an emotional and linguistic outsider the latter knew himself to be ("Affecting more emotion than I felt" among those "hissing factionists with ardent eyes," 9.71, 57), could hardly have been unaware of all this, nor unaffected by the broader Rousseauan enthusiasms all around them. This English liberal republican was also the most directly exposed to the French Revolution of all the great contemporary English-language commentators on it, apart from Tom Paine.

So our Lockean and Miltonic liberal republican was also a Rousseauan legislator-revolutionary, a young, sentimental "patriot" with his "heart . . . all / Given to the people" (9.124–25). As we shall see shortly, he was a chivalrous Spenserian dreamer too. The outcome of this complex amalgamation of influences was a sense of political reality quite different from any of theirs, with a corresponding sense of the loss of that reality also more devastating than any of theirs—apart, of course, from Milton, who was Wordsworth's most direct inspiration from the very beginning of his poem.

Burke
Intagliated Liberty

But there was one experience of the Revolution closer than any of these to Wordsworth's, if still not, like his, a first-hand one: that of Edmund Burke.[17] His sense of loss and threat, in particular, corresponded quite closely to the poet's, at least as Wordsworth was writing books 9 and 10, but probably much earlier. Indeed the political and post-political experience of *The Prelude* can be valuably understood as a clash in Wordsworth's mind between Rousseauan and Burkean conceptions of the self.

Here, in order of their appearance in the book, are some of the best-known passages from the *Reflections on the Revolution in France*, published in 1790 and certainly read by Wordsworth (and everyone else) soon after. Together they amount to one long quotation giving a fair impression, I hope, of the philosophical tendency of the whole book. For ease of reference in the following commentary the passages are numbered, with particularly important phrases in bold (i.e., emphases added).[18]

1. I flatter myself that I love a manly, **moral, regulated liberty** as well as any gentleman . . . But I cannot stand forward and give praise or blame to anything which relates to human actions, and human concerns, on **a simple view of the object, as it stands stripped of every relation, in all the nakedness and solitude of metaphysical abstraction.** (7)

2. You will observe that from Magna Charta to the Declaration of Right it has been the uniform policy of our constitution to claim and assert our liberties as an *entailed inheritance* derived to us from our forefathers, and to be transmitted to our posterity—as an estate specially belonging to the people of this kingdom, **without any reference whatever to any other more general or prior right.** (29)

3. **Our political system is placed in a just correspondence and symmetry with the order of the world** and with the mode of existence decreed to a permanent body composed of transitory parts, wherein, by the disposition of a stupendous wisdom, molding together the great mysterious incorporation of the human race, **the whole, at one time, is never old or middle-aged or young, but, in a condition of unchangeable constancy,** moves on through the varied tenor of perpetual decay, fall, renovation, and progression. Thus, by preserving the method of nature in the conduct of the state, in what we improve we are never wholly new; in what we retain we are never wholly obsolete. (30)

4. Far am I from denying in theory, full as far is my heart from with-holding in practice . . . **the *real* rights of men.** . . . If civil society be made for the advantage of man, all the advantages for which it is made become his right. . . . Men have a right to live by that rule; they have a right to do justice, as between their fellows . . . They have a right to the fruits of their industry.

. . . They have a right to the acquisitions of their parents, to the nourishment and improvement of their offspring. . . . **Whatever each man can separately do, without trespassing upon others, he has a right to do for himself**; and he has a right to a fair portion of all which society . . . can do in his favour. [But at the same time] . . . **each person . . . abdicates all right to be his own governor**. He inclusively, in a great measure, abandons the right of self-defence, the first law of nature. . . . **The moment you abate anything from the full rights of men, each to govern himself, and suffer any artificial, positive limitation upon those rights, from that moment the whole organization of government becomes a consideration of convenience** . . . The science of constructing a commonwealth, or renovating it, or reforming it, is, like every other experimental science, **not to be taught *a priori*. . . . The rights of men are in a sort of *middle*, incapable of definition, but not impossible to be discerned**. (51–54)

5. . . . the age of chivalry is gone . . . Never, never more shall we behold that generous loyalty to rank and sex, that proud submission, that dignified obedience, **that subordination of the heart which kept alive, even in servitude itself, the spirit of an exalted freedom** . . . **This mixed system of opinion and sentiment had its origin in the ancient chivalry** . . . produced a noble equality . . . subdued the fierceness of pride and power . . . But now all is to be changed . . . All the **decent drapery of life** is to be rudely torn off. All the superadded ideas, furnished from the **wardrobe of a moral imagination**, which the heart owns and the understanding ratifies as necessary to cover the **defects of our naked, shivering nature**, and to raise it to dignity in our own imagination, are to be exploded as a ridiculous, absurd, and antiquated fashion. . . . **In the groves of *their* academy, at the end of every vista, you see nothing but the gallows**. (66–68)

6. . . . we are generally men of untaught feelings, that, **instead of casting away all our old prejudices, we cherish them to a very considerable degree**, and, to take more shame to ourselves, we cherish them because they are prejudices; and the longer they have lasted and the more generally they have prevailed, the more we cherish them. **We are afraid to put men to live and trade each on his own private stock of reason, because we suspect that this stock in each man is small, and that the individuals**

would do better to avail themselves of the general bank and capital of nations and of ages. Many of our men of speculation, instead of exploding general prejudices, employ their sagacity to discover the latent wisdom which prevails in them . . . they think it more wise to continue the prejudice, with the reason involved, than to **cast away the coat of prejudice and to leave nothing but the naked reason** . . . (76)

7. **Society is indeed a contract** . . . It is a partnership in all science; a partnership in all art; a partnership in every virtue and in all perfection. As the ends of such a partnership cannot be obtained in many generations, **it becomes a partnership not only between those who are living, but between those who are living, those who are dead, and those who are to be born**. (84–85)

8. **The true lawgiver ought to have a heart full of sensibility**. He ought to love and respect his kind, and to fear himself . . . Political arrangement, as it is a work for social ends, is to be only wrought by social means . . . If justice requires this, **the work itself requires the aid of more minds than one age can furnish**. (148–49)

The first passage might be said to contain the essence of all the others. Human nature is to be understood as fluidly relational, almost metaphorical: not punctually conceptual, not abstracted. Liberty is the key political concept, rather than "equality" or "rights." It is not a naked abstraction, but a *regulated condition*. This is what makes it moral: that is to say, it is a part of our *mores*, of customs and habits. Outside this fabric, or weave, liberty is by implication *im*moral, or even not liberty at all, but just the *concept* "Liberty." Strictly what we have are liber*ties*, in fact, not Liberty. These liberties (second passage) are an "entailed inheritance," not an *a priori* right. They are precisely *tailored* (*taille*), intricately shaped (*intaglio*) inheritances, inherent practices with which their makers inform the political understandings of their descendants. In this way (third passage) a state persists and flourishes just as the natural world does. The parts may wither but the whole always remains as a "con-stancy," a standing-together in decay and renovation, in obsolescence and innovation. Rights are to be understood (fourth passage) in the light of this notion of liberty. The "real" rights of men are what we can do for ourselves without damaging the *intaglio*. You can see them but you cannot define them; indeed there might be a sense in which to define them is to weaken them. "Full" rights, the abstract or *a priori* or definable notion of governing oneself without reference to others, are what we have always already abdicated, "spoken away" (*ab-dicere*). Liberties and rights are not things we define, but what we practice together.

Crucially, government is a *convenience*, a coming-together (*con-venire*): not a set of definitions or even institutions. The social contract is a partnership or con-vention between all who live, have lived and will live in a society (seventh passage), not an abnegation of the individual's nature, certainly not a neo-religious transformation of the human condition. It assumes an ab*dic*ation of full rights, certainly, but an abdication giving us the right of entry into an immeasurably fuller and richer self, not a maimed and artificial one. How we are toward this convening, how we feel about it, does indeed rely (fifth passage) on "a subordination of the heart," a continued sense of that abdication. But in one of the profoundest of all insights into both political and ethical sensibility, Burke adds that this is a subordination that keeps "alive, even in servitude itself, the spirit of an exalted freedom." The very holding-back from full or original self-government, that constant self-subordinating restraint, indeed service itself, *is* freedom, the very spirit of freedom, the raising up (*ex-altus*) of freedom. Burke's model of the free self as a with-holding from self-government in conformity with established human practice is almost directly contrary to Kant's model of it as a spontaneous causality in conformity with a concept of reason. The origin of this spirit of freedom, for Burke, lies in chivalry, where the fiercest warrior becomes, of his own volition, the most abject servant. He puts on the decent drapery of civility, the wardrobe of the moral imagination, and leaves behind his fierce pride and power, now seen as the attributes of a naked shivering self. The revolutionary intellectual, by contrast, strips off the drapery, releases a ferocious abstraction, and reveals in all their starkness the gallows to which it will inevitably drive us. "Reason" is our mode of recourse to naked solitary abstraction, available to us only as a small private stock. Prejudice (sixth passage), on the other hand, is the "bank and capital" of the whole society and many other societies, accumulated only over long periods of time. "It is not so much our judgements as it is our prejudices that constitute our being," comments Hans-Georg Gadamer; our prejudices "are the biases of our openness to the world."[19] But Burke is less abstract about this moral fabric, this wardrobe of the imagination. Prejudice is for him a store of latent intagliated wisdom; we actively explore it, enlarge it, rather than just being constituted by it. And legislators, many of them, over many ages, are the best of us all at this task of unearthing, preserving, and tailoring ancient wisdoms (eighth passage): never presuming to remake human nature *de novo*, to redeem it from some primal deformation; but still always handling it, shaping it. The specter of losing this ancient rich store of wisdom is what terrifies Burke: "gone," "never more."

෴

Part of what this chapter proposes (not for the first time, by any means, although Wordsworthians for a long time seemed reluctant to say this out loud[20]) is that Wordsworth's deepest political and indeed moral instincts, although given freer rein by the time he wrote books 9 and 10 of *The Prelude*, were more Burkean than Rousseauan. He often seems to be groping for Burkean insights through a Rousseauan dazzle (that French dawn!). He is less metaphorically adept and consistent in his political thought than Burke, more inclined to follow Rousseau and his predecessors and followers in looking for spontaneous redemptions and conceptual certainties. And when his final crisis came, through the reading and rejection of Godwin's *Political Justice*, with its impoverished moral language and its differing debts to both Rousseau and Locke, he did not turn back to Burke, Godwin's adversary, for help. The encomium on the "Genius of Burke" at *Prelude* 7.512 was not added until 1832; the Burkean-Miltonic *Convention of Cintra* dates from 1808–1809; but the Godwinian *Letter to the Bishop of Llandaff* was written almost at the point of the crisis in 1793 (we shall return to Godwin later, in the last section but one of this chapter). But for all that, the broadly Burkean political self must stand behind Wordsworth's poetry as the principal alternative to the broadly Rousseauan one. Are we a spontaneous association of fallen souls, or a constant convenience of prejudiced inheritors? Do we work like sculptors with the ancient material of the state, or do we vaporize it and start again? Finally, and perhaps most importantly, Burke's metaphors are themselves both "intagliated" and "convenient." His model of the state and, by implication, of the self, *is* metaphorical, where Rousseau's, Locke's, Kant's, and (as we shall see) Godwin's are all conceptual. His thought is more congenial than theirs to any fundamentally metaphorical poetry. Wordsworth both felt this and resisted it. He wanted poetry to be poetry and not something else, but he also wanted his to be a new *kind* of poetry, full of conceptualized Rousseauan sentiment. Burke was a rival because he wrote about politics almost as a poet might.

History
Swarm of Locusts or Fragrant Spring . . .

. . . hissing factionists or merry crowds? Which of these two images best suited Wordsworth's France, in that critical epoch between 1790 and 1792?

> 'Twas in truth an hour
> Of universal ferment—mildest men
> Were agitated, and commotions, strife
> Of passion and opinion, filled the walls
> Of peaceful houses with unquiet sounds.
> The soil of common life was at that time
> Too hot to tread upon. Oft said I then,
> And not then only, "What a mockery this
> Of history, the past and that to come!
> Now do I feel how I have been deceived,
> Reading of nations and their works in faith—
> Faith given to vanity and emptiness—
> Oh, laughter for the page that would reflect
> To future times the face of what now is!"
> The land all swarmed with passion, like a plain
> Devoured by locusts . . . (9.164–79)

This was probably in the summer of 1792.[21] No Divine Reason or General Will here, apparently: certainly no Ancient Chivalry: only ferment, agitation, commotion, and strife, a widespread or general disturbance, a boiling (*fermentare*) or overheated general to-and-fro. "I saw the revolutionary power / Toss like a ship at anchor, rocked by storms" (9.48–49); the imagery was already, in late 1791 or early 1792, of violent but constrained movement, without direction or purpose, a febrile swarming of passion, a devouring of peace, fertile land, and common life. More of a cultural tourist than a patriot at this early juncture of his second visit, Wordsworth preferred Charles le Brun's Mary Magdalene to this swarm of locusts (9.75–80). This was the "fever of the world," the "fretful stir unprofitable" of "Tintern Abbey", the "Babel din" of London in *Prelude* 7 (7.157).

And yet—*this* was history, he realized, this disquieting, clamorous, anchored agitation: not the "historian's tale" of "Old heroes and their sufferings and their deeds" that used to excite him in earlier youth just as much as the "Tales of the poets" did (9.207–11). Indeed the historian's tale is *less* helpful than the poet's when reality confronts us. Such history strips events of "the life / Of manners and familiar incidents" that is their "humanizing soul" (8.775–76), whereas poetry at least retains these. This swarming passion, maybe, was how the Civil War had really been, or even the Glorious Revolution. So London in book 7 had turned out, chasteningly, to be an "endless stream of men and moving things" (7.158), a "perpetual flow of trivial objects" (7.702–3), not the romantic "Babylon or Persepolis" (7.85) he had imagined as a child, not a fairytale place of "gorgeous ladies, fairy cataracts" and "flowery gardens," of "processions, equipages, lords and dukes" (7.110–34). But from the later perspective of his rural seclusion this "real scene" became a "frequent daydream for my riper mind" (7.139, 153). Only a daydream now: but a dream of the real. The disenchantments of reality gave the political insights of this romantic dreamer a dimension missing from the thought of his more conceptualizing philosophical precursors. The world of the *polis* was always noisy and frequently unintelligible, but *this* was what, for him, had to be accommodated. The intensity of feeling with which he then accommodated it was commensurate with his dreamer's dismay when first confronted by the unaccommodated reality. And when the accommodation itself later failed he was, once again, commensurately dismayed.

The dazzling prospect of an accommodation to political humanity had first opened in the summer of 1790, at the time of Wordsworth's first visit to France with his friend Robert Jones:

> But 'twas a time when Europe was rejoiced,
> France standing on the top of golden hours,

And human nature seeming born again . . .
How bright a face is worn when joy of one
Is joy of tens of millions . . .
Among sequestered villages we walked
And found benevolence and blessedness
Spread like a fragrance everywhere, like spring
That leaves no corner of the land untouched . . .
Clustered together with a merry crowd
Of those emancipated, with a host
Of travellers, chiefly delegates returning
From the great spousals newly solemnized
At their chief city, in the sight of Heaven . . .
All hearts were open, every tongue was loud
With amity and glee. (6.352–409)

This was the first anniversary of what might be termed the Great Singularity of 1789, and human nature seemed to be realizing Rousseau's vision all by itself, without the intervention of any legislator. Every one of tens of millions of people shares a single emotion; the whole of humanity wears a single face; this is a spontaneous event, and yet it is not engineered. Basic moral emotions such as benevolence, even sacrificial ones such as blessedness, are as real, as sensory, as non-abstract, as if they were fragrances. Prague spring, Arab spring: human nature always seems to be "born again" at these times, as if the renewal were seasonal. But the rebirth in this great original case of political modernity seemed to be an apocalyptic or revelatory discovery (*apo-kalyptein* means "take the cover off"). Wordsworth's witnessing of revolution is itself originary for the English-speaking world; *this* is how we are henceforth to think of popular revolution—as apocalypse.

Perhaps the deepest source for this imagery of secular apocalypse is John's Gospel (3.3-8). "Except a man be born again," Jesus says to the rabbi, "he cannot see the kingdom of God." "How can a man be born when he is old?" asks Nicodemus incredulously; "can he enter the second time into his mother's womb, and be born?" This is the response (Authorized Version):

Except a man be born of water and of the Spirit, he cannot enter into the kingdom of God. That which is born of the flesh is flesh; and that which is

born of the Spirit is spirit . . . The wind bloweth where it listeth, and thou
hearest the sound thereof, but canst not tell whence it cometh, and whither
it goeth: so is every one that is born of the Spirit.

Behind Wordsworth's conception of human nature remade is the
Christian idea of the Spirit that is also the Word: a redeeming wind or
breath, a spring whose source is inscrutable, a unique, non-seasonal
annunciation in a beam of light from somewhere above and beyond our
world ("born again" is the expression used in the Bible to render the
Greek *a-nothen*, "from above" or "from further back"). This Christian
provenance enables for Wordsworth a vision of a spontaneous political
reality, a more human polity, unimaginable even to Rousseau. The two
young Englishmen walk among a people touched by the word, every
tongue speaking the same language of feeling, freshly returned from a
marriage between King and People not unlike that between Christ and
his Church, in a secular City of God.

This is something new in European experience, as Wordsworth
recognized: a vision of political life as blessed, as a visitation of the
spirit to a whole nation all at once, as universal rejoicing. His own rendering of this vision has become part of our political awareness, part
of our (often misguided) sense of how politics and especially revolu-
tions can or should be. Human nature is uncovered, as if for the first
time, and what is revealed underneath is *more real* than what appeared
before. This cannot be so, of course, but the sheer power of this illusion should tell us that despite its apparent affinities with his thought it
is not just Rousseau's illusion, but comes from somewhere much older
and deeper. Wordsworth imagines the annunciation coming spontaneously from something like a God: a Pentecostal speaking where everyone hears the same words but in his own language. In the *Profession
de foi du vicaire Savoyard*, for example, Rousseau does not imagine any
such connection between Man and the Supreme Being, the benevolent
will or intelligence that set the universe in motion. His is, if anything,
a *more* Stoic picture. The change in human nature is to be wrought by
human beings—but it is to be wrought *on* some *by* others. In Wordsworth's picture it happens spontaneously in all. This is closer to Locke,
if anyone, or at least to a Lockean conception of God's role in the
political realm, interpreted in biblical terms. Now everyone can play
an equal part in politics—but as one nation under God, so to speak

("under Nature, under God": 8.394; see the following section). Rousseau's picture may seem more humanist but it is also *less* egalitarian.

But of course any former witness to such an apocalypse, such a fragrant spring, must become fretful when the ferment and commotion of ordinary history resumes. He is desperate for renewed evidence, within that swarm of locusts, of redemptive political activity, of "dazzle." Wordsworth looked for this everywhere amid the "universal ferment" of Paris in the summer of 1792.

> But though untaught by thinking or by books
> To reason well of polity or law,
> And nice distinctions—then on every tongue—
> Of natural rights and civil . . .
> Yet in the regal sceptre, and the pomp
> Of orders and degrees, I nothing found
> Then, or had even in crudest youth,
> That dazzled me, but rather what my soul
> Mourned for, or loathed, beholding that the best
> Ruled not, and feeling that they ought to rule. (9.201–17)

The young poet feels out of place in the world of rational or theoretical political discourse, with its complex Rousseauan distinctions between natural and civil rights. Argument over this keystone of all Rousseau's thought can seem to him like mere agitation. But his "soul," what he might normally call his heart, rather than his fervent reason, knows that the best, the true *aristoi*, the ones he referred to earlier as "the wise and good," should "rule." They should be the ones against whom and by whom the state is measured (*regulare*). These legislators are anything but Rousseauan. They set standards, they see beauty and the good, but they do not engineer other souls. They may manage the stock but they do not try to change the nature of the beast. This is at least as Burkean, or perhaps Whiggish, as it is Platonic or Rousseauan. This was Wordsworth's "third way," so to speak: neither apocalypse nor swarm. In exploring it he moved fitfully toward his critical but partial insight into political agency.

London and Agency

To find the genesis of this "aristocratic way" we need to look back again, this time to 1791, the year of Wordsworth's "Residence in London" (the title of book 7), falling between his two visits to France. Book 7 shows us the details of this residence. Book 8, "Love of Nature Leading to Love of Mankind," sets the details in that broader life-context already sketched in "Tintern Abbey." We saw in chapter 1 that forms of natural beauty were supposed by Wordsworth to have the capacity to become forms of good, but that even in his own practice they did not do this. In "Tintern Abbey" love of nature may have led him to love of mankind, or at least of the music of humanity, but only by withdrawing him *from* mankind. Reality became in book 7's phrase a "daydream for his riper mind." In book 8 he thinks of Nature while he is in the city, rather than of the city while he is in Nature; but the outcome is the same.

> With deep devotion, Nature, did I feel
> In that great city what I owed to thee:
> High thoughts of God and man, and love of man,
> Triumphant over all those loathsome sights
> Of wretchedness and vice . . . (8.62–66)

In other words, forms of beauty provide elevated or noble *thoughts and feelings* to triumph over painful or ugly *sensations* ("loathsome" is cognate with both *leid* in German and *laid* in French). These unpleasant sensations are caused by one's perception of others' experience, not one's own direct experience, of misery or evil. Any good Lockean would seek to minimize this unpleasantness, which is both peculiar to those possessing an enhanced capacity for sympathy and, for the same reason, easily remediable in such people. This is one of those "Tintern Abbey" moments when Wordsworth's aesthetic hedonism presses rather too hard on his deeper moral philosophy. "Early converse with the works of God," the "virtue" in the "forms / Perennial of the ancient hills," shapes "the measure and the prospect of the soul / To majesty," the poet explains at the end of book 7 (719–26), making the transition to book 8. This is rather more attractive, but still all too clear: moral qualities are visible, palpable—are in fact sensory qualities—in Nature, and they can therefore inform and soothe a perceptive soul. Forms of beauty are forms of good. The informed soul is noble, aristocratic in its own virtue, like a mountain, feeling itself not so much above wretches and evildoers as beyond being distressed by them. *High* thoughts: to look up is to look in, and *vice versa.* The remedy is available only to those likely to be most affected by the disease, but the point of writing the poem is to make the remedy more widely available to such people.

Such a soul is almost Nature's companion as much as he is her disciple. But oddly enough, this moment of "proud humility" turns out to be less complacent than it seems. Now, as book 8 opens, Wordsworth's political sense deepens that broadly Lockean aesthetic hedonism into something altogether more original and appealing. The "dearest fellow-labourer" of the sun, the sky, the elements and seasons, is the "heart of man," beating or working in rhythm with Nature. "Man free, man working for himself" is a thing of "beauty, and inevitable grace." This is an important *political* step. The man or woman fully informed by and integrated into the life of the natural world is not just virtuous and beautiful but *free.* Not all country laborers work for themselves, of course, but those who do emit the true "fragrance . . . of humanity" (the phrase echoes both the fragrant spring and the music of humanity). They are the *most* human of all human beings (8.147–58).

The shepherd who "feels himself . . . / A freeman" was seen years before by the "rambling schoolboy" Wordsworth as almost superhuman:

> . . . thus
> Have I beheld him; without knowing why,
> Have felt his presence in his own domain
> As of a lord and master, or a power,
> Or genius, under Nature, under God,
> Presiding . . . (8.391–95)

This master is a natural aristocrat, a president or presiding genius of all his domain, a quasi-Natural "presence" or "power" (those key Wordsworthian annunciations of Being)—but of course under Nature and God, or Nature *as* God. He is, indeed, an Adam—or an Eve. Here is Milton:

> Two of far nobler shape erect and tall
> Godlike erect with native honour clad

In naked majesty seemed lords of all,
And worthy seemed, for in their looks divine
The image of their glorious Maker shone,
Truth, wisdom, sanctitude severe and pure,
Severe but in true filial freedom placed;
Whence true authority in men . . . [22]

The echoes are unmistakable. But the onlooker this time, the witness in Paradise, is the devout disciple Wordsworth, not the resentful, disdainful Satan. The experience was deeply formative:

> Thus was man
> Ennobled outwardly before mine eyes,
> And thus my heart at first was introduced
> ˋ To an unconscious love and reverence
> Of human nature; hence the human form
> To me was like an index of delight,
> Of grace and honour, power and worthiness. (8.410–16)

Blake's "human form divine" has the same Miltonic ring; so, notably, has Kant's self-legislating person of *Würde*, of free will, of causative agency. These are beings of "true authority," fit to govern not just themselves but others.

Wordsworth describes these aristocrats most famously in book 13, in the passage referred to in chapter 2, his culminating account of the imaginative person:

> They need not extraordinary calls
> To rouze them—in a world of life they live,
> By sensible impressions not enthralled,
> But quickened, rouzed, and made thereby more fit
> To hold communion with the invisible world.
> Such minds are truly from the Deity,
> For they are powers; and hence the highest bliss
> That can be known is theirs—the consciousness
> Of whom they are, habitually infused
> Through every image, and through every thought,
> And all impressions; hence religion, faith,
> And endless occupation for the soul,

> Whether discursive or intuitive;
> Hence sovereignty within and peace at will,
> Emotion which best foresight need not fear,
> Most worthy then of trust when most intense;
> Hence chearfulness in every act of life;
> Hence truth in moral judgements; and delight
> That fails not, in the external universe.

> Oh, who is he that hath his whole life long
> Preserved, enlarged, this freedom in himself?—
> For this alone is genuine liberty. (13.101–21)

This imaginative person is also the political person, possessing genuine liberty. He is an aristocrat on his Edenic estate, a human form of near-divine power. He is an Adam, an "index of" (literally "pointer to") the highest, Paradisal bliss, the "delight / That fails not." More: he is actually a kind of angel. He occupies himself not just in that "discourse of reason" which for the Renaissance had marked the human, but in the practice of that "intuitive" or "right" reason which Milton's Raphael ascribed to the angels: "discourse / Is oftest yours, the latter most is ours, / Differing but in degree, of kind the same" (5.488–90). His "communion with the invisible world" or "world of life," as opposed to the sensible world, is like an angelic discourse of this kind. Such angelic and aristocratic minds "are truly from the Deity," their authority being derived directly not so much from God as from Nature. "For they are powers," just as the angels addressed by God a few lines later in *Paradise Lost* are "Thrones, Dominations, Princedoms, Virtues, Powers" (5.601).[23]

Inner sovereignty or autonomy, peace as a matter of will, truth in moral judgment as delight in forms of beauty, inner freedom as genuine liberty: this free shepherd, his self-consciousness enhanced by his imaginative powers, looks for a moment as much like Kantian or Miltonic Man as he does the engineered Rousseauan or chivalric Burkean models. "We are still living in the age of the Kantian man, or Kantian man-god," says Iris Murdoch.

> This man is with us still, free, independent, lonely, powerful, rational, responsible, brave, the hero of so many novels and books of moral philosophy . . . In

fact Kant's man had already received a glorious incarnation nearly a century earlier in the work of Milton; his proper name is Lucifer.²⁴

Wordsworth's version, though, is in transition from Enlightenment to Romanticism, from Reason to Imagination. This "Man, inwardly contemplated, and present / In my own being," "instinct / With godhead," "rapt away" by "the divine effect of power and love" (8.632–39), is an enlightened angel-aristocrat, a visitor from a higher world, a benign, secular Lucifer. "As when a traveller hath from open day / With torches passed into some vault of earth" (8.711–12), but "gloomier far, a dim / Analogy to uproar and misrule" (8.662–63): so Wordsworth arrived in this infernal bedlam called London. "A dungeon horrible . . . of mournful gloom" is what Milton called Hell, that other, analogous place of uproar and misrule (1.61, 1.244²⁵). But Wordsworth in London was neither a Satanic ruler nor a Dantean witness: more benevolent than one, more *engagé* than the other.

Crucially, this instinctive godhead or angelic autonomy did not merely insulate him from humanity, did not just guarantee him a world of delight by "softening" and "solemnizing" the "vulgar light / Of present, actual, superficial life" (8.651–52), as at the end of book 7. His residence in London saw the awakening in Wordsworth of a genuinely beneficent, not just a benevolent, consciousness:

> . . . seeing, I essayed
> To give relief, began to deem myself
> A moral agent, judging between good
> And evil not as for the mind's delight
> But for her safety, one who was to *act*—
> As sometimes to the best of my weak means
> I did, by human sympathy impelled,
> And through dislike and most offensive pain
> Was to the truth conducted—of this faith
> Never forsaken, that by acting well,
> And understanding, I should learn to love
> The end of life and every thing we know. (8.666–77)

This "seeing" does not prompt a mere *wish* to "give relief," but an essay, an attempt. This is no doubt a fairly unremarkable impulsion, deriving straightforwardly from sympathy, as he admits ("wherefore speak of things / Common to all?," 8.665–66). But this impulsion actually to *do* something, to *give* relief, is what saves him from his habitually hedonistic or aestheticizing withdrawal: "not as for the mind's delight," but "to *act*." *Salvus* is "whole" or "healthy," and gives us not only "safe" but also "salvation." The metaphor is the familiar Wordsworthian one of restoration, of renewed spiritual health. Moral judgment, the act of judgment, is what sound people *do*, not what pleasure-seekers *think about*: after all, it can bring "offensive pain." And to judge means not only "to *act*" (in Wordsworth's emphasis) but also "acting *well* " (in mine). Wordsworth even implies that *only* acting well brings real understanding of a moral case: "and [*thus*] understanding." Moral agency, not just forms of beauty, not just, as Satan says, "the mind . . . in itself," will make "a heav'n of hell" (1.254–55[26]). All this is much better than withdrawal; indeed it is the single most important step on Wordsworth's path from a generalized, vague, almost abstract sympathy, to some kind of real political agency.

And yet there is always the half step back, or even two steps. It still is not entirely clear what acting well amounts to, apart from learning to understand and love. Acting well *how*? Understanding *what*? What "end of life"? Love *everything* we know?

Wordsworth's next important moment of political recognition has very little to do with agency. It happens, properly enough, when the full reality of London, which he calls his "Preceptress stern" (8.678), is first borne in upon the young country traveler, arriving on the roof of the coach. "Never shall I forget the hour" (8.689). At the exact moment when he crosses the "threshold" from suburbia into "the great city," he says, then "great God! / That aught *external* to the living mind / Should have such mighty sway":

> A weight of ages did at once descend
> Upon my heart—no thought embodied, no
> Distinct remembrances, but weight and power,
> Power growing with the weight . . .
> All that took place within me came and went
> As in a moment, and I only now
> Remember that it was a thing divine. (8.689–710)

The "thing divine" is the *polis* in its entirety. The emphasis on *external* draws our attention to the fact that this is the human world breaking in, that external living minds are making themselves felt. After this moment of encompassing vision, when the threshold between his mind and the external world is at last crossed, he is submerged in the confused uproar of the "vault of earth" (8.712). This is the infernal cavern familiar from *Aeneid* 6 and *Paradise Lost* 1, which at first glance overwhelms and then immediately, strangely, disappoints the traveler, as if in that first panoramic glance he had seen everything and reached the end of what there was to see within an instant. After that he loses himself once more in the close details of a "spectacle to which there is no end" (8.741). But at that first moment he feels he has been moved by "a swell of feeling, followed soon / By a blank sense of greatness passed away" (like the wave breaking just after it has passed under the surfer). The moment is identical with the one in book 6 in which Wordsworth and Jones find they have crossed the Alps; indeed Wordsworth originally used parts of this London passage in the Alps episode. "Something evermore about to be" was his expression for that earlier experience of imaginative rebound from an anti-climax that makes the mind "Strong in itself" (6.542–47).

The moment of arrival in London is like the moment of crossing the Alps. The traveler feels the power of the external world, a sense of the divine or sublime, a mood of expectation, a moment of disappointment, a rebound into activity. But this time the sublime presence is a vast city, not mountains; this is the human sublime. The activity is social. Instead of seeing river, crags, and clouds as "Characters of the great apocalypse, / The types and symbols of eternity" (6.570–71), the reinvigorated mind contains "elevated thoughts / Of *human* nature" (6.801–2, emphasis added); "new objects, simplified, arranged, / Impregnated my knowledge, made it live."

> Neither guilt nor vice,
> Debasement of the body or the mind,
> Nor all the misery forced upon my sight . . .
> . . . could overthrow my trust
> In what we may become . . .
> Lo, everything that was indeed divine

Retained its purity inviolate
And unencroached upon, nay, seemed brighter far
For this deep shade in counterview, the gloom
Of opposition, such as shewed itself
To the eyes of Adam, yet in Paradise
Though fallen from bliss, when in the East he saw
Darkness ere day's mid course, and morning light
More orient in the western cloud, that drew
'O'er the blue firmament a radiant white,
Descending slow with something heavenly fraught.' (8.799–823)

The quotation from *Paradise Lost* (11.203–7[27]) is all but verbatim now, even preceding Wordsworth's own quotation marks (see my italics); and its implications are many. London is a sublime hell, or at best a fallen Eden; but the mind of this wanderer (an Aeneas or Dante, maybe an Adam—not quite a Satan), though "fallen from bliss," though beset by sin, finds itself rebounding from a flat or blank sense that even the sublime is not really all that sublime, to a new sense of redemption from guilt and vice, a new hope of the divine, a new angel hid in a cloud. The hope, that forlorn hope mentioned at the start of this chapter, takes the shape of "what we may become":

Add also, that among the multitudes
Of that great city oftentimes was seen
Affectingly set forth, more than elsewhere
Is possible, the unity of man,
One spirit over ignorance and vice
Predominant, in good and evil hearts
One sense for moral judgements, as one eye
For the sun's light. (8.824–31)

"The starry heavens above, the moral law within": again it is Kant who has the same sense of what is at the heart of the ethical and political realm—namely, that "sensation" of "union or communion" that gives the soul its "highest joy," its sense of being one not just with Nature and God (831–36) but also with all of humanity. Wordsworth has been able to transfer his sense of human oneness from France on top of her golden hours to a still unredeemed London.

This was Wordsworth's deeply qualified reconsideration of his new belief in agency: the point where he retreated from its genuinely novel implications into an older habit of thought disguised as another discovery. The natural aristocrat is the only one who can make redemptive sense of the loathsome sights of the city, its wretchedness and vice. He sees on behalf of us all that we are *one* spirit, *one* sense, *one* city. Each of us is not just one with nature, but one with all humanity. Love of Nature leads to love of Man—but not men. The human form in general is indeed a *form*, an index of delight as God's finger points to it. That is the light in the cloud, that is what Wordsworth's imagination rebounds into, and that is now the shaky ground of his belief in agency. He will act for *that*, not just out of ordinary sympathy—or rather, this is what ordinary sympathy *is*, for him. He will see *that* in ordinary people; he will see them like *that*, as types, as souls perhaps.

He looks at a workingman sitting in a square holding a "sickly babe" on his knee and notices the man's expression as he gazes at the child: he "eyed it with unutterable love" (8.844–59). The feeling is so universal that neither the man nor the poet can articulate it; it is the meaning of the man and the child. In seeing humanity that way lies safety or salvation for the poet's mind; and "in seeing I essayed to give," to act. Giving turns out to be just seeing, after all. Essaying is still not actually doing. But further: this is the perspective of the "best" who "ought to rule"; those who can look as if they were Adam on ordinary fallen people, or who can look on Adam as if they were angels. They do not seek to change human nature: only to represent and thus "manage" it, its impact on them. And in the end, for Wordsworth, the poet is the epitome of such minds; his poetry is his agency. This is a peculiar conception of agency, not just because it denies full identity to other people, but because it is undertaken primarily for the safety of the actor's mind rather than the benefit of the one acted on: for the salvation, not just delight, of higher minds, not lower bodies.

Still, the story was not yet over. London in 1791 had at least brought Wordsworth a glimpse of a new agential possibility, even if it was then obscured by older and more powerful models of thought. France in 1792 delivered an experience that was harder to obscure in this way.

Sources of Power
Disposition or Zeal?

Wordsworth's political epiphany occurred in the spring and early summer of 1792, while he was living in Orléans and Blois, in conversations or interactions with Michel Beaupuy and other officers. He was also at this time deeply involved with Annette Vallon, whose family lived in Blois. Not that Wordsworth ever puts it so straightforwardly. Fact, notoriously in short supply during this period of his life, is never his principal business anyway. On that autobiographical continuum running from evidence-based historiography at one end to poetry's metaphorical kind of moral thought at the other, *The Prelude* and its companion poems are very much at the latter end.

The poem's principal business, as Wordsworth makes perfectly clear in the original 1799 two-book *Prelude*, is with "spots of time":[28] those mysteriously renovating or restorative singularities, whose spontaneous emissions alone shed the light of meaning on the teeming mass of otherwise unintelligible trivialities we call our lives. (Physicists refer to the phenomenon in which an atom or nucleus suddenly changes state and emits a photon, a unit of light, as a "spontaneous emission.") The poem is a kind of palimpsest of such quantized or punctual moments of meaning-giving, layered onto and superseding each other: such as the ones on the outskirts of London and on crossing the Alps referred to just above. The various versions of the poem themselves have this character. Writing the poem is a matter of assembling the moments so as to allow the palimpsest to shed its own new light on the poet's life, or rather to *make* the meaning-laden, poetized life. This was not just a "poem on the growth of my own mind," which was the only name Wordsworth himself ever gave to what we now know as the *Prelude*, but a poem *as* the growth of his own mind. Some aspects of the Wordsworth of 1792, the one who had these primary experiences, are recreatively represented by the Wordsworth of 1804, who narrates them. The outcome is a layered composite self accessible only through the poem.

As we saw in chapters 1 and 2, Wordsworth's poetry proposes this way of poem-making as a model for all human life-making. In addition to being an aesthetic model of how life is, it is also an essentially dualist one. On the one hand there is all the inert material, and on the other hand there are a few highly charged particles. On the one hand so many inert minds, on the other a few highly charged individuals. (This is still an operative model today in many progressive, redemptive circles: the charged or saved redeem the inert or fallen.) What made those spring and summer days in 1792 so crucial was that then, for the only time in his life, Wordsworth escaped this aesthetic-dualist model and glimpsed another one: agential and integrated. Indeed it is hard not to think that the collapse of this briefly glimpsed alternative, in which all of us are equally charged members of an active political world, was what drove him to construct the palimpsestic, quantized, Pauline-Augustinian-Rousseauan model of the single self in nature for which he is now so famous, and which became so enormously influential in the post-Christian English-speaking world of the nineteenth and twentieth centuries.

This period in 1792 (we are now in book 9) was when Wordsworth experienced in himself the apocalypse he had first witnessed in the French people in 1790. He came to understand more fully, he felt, the nature of that "uncovering" he had seen in them. Then human nature had seemed reborn, as if spontaneously, both of itself and by the grace of God; now, from his first-person viewpoint, human beings seemed to have it in their own power consciously to remake their circumstances. But if this model was more agential it was still surprisingly inegalitarian. Some had more power, or access to better sources of power, than others: some may have been, if not more equal, then more open to *ideas* of equality. Wordsworth even saw himself as one of these special ones—though by virtue of his upbringing rather than of his reason.

The sources of his political power, as he describes them, were three. First, paradoxically, there was the natural egalitarianism of his boyhood surroundings in the Lake District. Noone there, or so it seemed to him, was "vested with attention or respect / Through claims of wealth or blood" (9.218–26). Second, there was Cambridge, where on Wordsworth's somewhat ingenuous (or perhaps disingenuous) account he found that academic life resembled a "republic," in that "talents" and "industry" conferred more "esteem" than "wealth and titles" (9.226–36). Third, a "mountain liberty" had been conferred on him since birth by the landscapes of his home. Like a mountain himself, perhaps, or else moved by the mountains' scale to discount human pretention, he recognized only "God and Nature's single sovereignty" (9.237–42). His sense of "subservience" to this sovereignty is coeval with his sense of liberty, making it sound closer to a Burkean service than a Rousseauan subjection.

Liberty, republic, sovereignty, privilege, talent: several of the master-concepts of political theory crop up in this story. Wordsworth's original insight is that to someone of his upbringing, his constitution, the Revolution or "government of equal rights / And individual worth" (9.248–49) at first seemed an obvious and *natural* outcome. It was the outcome, not of a triumph of reason in these political concepts, as if, in Kantian manner, to feel reason's imperative *is* to act on it, but of "nature's certain course" (9.253). At one level this looks like mere naïveté: are all human beings naturally equal under God in just the way William Wordsworth's own upbringing has suggested to him? Are all human beings born into mountain communities naturally egalitarian? But at another level this acculturated and aestheticized way of accounting for political dispositions and modes of agency points to an important naturalistic alternative to either a conceptual (Kantian, Platonic) or an appetitive (Hobbesian, Thrasymachian) way. Wordsworth thinks of his political self as continuous with his whole self. The confessional, life-writing approach here is obviously Rousseauan; but the anti-conceptualism is not.

This dispositional confidence, rather than any sort of superior reason, enabled Wordsworth to defeat in political argument the group of anti-revolutionary military officers he chiefly associated with:

> Zeal which yet
> Had slumbered, now in opposition burst
> Forth like a Polar summer. Every word
> They uttered was a dart by counter-winds
> Blown back upon themselves; their reason seemed
> Confusion-stricken by a higher power
> Than human understanding, their discourse
> Maimed, spiritless—and, in their weakness strong,
> I triumphed. (9.259–67)

This was a moment to rank with his discovery of agency in London. It was his own first political triumph, his real arrival as a political *actor*, and it marks an epoch in Wordsworth's represented life. His political self had been a polar waste, not a "Polar summer," up to now; the knowledge of this previous emptiness was the legacy of 1790. Sadly, though, the summer was to be as short as a polar one, as he was soon to find out, and as he certainly knew by the time these lines were written. But for now, impelled more by the whole warp of his personality than by any recent ideas, feelings, or experiences, he was, at last, a player. Their words became his weapons. His power overcame their reason.

Yet the moment is heavily qualified, as so often in Wordsworth, and the qualification occurs apparently without his intending it, as also happens often. What emerges as decisive in the struggle, out of this deep chasm or contour of the self, is something he chooses to call "Zeal." The Greek *zeilos* is also the source of our "jealousy," and Hebrew too has one word for the two concepts (*kana*). The jealous person is over-zealous in defense of what he sees as his own. But even the zealot may already be seen as over-zealous. The original Jewish zealots, including the disciple Luke calls Simon Zelotes (6.15) and Matthew brackets with Judas (10.4; Matthew's "Canaanite" is probably cognate with *kanan* or *qan'an*, not Canaan), were fanatical, without restraint or compunction in their hostility to non-believers. This is a feeling that comes straight from that inaccessible inner place where a god dwells. This is a higher or deeper power than *any* human understanding can reach. Virtue as character has once again morphed into virtue as spontaneity; emission once again trumps disposition.

This may rather undermine our confidence in Wordsworth's judgment in book 9 regarding either the rural or the academic equality of rights. His insight into the "politics" of rural life was certainly deeper on other occasions, when his real business was with civil not political society: with ethics, really, rather than politics. The most celebrated example of this deeper insight is "The Old Cumberland Beggar," first published in the 1800 edition of *Lyrical Ballads*.[29] The old man of the title, simply by pursuing his endless round from door to door, "keeps alive / The kindly mood in hearts" (lines 83–84) which might otherwise relapse slowly into selfishness.

> Where'er the aged Beggar takes his rounds,
> The mild necessity of use compels
> To acts of love; and habit does the work

Of reason, yet prepares that after joy
Which reason cherishes. And thus the soul,
By that sweet taste of pleasure unpursued
Doth find itself insensibly disposed
To virtue and true goodness. (lines 90–96)

As moral thought this is a great deal more sophisticated and less sentimentalized than the equivalent passage from "Tintern Abbey" about
nameless unremembered acts of loving-kindness. Aquinas' sense of the
transition from *actus hominis* to *actiones humanae*, using *habitus* as the
bridge between *appetitus* and *amicitia*, between appetite and human
love, is one of the profoundest of all ethical understandings, and
Wordsworth here shows himself capable of it, although he knew little
of Aquinas. His own sense of habit, "havour" (from *habere*), as "the way
in which one holds or has oneself, the mode or condition in which one
is" (*OED*), fully deserves consideration as that alternative to a Kantian
or deontological model of the moral self which neither Mill nor even,
perhaps, Burke ever quite managed to articulate. The "mild necessity
of use" is anything but the harsh necessity of utility. Habit does the
work of reason, and reason can value it only later.

What matters about these acts of love is that they are *acts* rather
than *feelings*, and that they are *compelled* rather than *willed*. Virtue on
this model is a habituated disposition, not a series of choices, although
what disposes us to virtue, as so often in Wordsworth, everywhere in
Locke, but never in Aquinas, is *pleasure*. Still, Wordsworth's hedonic
eudaimonism here is profounder than his usual aesthetic hedonism. It
gains immeasurably from the subtle claim that *unsought* ("unpursued")
pleasure is the really effective disposing agent; intentional impulsion
toward a merely appetitive goal is not likely to build a wide or enduring
pathway to virtue. This adaptation of an Aquinean or Aristotelean conception of virtue to the hedonic Lockean model may be Wordsworth's
finest single piece of moral thought; *this*, not book 9's lines about the
natural equality of shepherds and farmers, is the core of what he has to
say about rural "politics."

Even so, this passage from "The Old Cumberland Beggar" does
go on to say that "Lofty minds," those minds of imaginative power
described in book 13 of *The Prelude*, will especially receive their "first
mild touch of sympathy and thought" here. *In*equality is the burden

of these insights. It is not that the rest of us, even the poorest, need beggars to remain beggars, as a motivating "record" of "past deeds and offices of charity," so that we can go on congratulating ourselves on how virtuous we are just because we offer them alms. Such a hypocrisy of "inevitable charities" and "virtuous decency" is one of the poem's own targets. Its purpose, if anything, is to evoke a powerful morality of ser-vice close to the one Burke calls chivalry. There are those who are worse off than we. To be able to give to them is both affiliative and liberating, and this is "exhilarating," as the poem has it. The problem, just as with "Simon Lee," and despite Wordworth's keen awareness of the dangers of such a complacency, is that it is the narrator's feeling, not the old huntsman's, nor the poor man's, nor the beggar's, that ends up being the point of the poem. The exquisite sensibility of lofty minds: this hierar-chy or aristocracy of sentiment is from Rousseau, not Burke.[30]

But our passage from *Prelude* 9 has less to offer than "The Old Cumberland Beggar" as an insight into the formativity of rural poli-tics for the individual. Burke's "petty war of village vexation" seems closer to the mark here.[31] As for the claim that academic life supplies a model for a kind of natural republicanism, that is possibly even more laughable today than it was in 1790. Here is Burke again: "when men are too much confined to professional and faculty habits . . . they are rather disabled than qualified for whatever depends on the knowledge of mankind."[32]

In fact what is most striking about both the rural and the academic worlds is precisely that they are *not* political. They flourish, indeed, only as an *absence* of a genuine politics, being rather a shared set of activities constituting a common interest. A full-fledged egalitarian polity, whether rights-based or talent-based—and those are obviously inconsistent principles—cannot arise naturalistically out of either country or university life. What is important about these two accounts of his political formation is only that Wordsworth *thought* they mat-tered. He offered them *as* mattering—that is, his mind turned to con-stitutive sources of political consciousness outside the usual Kantian or Lockean ones ("we feel Reason"; "we feel Pleasure"). His inclination here was to find the sources of agency in disposition, rather than in fathomless, ineffable moments of either zeal or appetite (Burke). But also some dispositions are just *better* (Rousseau).

The third source of power was the sense of natural liberty under God or Nature, conferred by mountain landscapes. We are returned to the "Tintern Abbey" problem, as well as to the lines about "Man free, man working for himself" in book 8. Can forms of beauty or of sublimity, as opposed to the necessity of human use, cause such a sense of liberty, any more than they can cause good acts? Is there this kind of political virtue in the forms? We may feel that we can subserve the "awful power" of nature (239), but is this in any sense comparable to a political recognition, as in serving a person or institution? Is the sense of liberty we may feel before Being in any way analogous to what we may feel before The Nation, or The Leader? Perhaps it is. People do love and serve their countries and leaders, after all. But the Being-feeling is more like a loss of self in worship than an expression of self in service. "Mountain liberty" consists more in an independence from other human beings than in collaborative activity. What we feel before Being is quite likely to evoke Zeal, the sense of "a higher power than human understanding," of an inner fountain of energy that may even lead one to attempt to change human nature itself. But is this what we want to feel *before* Nation or Leader (as opposed to feeling *about* Queen and Country, say)?

Wordsworth did become something of a career zealot on the subject of Being and Nature, but his excursion into political zealotry was short-lived and unhappy, as we shall see. In both respects he differed from Rousseau, an angrier outcast who for all his reverence toward Nature and the Supreme Being was no zealot on those subjects, whereas he thought that human nature would have in the end to be invasively and zealously remade by the supreme beings called legislators. Wordsworth does not tell us what "discourse" he used against the monarchist officers, but if he borrowed any of Rousseau's discourses they were less important to him than his feeling of being the emissary of some higher non-human power. Love of Nature led him to the love of Man. In Rousseau's case it was love of Rousseau that did this. The result was that he wanted to remake human nature in his own image. But alongside his natural pieties Wordsworth had just begun to find a sense (although it was really more of a fleeting insight) that politics is made of people, other people, and that *he himself* was also made of other people. This was a dispositional matter, however zealous he might have felt about Being.

Michel Beaupuy
Hero of Romance

Now more than ever before, or later, Wordsworth needed another person to remake him, to help him find this new self, whether dispositional or zealous. There is no sign of such a need on the erotic or domestic level, as we remarked earlier. Even after his breakdown, when he so badly needed Dorothy and Coleridge, they merely returned him to a familiar self (this is why he was so effusively grateful to them). This makes the key figure in his discovery of political agency, his friend Michel Beaupuy, someone of unique importance in Wordsworth's life. As noone else does, he stands for the reality of other active people: for the true friend, the *philos*. The only "patriot" among the officers in Blois is presented as the chief protagonist, the Knight, in this provincial political drama, with Wordsworth as his young squire. And yet it is Wordsworth's drama, his life, his poem; and the provincial scene also serves as a microcosm.

Romance is a genre of great importance in the *Prelude*; it amounts to a fourth source of "power." Beaupuy is presented, crucially, as both a character from Romance, a Spenserian knight-errant in search of Truth; and a revolutionary figure in contemporary political France.

> He through the events
> Of that great change wandered in perfect faith,
> As through a book, an old romance, or tale
> Of Fairy, or some dream of actions wrought
> Behind the summer clouds. (9.305-9)

Like the perfect faith that never exists, the dream of action that is not really action, and the old romance that has long lost its currency, Beaupuy's political conviction seems to exist in a bubble out of time, protecting him from reality. Almost randomly he wanders through this modern apocalypse, this momentous change in human nature and institutions. Wordsworth seems to present this impersonation of all that was good about the early Revolution as a pious, bookish dreamer.

He had already said something similar about himself in London, in book 7, when he found the city quite unlike the Babylon or Persepolis of his romance imagination, or when he listened to a lawyer orating "like a hero in romance," a Roland winding his horn (7.538). These and numerous other examples through the poem are usually designed to suggest how romance thickens or deepens his sense of reality, so that what is happening is either enriched by the extra layers or seen as archetypal, true of all epochs, including imagined ones. Sometimes they suggest that reality is not like romance, but more difficult and important: or, conversely, that it is equally unreal, illusory. But this is the Revolution. Surely when even *that* is turned into romance something politically important is being claimed about the genre, or about books in general? How is Beaupuy's status enhanced by being a Quixote or a Red Crosse Knight?

We need to turn to *Prelude* 5, "Books," to understand this better. Books are represented there as supremely man-made things, "worthy of unconquerable life" (emphasis on *worthy*), but certain to perish (5.19–21). If forced to choose, we must always let Nature be our teacher, not books. The dream of Wordsworth's friend, about an "arab of the desart" (5.49–165), a "semi-Quixote," shows "poetry and geometric truth" (5.64) symbolically as twin uncoverers of nature's greatest truths, yet doomed to be drowned in a great flood or buried under the desert sands. The contrasted stories of the Infant Prodigy, crammed with book-learning (5.294–369), and the Boy of Winander, educated only by Nature (5.389–449), constitute a two-pronged frontal attack not just on the regimentation of post-Rousseauan education theory, as in the *Practical Education* of Maria Edgeworth and her father, which Wordsworth read in 1798,[33] but also on the broader moral damage that is done when books become merely repositories of learning, not so much forming the mind as infesting it. We should only "teach as nature teaches" (230).

But some books are different. They are not "barren leaves," as "The Tables Turned" put it in 1798, but friends. Rousseau was wrong, apparently, to ban *all* books from Émile's education (apart from *Robinson Crusoe* which, he thought, offered some useful outdoor survival tips). The genre Wordsworth most admires, it turns out, is indeed romance, especially when written to be read in childhood. *Gil Blas*, Robin Hood,

Don Quixote, *The Faerie Queene*, Jack the Giant-Killer, the Arabian Nights, St. George, Gulliver (*Robinson Crusoe* is not mentioned): here are "the shining streams / Of fairyland, the forests of romance" (5.476–77); "tales that charm away the wakeful night / In Araby—romances, legends . . . Fictions . . . adventures endless"; the Stephen Spielberg or Harry Potter world of "the marvellous" (5.520–24, 564). This "golden store of books" (5.503) or something like it "will live till man shall be no more" (5.529). Just as liberty grows out of early experiences of equality, so romance lays the foundation for our later responses to the real, to "what we have seen," not read (5.565). But it also introduces us to "words themselves," "For *their own sakes*" (5.567, 579, Wordsworth's emphasis): to that aesthetic appeal out of which grows the "wish for something loftier, more adorned, / Than is the common aspect, daily garb, / of human life" (5.599–601). Further down that track lies "the great Nature that exists in works / Of mighty poets" (5.618–19), the place where poetry re-creates Nature so powerfully that it becomes itself a parallel Nature. But romance is even more important to Wordsworth than great poetry. "Our childhood sits, / Our simple childhood, sits upon a throne" (5.531–32). When we read romance we are not in the presence of what "the ape / Philosophy" calls "Impostors, drivellers" (5.549–550). Instead, "oh, then we feel, we feel, / We know, when we have friends" (5.546–47). This defense of romance sounds more like a defense of poetry in general. Wordsworth was writing the Immortality Ode at about this time, and these childhood friends are still appareled in celestial light, like a glory that has not passed away. When Beaupuy walked out of one of these stories into Wordsworth's life it was as if the glory itself came alive.

As for the great poets, Homer, Shakespeare, Milton, and the Old Testament prophets, one feels that they are named almost dutifully, as "labourers divine" (5.165, 203–4) in this great vineyard of parallel nature. But these greater and more powerful "friends" were not part of the visionary gleam; they did not make the growing boy. Now that he is grown, his philosophic mind has learned better to appreciate the power of words, that words *are* "powers." But it is utterly characteristic of Wordsworth that he does not value them for what Hazlitt calls "the trappings of verse." "His Muse," after all, "is a levelling one." Part of what Hazlitt meant in that shrewd phrase from his shrewd essay[34] is that Wordsworth's poetry is leveling in its attitude not just to politics or society but to poetry itself. It "proceeds on a principle of equality" according to which all poetry is finally to be judged only by its power to save us. His own poetry was the first (or so he felt) to be written entirely according to this principle, including Milton's. It was intended to remake all poetry, especially Milton's. It is more equal than anyone else's. It is that essence of poetry that alone rebuts the criticisms of the ape Philosophy, which alone has the capacity to compete with nature or, remade itself, to remake human nature. It will be a second nature.[35] In this respect Wordsworth is indeed Rousseau's disciple; Hazlitt's sense of his egotism corresponds to Burke's sense of Rousseau's vanity.

To do what he had to do, to become what he had to become, Wordsworth needed Robin Hood and *Gil Blas*, not Shakespeare. Much as he says he values the example of his fellow laborers in the vineyard of poetry, they cannot be *friends* (nor, finally, could Coleridge). Their task cannot be as important as his. His is of a different kind. His account of books, which is implicitly a critique of all previous poetry, is designed so to level the playing field that what one might call "level" poetry will best suit it: no cloud-capped towers: hardly raising its wing from the ground (again, Hazlitt's metaphor). Robin Hood was something of a leveler himself, of course, but he is not a rival. He is something more like an energy source; he and his peers are the true friends. Homer and the rest may be the conch shell in the desert, from the semi-Quixote dream: mysterious, spontaneous. Wordsworth's friend in the dream fears that they may be drowned (i.e., by nature); but there is also a sense in which Wordsworth himself wants them buried. Perhaps, even, he sees his own work as more like the cleansing flood, nature itself, than the worthy but perishable shell. This is true Rousseauism.

Beaupuy himself, then, to return to book 9, is no rival but a true friend, a hero in the great redemptive natural romance Wordsworth himself is writing. He is no ineffectual Quixote, but a real Robin Hood. He may be a character in a dream or book, a Red Crosse Knight or Galahad, but he is not really a dreamer himself. Chiefly he looks like a knight militant, an agent. "By birth he ranked / With the most noble," but "fondness, and a kind of radiant joy . . . covered him about when he was bent / On works of love or freedom" (9.309–10, 322–24). In most of the Beaupuy passages Wordsworth merges romance and real nobility, or aristocracy. Old-fashioned bookish gallantry co-exists with modern political agency. Those who read romances, he almost suggests, those who behave romantically, are natural reformers. As the two friends continue their "earnest dialogues" (9.446), during walks by the river or in the forest, Wordsworth's mind turns to hermits in caves, or Ariosto's Angelica on her palfrey, or knights jousting and satyrs dancing. "Within the groves of chivalry I pipe," he wrote in book 1 (1.180), describing his preliminary search for a poetic subject, here the Arthuriad Milton also never wrote. But now Wordsworth is able to interweave his reveries of the heroic past with the politics of the revolutionary present in such a way that the two itinerant reformers become characters in an old story. When Beaupuy shows Wordsworth castles or ancient villages with chivalric associations he is like a courtly host himself, while his guest gazes around with "chivalrous delight" (9.503).

These romance imaginings are not idle. They arouse a bivalent political emotion. On the one hand they moderate "the force / Of civic prejudice, the bigotry . . . of a youthful patriot's mind." On the other, they feed his "Hatred of absolute rule, where will of one / Is law for all" (9.500–505). Chivalry can motivate the reformer by offering its own reminder of those inequalities built into its system that, unchecked, could grow into an *ancien régime*. This is the fallen political condition diagnosed by Rousseau, the obverse or reflex of the one Kant later advocates (that is, of the same model), in which the good wills of the many are subordinated to the bad will of the one: a bad will being one that is determined not by respect for the moral law but by a monstrous, malignant *amour-propre* that becomes coercive law for everyone else. But chivalry is not therefore to be dismissed as a proto-autocracy. It also moderates bigotry and prejudice, republican or revolutionary, by showing us "gallantry" and "courtesy," displayed now not by men to women but by such chivalrous reformers, progressives and "ardent hearts" as Beaupuy (9.437) to the "mean," the "poor," the "obscure" and the "homely" (9.313–18). "Radiant joy," "love or freedom," "the progress of a cause" (9.322–25): there can be, Wordsworth is careful to point out, "no air / Of condescension" here. The joy and courtesy found in service are emotions of equality and leave no scope for some appearance of descent to a lower level. As in "Simon Lee" and "The Old Cumberland

Beggar" he is acutely aware of the lapses he is so subject to himself, and even manages to recast them as virtues.[36]

Criticism of the "will of one" as "law for all" is Rousseauan; but this brand of Romantic progressivism is utterly contrary to the spirit of Rousseau, for whom (as for many progressive thinkers since) Beaupuy's gallantry to the poor would have seemed the very seed of social degeneration. Wordsworth's quite remarkable return on Burke, meanwhile, is to suggest that the age of chivalry is *not* dead, but that, despite the abuses it countenanced, the noble-born themselves, patriotic reincarnations of romance gallantry, are still political reform's best hope. This is a remarkable piece of political thinking, although it is not one that socialism would approve of. Beaupuy is imagined as both an aristocrat and a revolutionary, retaining the chivalric ethos of one (leadership as service) while embracing the egalitarianism of the other. There could hardly be a better example of how to combine the two most celebrated ingredients of Romantic literature: romance and revolution.

The two friends continue their conversation. Beaupuy, an "upright man and tolerant" (9.337), is chivalrously determined to put the royalist point of view:

> Oft in solitude
> With him did I discourse about the end
> Of civil government, and its wisest forms,
> Of ancient prejudice and chartered rights,
> Allegiance, faith, and laws by time matured,
> Custom and habit, novelty and change,
> Of self-respect, and virtue in the few
> For patrimonial honour set apart,
> And ignorance in the labouring multitude. (9.328–36)

So good a job does Beaupuy do that the lines really do sound genuinely Burkean. Ancient prejudice and chartered rights are not despised here as Rousseau or Blake had despised them, nor custom and habit as Shelley was to. Indeed these, the lines suggest, may be among the wisest practices in civil governance. Virtue and honor seem for a moment here to belong chiefly to the aristocratic and masculine few: ignorance to the laboring many. The "experience of past ages" is invoked (343). These are not what we would normally call progressive views. This is certainly not the Wordsworth of the *Letter to the Bishop of Llandaff*. The following lines on the "voluptuous life / unfeeling" (9.353–54) of royal courts carry far less rhetorical weight. Wordsworth even suggests that he felt then (as of course he feels now) a good deal of sympathy for the case Beaupuy was so fair-mindedly arguing, avowing that he then "had a sounder judgement / Than afterwards" (9.340–41).

It hardly seems adequate simply to read all this as the conservative thinker of 1804 discounting or re-inventing an earlier, more radical, and somehow, therefore, *more real* self. We are reading *this* poetry, not the *Letter to the Bishop of Llandaff*, or the *Salisbury Plain* poems. The political reality *this* poetry gives us is a conflicted, unconventional one: perhaps more so than it knows. In both men, it says, revolutionary zeal was tempered by Romantic chivalry (as it was not to be in others). The management of nations may be as much a matter of husbandry, service or prejudice as of social engineering *de novo*. And yet this does not stop it from being progressive. Their long conversation ranges over the formation of many nations, through all "recorded time," until it finally arrives at their own inchoate "aspirations." Looking up, they

> beheld
> A living confirmation of the whole
> Before us in a people risen up
> Fresh as the morning star. Elate we looked
> Upon their virtues, saw in rudest men
> Self-sacrifice the firmest, generous love
> And continence of mind, and sense of right
> Uppermost in the mind of fiercest strife. (9.389–96)

It is as if the political model they were fumbling for has suddenly risen brilliantly up out of an all-night conversation. The morning star heralds that blissful dawn they were and we are about to witness (although it is a typical Wordsworthian slide to call the star "fresh" instead of "bright," or to call the *star* "fresh" rather than the morning); this way of seeing "a people" is precursive of that way of being part of one. Out of the romance courtesy of Beaupuy arise truly demotic virtues; the "labouring multitude" are ignorant no more. They are as capable of self-sacrifice and continence, of fair-mindedness even in the fiercest combat, as any Red Crosse Knight. It is a glimpse of an unlikely bridge between aristocracy and democracy. Rough peasants absorb the liberal sentiments of an upper-class military officer. In the introduction to his edition of the *Reflections*, J. G. A. Pocock points out that Burke uses the idea of chivalry as shorthand for a complex system involving "a learned and charitable clergy" and "the enlightened townsmen of the age of commerce," as well as the nobility.[37] Through chivalry the knightly class acquires a sense of responsibility, of a society with which it interacts. In Wordsworth's remarkable passage the "rudest men" do just the same.

But as we saw with "Tintern Abbey,", and again just a moment ago, Wordsworth's metaphors tend to slide at crucial moments. Other possibilities inherent in them emerge. In this case, too, Wordsworth is in the unfamiliar territory of political thought, tugged in opposite directions by two very different guides. He is also dealing with true friendship: again, not his forte. Under such pressure the Knight of Romance turns into a kind of Rousseauan Engineer. One minute the multitude have risen up into reality, inspired by this gallant example; the next the figure of the Knight has once more become the primary agent, the hero, the focus, the only true actor, the "one paramount mind" (10.180) that Wordsworth so ardently wishes had saved the Revolution at any time during the period from 1793 to 1795. He could not possibly have meant Napoleon (as Byron did later), but perhaps we have to be careful what we wish for. Even the *good* will of one can easily become law for all. Beaupuy seems like one of those "whom circumstance / Hath called upon to embody his deep sense / In action, give it outwardly a shape" (9.407–9). As soon as he has this thought, Wordsworth's mind turns almost by reflex to Dion and Plato, and their Sicilian "philosophic war Led by philosophers" (9.423–24). Action informed by and implementing the concepts of reason (or embodying a deep sense: much the same here) is a Platonic and Rousseauan business, and a powerful current of concept-driven Western philosophy is now sweeping his mind along. In such a case, Wordsworth says,

> . . . truth is more than truth—
> A hope it is and a desire, a creed
> Of zeal by an authority divine
> Sanctioned, of danger, difficulty, or death. (9.411–14)

Maybe even the Spenserian knight-errant was similarly driven, by authority divine, by a creed beyond reason, by a hyper-truth. Beaupuy, like Wordsworth himself earlier, is now seen not just as a philosopher-warrior but also as a zealot. Chivalry itself is no longer a courteous service but a fanatical creed, welcoming danger and death as parts of that creed. Service respects persons; creeds do not. Without fully seeing it, Wordsworth has conceptualized his friend.

In the last and most generally admired of the Beaupuy passages in book 9 the hero appears to greater advantage, or so it seems at first:

> And when we chanced
> One day to meet a hunger-bitten girl
> Who crept along fitting her languid self
> Unto a heifer's motion . . .
> . . . and at the sight my friend
> In agitation said, "'Tis against that
> Which we are fighting," I with him believed
> Devoutly that a spirit was abroad
> Which could not be withstood, that poverty,
> At least like this, would in a little time
> Be found no more . . .
> All institutes for ever blotted out
> That legalized exclusion, empty pomp
> Abolished, sensual state and cruel power,
> Whether by edict of the one or few—
> And finally, as sum and crown of all,
> Should see the people having a strong hand
> In making their own laws . . . that henceforth
> Captivity by mandate without law
> Should cease . . . (9.511–39)

There is no doubting the generosity, the sympathy or the ambition here, facile or pious as the feeling may at first appear (of *course* they are fighting whatever causes *that*). In this wretched girl the two patriots see all poverty, and behind that they see the institutions and appetites causing it, and behind *those* they see a vacuum or an inertia where popular political activity should be. The general political model is attractive, even if the economics is questionable (is it conceivable that if we all make our laws together noone will ever be poor again?). *Habeas corpus* is rightly seen as the single indispensable constituent of all political liberation. It is *that*, or something like it, for which they are fighting, surely? So should the starving girl really be seen as the single unmistakable token of all political motive? Beaupuy is "unto the poor . . . in service bound / As by some tie invisible, oaths professed / To a religious order" (9.310–13). An irresistible spirit fills this devout Galahad, engaged in his holy war against poverty. The girl's "languid self" is transformed by his very zeal into a "that" ("against *that*"): a symbol of poverty, not a person. (The same thing happened to Simon Lee and the old Cumberland beggar.) This kind of knight is in the business of killing concept-dragons, not rescuing real damsels in distress.

It seems as if the rare, hard-won insights glimpsed earlier, into political making as the true heaven of dispersed or collective agency, and chivalry as the bridge between aristocracy and democracy, are all but buried, for now, under a pile of sentiment and slipped metaphors. But one of these insights, at least, was about to find its most celebrated expression.

The Bliss of Politics

Here, then, is the famous passage, occurring halfway through book 10. Following several hundred anticipatory lines on the "bitter truths" (10.657) he has learned from the terrible events and destructive emotions of 1793 and 1794 (see chapter 5), Wordsworth returns for the last time to 1792 and the Beaupuy period.

> O pleasant exercise of hope and joy,
> For great were the auxiliars which then stood
> Upon our side, we who were strong in love.
> Bliss was it in that dawn to be alive,
> But to be young was very heaven! O times,
> In which the meagre, stale, forbidding ways
> Of custom, law and statute took at once
> The attraction of a country in romance—
> When Reason seemed the most to assert her rights
> When most intent on making of herself
> A prime enchanter to assist the work
> Which then was going forward in her name.

Not favoured spots alone, but the whole earth,
The beauty wore of promise, that which sets
(To take an image which was felt, no doubt,
Among the bowers of Paradise itself)
The budding rose above the rose full-blown.
What temper at the prospect did not wake
To happiness unthought of? The inert
Were rouzed, and lively natures rapt away.
They who had fed their childhood upon dreams—
The playfellows of fancy, who had made
All powers of swiftness, subtlety and strength
Their ministers, used to stir in lordly wise
Among the grandest objects of the sense,
And deal with whatsoever they found there
As if they had within some lurking right
To wield it—they too, who, of gentle mood,
Had watched all gentle motions, and to these
Had fitted their own thoughts (schemers more mild,
And in the region of their peaceful selves),
Did now find helpers to their hearts' desire
And stuff at hand plastic as they could wish,
Were called upon to exercise their skill
Not in Utopia—subterraneous fields,
Or some secreted island, heaven knows where—
But in the very world which is the world
Of all of us, the place in which, in the end,
We find our happiness, or not at all. (10.689–727)

It is hardly an exaggeration to call this passage, along with its contrary less than a hundred lines later, the source and origin of Wordsworth's vocation, of his entire poetic career. The destruction of this vision by subsequent events in France and Britain, and his own dysfunctional response to those events, led to his retreat from political and social life and his rationalization of that retreat as a redemptive restoration. So it is worth clarifying what he saw or learned in this "moment": so unlike those other moments of epiphany, called spots of time, in the poem.

What Wordsworth experiences in the spots of time is something like a punctual, individual *connection with a deity*; what he experiences here is a collective *human exercise*, an unleashed activity between human beings. (Neither of these experiences, notably, is of an individual connection with another human being.) Hope, joy and love are not spontaneous emissions here: they are more like activities. The spots of time, those "favoured spots," occur when we "have had deepest feeling that the mind / Is lord and master, and that outward sense / Is but the obedient servant of her will" (11.270–72). Here, on the other hand, the mightiest minds, those accustomed to treat even the grandest objects of the sense as their servants, are as it were reproached with their assumption of some lurking right to behave in this way, and have no advantage over the gentlest, mildest and most peaceful selves, gentle readers, not poets. All alike can exercise their skill on this *stuff*, like children in the pottery class. The Greek *plassein*, "to form or mold," is not quite *prattein*, "to act or achieve," nor quite *poiein*, "to make," but the idea behind the lines is nevertheless of politics as the active making or shaping of some existing material or fabric, done together by all kinds of co-operating human minds—the plastic stuff of politics is not really material, but is thought of as if it were an object of the sense ("moulds it and remoulds," 10.733). "The best legislators," says Burke, using as ever his metaphor of shaping the stuff of the state, "have been often satisfied with the establishment of some sure, solid and ruling principle in government—a power like that which some of the philosophers have called a plastic nature."[38]

The workshop in which this happens is not a divine one, not the light of setting suns or the round ocean or the living air, but that very world of trivial intercourse we normally find (Wordsworth finds) so enervating. The solution to the meaningless din of towns and cities is not something to be found in a moment of quasi-religious meaning. Instead it consists in a sustained human activity in the very world of all of us. We find our happiness not just in this world but in *making* it, for ourselves. (This insight was originally Vico's, but noone knew of him then.) This world is not some ideal Platonist nowhere, some Elysian field or Ultima Thule, some as yet undiscovered version of Britain, known only to God. It is Paris, or London, now. And the making is not a solitary redeeming but a collective shaping. Although the passage starts by saying that "we" have great auxiliars, by its end *all* of *us* (the meter emphasizes the two words; now "us" is everybody) are helpers, the inert as well as the lively. This heaven is not really a new place at all, in fact, but a better way of being in the places we already have. It is an unredeemed human condition, and here it has spread to everyone, even those who would normally know nothing of it. Bliss, the condition of feeling and being blessed, is not reserved here for saints or the saved; everyone is blessed just by being alive. *Life* is bliss; if we do not find happiness here (not redemption or salvation, just happiness) we never will, although this is a kind of happiness unthought of, something that never occurred to Wordsworth before, and rarely to any political thinker. The etymology of "bliss" connects it with "bless" on the one hand and "blithe" on the other. In *Paradise Lost* "bliss" is what is felt in Heaven and its mortal copy, Eden; the word recurs throughout book 4, for example. Milton is very much in Wordsworth's mind as he reaches this place. But this is a Paradise that really exists, here and now, its meaning deriving simply from what we are all doing together, not from some visionary re-imagining.

Inertia is the greatest enemy of political responsibility; evil will triumph if the good do nothing. Here inertia is defeated. The Latin term means "want of art"; even the artless, the unimaginative, are blessed by this new condition. Politics no longer seems just a mechanism for delivering justice; it is not a matter of meager custom, stale law, forbidding statute (the adjectives and nouns in the two lines balance). *Makros* is "long and thin"; "stale" water (the root is probably "stand") has been there too long; to forbid is to "fore-bid," to anticipate and prohibit, already to disallow change. Politics, in short, used to look like an old but attenuated barrier: a Berlin Wall. But *now* ("O times": this is the very hour) these mechanisms suddenly look enchanting.

This is, critically, a country *in romance*. Beaupuy and his fellow knights are in their element, for once. It is the element of all of us; it *is* all of us. Reason, political concepts, such as the Rousseauan idea of the general will, now seem most self-evident, just as they become most helpful. The rightness of reason becomes manifest just as its concepts become useful; it serves the exercise instead of driving it. Reason is a tool, not a master. Some might say that this was precisely the Rousseauan paradise, in which each gives himself to "all of us." But there is no hint here of any *loss* of self *in* the collective. Each remains himself. And in sharp contrast to the rest of the *Prelude* any isolated "spots" of time and place are relatively unimportant. The *whole* earth, the whole of life, and not just a few favored forms, wears beauty, and precisely *wears* it, rather than manifesting it in select places: or again, wears *it*, rather than being worn *by* it. There is a subdued background note of warning, of course. This was all just an enchantment; the promise of the budding rose was not to be fulfilled; Reason *seemed*. But this was no mere Rousseauan fantasy. It was a real promise, a real dawn; things really could have been like this, and, briefly, they *were*. *Promittere* is a putting forth, a tender or proposal of something that is still being made. This was the joy of politics. It was Wordsworth's own dawn, heaven, or morning star. The emotion is as powerful as anywhere in the *Prelude*. *This* was what they were fighting for. *This* was the earthly Paradise he lost.

5

WORDSWORTH AND
POLITICAL REDEMPTION II

Paradise Lost

Nameless Moral Shock

Wordsworth speculates that had he not been obliged by lack of funds to return to England in late 1792 he might have perished in the Terror, fighting for the lost vision of those lines, "A poet only to myself" (10.199). Instead he lived and became a poet, but he became the poet he did become *because* of these lines and what they represented for him. The condescending, bookish liberal had become, briefly, an active participant in political creation. Nothing was ever the same for him again.

But all this fell to pieces—for everybody, of course, but our concern is with the collapse of Wordsworth's own personality. Why did that collapse take the form it did? Why did it lead to *that* kind of recovery?

We are now in book 10. Wordsworth left Orléans in late October 1792 and remained in Paris for a month or so. The king was in prison, the republic was threatened by the armies of the Coalition, the September massacres had come and gone, and the hissing factions were disputing power. Robespierre's star was rising. For now he is just a tiger; Wordsworth later likens him to Moloch. Paris "seemed a place of fear" (10.80). But so far all this merely provoked him to thoughts of action and service. He himself was "all unfit . . . for tumult and intrigue" (10.133), but as we have seen he was obsessed by the thought that "the virtue of one paramount mind" would have "cleared a passage for just government . . . according to example given / By ancient lawgivers" (10.179–88). His liberal, aristocratic, and romance instincts were still undaunted, in other words. Virtue could have been imposed by a paramount mind informed by ancient laws. This, he insists, was a "Creed which ten shameful years have not annulled" (10.178). But Wordsworth himself has taught us to be wary of creeds of zeal. Truths about chivalrous service grasped in that joyous popular exercise of 1792 narrowed and hardened into something relatively illiberal and inegalitarian under the influence of what happened soon after, as he half-perceives, from the vantage point of 1804, in his very choice of the term "creed."

In any case, he was now hit by a double blow or shock. The first impact came not from events in France, from the Revolution itself, but from what he found on his sudden return home. This is the experience that in biographical or chronological terms, though not in the narrative, succeeds and counterbalances the "Bliss was it in that dawn" passage. We are now in spring and summer 1793.

> And now the strength of Britain was put forth
> In league with the confederated host;
> Not in my single self alone I found,
> But in the minds of all ingenuous youth,
> Change and subversion from this hour. No shock
> Given to my moral nature had I known
> Down to that very moment—neither lapse
> Nor turn of sentiment—that might be named
> A revolution, save at this one time:
> All else was progress on the self-same path
> On which with a diversity of pace
> I had been travelling: this, a stride at once
> Into another region . . . for I felt
> The ravage of this most unnatural strife
> In my own heart . . . I rejoiced,
> Yes, afterwards, truth painful to record,
> Exulted in the triumph of my soul
> When Englishmen by thousands were o'erthrown,
> Left without glory on the field, or driven,
> Brave hearts, to shameful flight. It was a grief—
> Grief call it not, 'twas any thing but that—

A conflict of sensations without name,
Of which he only who may love the sight
Of a village steeple as I do can judge,
When in the congregation, bending all
To their great Father, prayers were offered up
Or praises for our country's victories,
And, 'mid the simple worshippers perchance
I only, like an uninvited guest
Whom no one owned, sate silent—shall I add,
Fed on the day of vengeance yet to come! (10.229–74)

For Britain to join the coalition of Continental powers against the French revolutionary republic was, Wordsworth says, a shock to "all ingenuous youth," not just to him. The collective consciousness Wordsworth had discovered in France was still with him. So was the trace of liberal-aristocratic blood-consciousness; *ingenuus*, like its derivative, means "of the same *gens*," and thus by definition free-born, and therefore noble in bearing, upright, frank—like Beaupuy, in short. These are "the best youth in England" (10.277). The implication is that anyone of that sort, any *gentle* person, was as distressed as Wordsworth. To be young in that hour was very hell—that is, if you were free, frank and a gentleman.

Indeed to be all these things was to be not just changed but *subverted*. To be changed is to have one quality or disposition replaced by another. The ingenuous become disingenuous, ignoble or dissembling (the proto-Indo-European root of "change" means "crooked"). But to be subverted is to be turned upside down, with the underside uppermost. So love of one's country takes the form of not just inwardly rejoicing but exulting, as if leaping up (*ex-salire*), at its defeats (its defeats are his triumphs). Conversely, one sits mute amid the praise, vengefully refusing to pray for or rejoice in its victories. Turning upside down is literally a revolution: this, not what happened in 1790 or 1792, was Wordsworth's. Change *and* subversion means conversion *and* inversion, alteration *and* revolution, becoming another person but one who is also completely disoriented—a far cry from redemption. What happened to Wordsworth in France, as we saw before, was "progress" for him, a natural evolution of the self, or evolution of the natural self, into something no longer single: an auxiliary. There was no lapse nor turn of moral sentiment in that—no slip (*lapsus*) in the carving of the self on the lathe (Greek *tornos*).

The fact that *this*, now, in Britain, was the primary "moral shock" tells us a good deal about Wordsworth's trajectory from bliss to collapse. The phrase is popular now among sociologists. It was coined, or re-issued, in the 1990s, to explain the phenomenon by which people join mass social movements after a triggering event. But Wordsworth was the one who really coined it, two hundred years earlier, anticipating the experience of many a young person closer to our times, in the 1960s and 1970s, taking his or her own stride into another region. To be a "patriot" was to be a French revolutionary, as we saw earlier, so the shock of war against the nation of patriots is felt as a revolution itself. The evolution charted in the preceding books, leading up to the political revelations of 1790 and 1792, veers sharply off into another region of moral sentiment: another dimension, really, since one step off the familiar path takes the traveler into an entirely different kind of landscape. We spoke of the "fragrant spring" of 1790 as apocalyptic, and of the Revolution as the Great Singularity. But a benign consequence of the later "blissful dawn" was that Wordsworth was able to assimilate that earlier apocalyptic experience. He had actually moved closer to a homogeneous model of the self, whether moral or political, as equally active throughout, and away from a more dualist model, with one or a few active or charged particles (spots of time, spontaneous emissions, even chivalrous leaders) and an inert remainder. He was hardly aware of the importance of this change, or how much further it could have taken him down his self-same, *bildungslich* path. The excited discovery he made was as much about a model of the self as about politics, though he hardly saw this. So when the politics was utterly repudiated in his own homeland he took the rebuff as deeply personal: as a blow against his very self. He took *this* as the change, not what had happened in France; and indeed it was a change of an entirely different kind, a moral shock, not just a conflict. In the end he was to react by trying to get back onto the path at an earlier or "upstream" point, avoiding or redeeming himself from the contentious section, and going back to his more dualist model.

He returns to the metaphor in a later passage, but shifts the medium from path to river:

This threw me first out of the pale of love;
Soured and corrupted upwards to the source,
My sentiments; was not, as hitherto,
A swallowing up of lesser things in great,
But change of them into their opposites . . . (10.760–64)

The 1850 text was to replace "opposites" with "contraries"; but Wordsworth is not looking for a Blakean, or Hegelian, progression. He has
experienced total inversion and col-lapse. The earlier "lapse" is related;
cor-rumpo is something like "burst inward" or "implode." The clear
stream of feeling familiar from "Tintern Abbey" and elsewhere has
flowed from its pure source onward into a life, and has become a life.
Life itself can be seen differently from the place it has carried him to.
But it is as if in that place he was exposed to a blight or pollution ("that
strong disease," he calls its terminal stage in the 1850 edition), which
has now worked its way, unnaturally, back up the stream, and poisoned
or tainted the well. Inside that sacred place, inside the "pale," was love:
that was the source, in fact. But now he is beyond the pale, lapsed,
imploded, an outcast from love, including from the social love he felt
among the blessed youth of Blois and Orléans, itself an outgrowth of
everything he had been since birth. Cut off from his life-sources, his
very feelings, by this moral shock, he no longer knows what name to
give them. This is the antitype of redemption.

Because his self had been changing, of course, he also took the
shock partly as a blow *by* himself *against* himself. This is a "most unnat-
ural strife." Rejoicing at his brave countrymen's inglorious defeat and
shame itself seems shameful, painful to record, from the perspective
of 1804. But in 1793, with no moral center, he could give no name to
this conflicted moral sentiment: neither grief nor shame, neither joy
nor triumph. "What had been a pride / Was now a shame" (10.768–69).
The pride and joy felt in their country by the "best youth," the *aristoi*,
are "torn" or "rent" from them (10.275–78), but who knows what the
replacement feelings are to be called? The emotions are so powerful
as to be sensations, but so corrupted or lapsed as to be unidentifiable.
Concepts do not work at all. This is that moment of collapse, regis-
tered in "Tintern Abbey," when the language of the sense fails him,
when a nameless "something" treads close behind.

The shock was a double one, however. This is partly what made the sensations so hard to identify: they overlapped. Government policy and the attitudes of most ordinary people in Britain, in 1793 and onwards into the mid-1790s, like the congregations in those churches, made the "ingenuous youth," and educated liberal opinion, feel as if they lived in a different moral universe. But what made it impossible for them to find their bearings in this new universe, the one Wordsworth had glimpsed, he thought, in 1790 and 1792, the one in which everybody could "do politics," was what was happening on the other side of the Channel, where the Terror began in June. These events seemed to suggest that the repressive behavior of the British government and the apparently docile complaisance of its people might even have some justification. The land of the blissful dawn now looked like a blind alley at night with an axe-murderer lurking at the end. Here was the unbearable human sublime in all its awfulness; this was what Wordsworth was fleeing in "Tintern Abbey."

> In France, the men who for their desperate ends
> Had plucked up mercy by the roots were glad
> Of this new enemy . . .
> The goaded land waxed mad; the crimes of few
> Spread into madness of the many; blasts
> From hell came sanctified like airs from heaven . . .
> Domestic carnage now filled all the year
> With feast-days: the old man from the chimney-nook,
> The maiden from the bosom of her love,
> The mother from the cradle of her babe,
> The warrior from the field—all perished, all—
> Friends, enemies, of all parties, ages, ranks,
> Head after head, and never heads enough
> For those who bade them fall. They found their joy,
> They made it, ever thirsty . . . (10.306–37)

This was hell. The "very heaven" of book 9 was not just inverted but also perverted. What the ingenuous youth faced in an English church was nothing by comparison—although the juxtaposition of these unlike categories is partly what constituted the moral shock. It was not pride or joy that were torn and rent now, but mercy. Sanctity, holiness, has become a mask for carnage, for ritual or festive everyday feasting on the flesh of the household itself. The domestic sphere, each family member's most private and characteristic sanctuary, is desecrated. Noone's public status, whether rank, party or affiliation, matters either. Every person has become just a head, to feed an insatiable machine. *Perire* is "go through" or "utterly pass away," as one might pass through a gate—or a guillotine—to non-being. All of them, all, just vanish, all are disappeared. The passage might be describing the killing fields of the 1980s, or any other of those dreadful mass psychopathological, repellently "sanctified" episodes of modern times that seemed and seem to have their deepest roots in this one. Whereas the blissful youth of 1792 found happiness in making politics, the monstrous tyrants of 1793 found joy in unmaking people. The appalling thought lurking behind this is that one might have given birth to the other as its perverted opposite. What if any collective attempt to remake the political world (such a dynamic idea) leads inevitably to mass slaughter?

This of course is the utterly Burkean question that so haunted Wordsworth and his liberal peers. Those who continued to hope most for and trust most in humanity were precisely those who most deeply and lastingly felt the double shock (10.357–60), the two impacts fused into a single one more than twice as bad as either:

> Through months, through years, long after the last beat
> Of those atrocities (I speak bare truth,
> As if to thee alone in private talk)
> I scarcely had one night of quiet sleep,
> Such ghastly visions had I of despair,
> And tyranny, and implements of death,
> And long orations which in dreams I pleaded
> Before unjust tribunals, with a voice
> Labouring, a brain confounded, and a sense
> Of treachery and desertion in the place
> The holiest that I knew of—my own soul. (10.370–80)

The bare truth of private talk with a friend stands in sharp contrast to the confounded brain and laboring voice of public oration to an unjust tribunal.[1] The passage prefigures Wordsworth's eventual retreat into private talk with his friend Coleridge—the mode of all his poetry henceforth, with its common-language tone, as of one treating all its gentle readers as his private friends. Public talk with his friend Beaupuy and others has failed; the fluent, interactive, and justice-creating speech of 1792 has now and forever in his mind been perverted by visions of despair and death, by the savage metronome of the Terror (drumroll, blade's drop, fall of heads), into a labored pleading that knows already that its appeal is only to tribal injustice, not political justice. And the worst thing about this tribunal is that the most unjust tribune is the accused himself. Unjust as they both are, neither the "gravest heads" and "scoffers in their pride" in Britain "watching in their hate of France for signs / Of her disasters" or saying "Behold the harvest which we reap / From popular government and equality" (10.430–32, 622–24), nor the inhuman "tigers" roaming the Paris jungle (10.82), are as unjust to himself as he is. The tribune is his own treacherous self-deserter of a soul, desecrating its own sanctuary. Maybe Wordsworth's sense of self-betrayal lay partly in that he left Paris (and surely in that case some of his guilt must have been domestic), partly in that he did not do more to fight the injustices he found at home. But more than these, it lay in the experience of subverted and corrupted sentiment described earlier. He feels *both* like an alien in *and* like a traitor to *both* his own country *and* France. His own self is soured to its source; this means that it *is* corrupt. Here is the germ of that terrible moment in "Tintern Abbey" when it turns out that the dreadful thing he has been fleeing is himself. Somehow he now carries everywhere in himself the seed of alienation and treachery. Thinking he was participating in a wonderful collective activity, had he actually been helping to make something monstrous?

This self-doubt makes even Wordsworth's attempts at self-justification in the poem itself fall rather flat, turning us, his very readers, into the unjust tribunal he most fears. He tells us of his hopes that from the deepest affliction will grow a still greater honor and faith. Thus those who taunted him and his ilk with the Paris horror merely taught him that "popular government and equality" are not to blame,

> But that it was a reservoir of guilt
> And ignorance, filled up from age to age,
> That could no longer hold its loathsome charge
> But burst and spread in deluge through the land. (10.436–39)

But the brief Rousseauan proposal is unconvincing because it is undeveloped. It is not anchored anywhere in the metaphorical structures of the poem. What it claims is familiar enough, certainly: these people behave badly because they know no better and because they feel a sense of unacquitted crime or sin, theirs or someone else's. But it is not clear who feels the guilt here, or for what. That lack of clarity vitiates the whole passage. He seems to protest too much.

There is a somewhat more convincing suggestion offered soon afterwards, however:

> To Nature then,
> Power had reverted: habit, custom, law,
> Had left an interregnum's open space
> For her to stir about in, uncontrolled. (10.609–12)

The idea that habit and custom may provide checks to uncontrolled appetitive impulse, here seen as a faintly sinister, reptilian "stirring about," has its provenance somewhere between Aquinas and Burke. It is certainly far from Rousseau, or indeed from most of Wordsworth's own views about Nature. The phrase is oddly reminiscent of his "Creature / Moving about in worlds not realized," from the contemporary "Immortality Ode." It also strangely prefigures the Tennysonian and Darwinian Nature, "red in tooth and claw." Unlike the earlier "pleading" passage, this one has the ring of confident political diagnosis, probably because the immediate context here is of triumph, not despair. "*Robespierre was dead*" (10.535; emphasis in original): the news, heard on a beach, sends Wordsworth back both to exultant childhood, repeating a line from book 2 ("We beat with thundering hooves the level sand," 10.566 and 2.144); and to 1790, as he prophesies a return of the "golden times" (10.541). In his relief at the destroyer's death he briefly recovers his 1792 sense of political space and possibility. But it is still not a metaphor Wordsworth develops anywhere else in the poem. The moment passes, and he does not connect his two diagnoses of the Terror: for example, by suggesting that the open space of power is not a reservoir but an expanding sphere, which needs to be filled up from age to age—with agency. Instead he undercuts his own just-renewed belief in "the people" and "the young Republic" (10.577, 582), qualifying this belief first as a "dazzling . . . faith" and then, worse, as "zeal" (10.586–88). This dazzle prevented him, he says, from seeing either that France had once again changed its nature, had suffered a "transmigration" and a "fall of being" (10.599–600), or that Britain had not (10.591–92), its own rulers working as hard as France's, though in a childlike and imitative mode, to "undermine Justice, and make an end of liberty" (10.647–56). The moral shock continues, but the brief return of his French enthusiasm seems only to weaken his judgment and self-confidence.

Wordsworth's double shock left him, and all like him, without any recognizable moral sentiments—not even love. He did not know what the words denoting those feelings meant. He was turned inside out, unrecognizable to himself. His great discovery was repudiated, vitiated. Hating what he saw happening in the two places he derived his identity from, one recently and one all his life, and yet powerless to stop it happening, he had lost all faith in himself. He was in neither heaven nor hell, but limbo. (This is a depression straight out of the psychology textbook.) He could not even speak: he had no terms. What *was* Justice, or Liberty? If they derived their meaning neither from Nature, as he had thought before 1790, nor from practice and agency, as he thought in 1792, then where *did* they get it from? If sentiment was soured and corrupted, maybe he could take refuge in concepts, since they had neither natural nor agential roots.

> And thus a way was opened for mistakes
> And false conclusions of the intellect,
> As gross in their degree, and in their kind
> Far, far more dangerous. What had been a pride
> Was now a shame, my likings and my loves
> Ran in new channels, leaving old ones dry;
> And thus a blow, which in maturer age
> Would but have touched the judgement, struck more deep
> Into sensations near the heart. (10.765–73)

This way of the intellect was to lead Wordsworth into his final moral and political dead end. The stream of his feelings, his life, had been corrupted, so he tried to re-channel it. The metaphors are slippery, as so often; the new channels, it seems, are fast but shallow, whereas the old ones are deeper but dry. The "blow," either the double moral shock we have already discussed or, more likely, the coming intellectual shock, is no longer mediated through the deep old channels of judgment and pride, but travels quickly through the shallow new ones of shame, to the heart (it is hard to make complete sense of a "blow striking into sensations"). The usual defenses and strategies of the self having collapsed, political confrontation, and then political concepts, found their way unmediated into the psyche, the heart, like an enzyme it was not meant to assimilate directly.

Political Philosophy as Moral Despair

One short passage of 130 lines or so from book 10 is important out of all proportion to its size. It is one of the most important passages in the poem, which is to say in all Wordsworth's poetry. Along with the "bliss was it in that dawn" episode, less than a hundred lines earlier in the narrative though several years earlier in his life, it constitutes the core of Wordsworth's represented political experience. It is originary to a high degree; it best represents the immediately precursive "fallen" state out of which grew the recognition of his need for redemptive poetry. This was a state of *failed language*, and the rest of Wordsworth's life was then spent devising and practicing a higher or more successful form of language, or form of words: one that would not fail to convert his readers to, and reassure himself about, his point of view.

But wasn't the fallen or failed state the one he found himself in *during* the twin moral shocks? Wasn't *that* when he lost his identity both as an English liberal and as a French radical: both as a natural and as a political being? Hadn't he been soured and corrupted all the way to the source already, *before* embarking on this fool's errand? Yes—but he was walking wounded, so to speak. The shock had not actually felled him yet. This third and decisive phase revealed the true measure of the other two. They opened the way for the final blow, which was an intellectual one. Events in France and England were social and outward, part of the world of action Wordsworth thought he had joined but now felt a failure in and rejected by. The third blow was inward, to do with how he *thought*. It "struck more deep."

The psychology should be familiar enough to any intellectual. A sensitive and articulate person is defeated, or is one of those defeated, in a political or power struggle (in this case two related struggles). The person's response is to rationalize this failure and in doing so, he or she hopes, to redeem it: to win back by argument, with conceptual weapons, what he or she lost in action. "I was right and should not have been defeated and for these reasons," someone in this position is saying. As if *reasons* were why the person lost and how he or she might now win. (At a more subliminal or animal level the argument is felt as a continuation of the struggle by other means. One thinks of the defiant barking of the retreating dog.) This is in fact the very dream of pleading before unjust tribunals that Wordsworth has already described. He knows he has already lost. This is at some level or other *the* dream of the disempowered intellectual: that the political arena is always a Manichaean struggle between oppressive force and liberating ideas (or, if force can be dissolved into ideas, between ideologies). In fact insofar as there is such a struggle it often leads to success for the ideas, even to zealotry, which is a worship of the ideas in themselves. Since the seventeenth century, indeed, we have too often been convinced that human reality *is* conceptual. This later became the great and in many ways still powerful Hegelian illusion. For all the subsequent rebuttals of this illusion—for example, by Marx, Nietzsche, Kierkegaard or Wittgenstein—the most important response is still Vico's, even though he was talking to Descartes, not Hegel: that history is what we make together, not a set of concepts. This was Burke's answer, too. Most modern intellectuals still prefer a neo-Hegelian view: that instead we can change what people think *about* what they made, by changing their concepts. But Wordsworth's own attempt at concept-response failed wretchedly, as we are about to see. His only recourse after that was a life-response: "I lost but I am a *good person* and the meaning of this good life trumps political power and its effects." To make *this* response, though, he needed a new kind of life-writing, a new model of poetry as life-*making*. He needed to *become*, or once more become, that good person. Poetry would be the redemptive agent.

So what was this "failed language"? It originated in the seventeenth century, in the rationalism of Descartes and the empiricism of Locke and Hobbes, as a way of describing the self. More recently it was adopted as a variant, as a combination and extension, of these two traditions, by the French *philosophes*, followers of and/or contributors to the great Enlightenment dictionary/encyclopedias of Bayle, Voltaire, and Diderot. The resulting amalgamated language manifested a kind of sentimentalized sensationism from which the Cartesian immaterial inner soul was omitted, leaving only a sentient body as the blank receiver (or reflex avoider) of all impressions. The impressions nevertheless collectively coalesced into a self in which the "reason" acted merely as a calculator of the discounted present value of various possible future sensations (the root of utilitarianism). It was developed, for example, by Condillac, for whom *le moi* is the sum of all my sensations; by Helvétius, for whom all ideas, behavior, and motives are reducible to the reflex pursuit of pleasure and avoidance of pain, in which the public interest is valuable only because it produces more pleasure and less pain than immediate self-gratification; and by Holbach, for whom life is just sentient matter, an oscillating machine or *machine sensible* in which the *moi* is the sum of all its impressions. There *was* still a *moi*, though, a kind of node of moral feeling. Vauvenargues, Cabanis, and La Mettrie all developed versions of this language of the self. For all of them feeling and sense are blurred together partly by the double meaning of *sentir*: but of course the language was not only French. David Hartley's "vibrations" theory of sensation and psychology is very close to Condillac. Rousseau's Émile represents the selves of its young protagonists as infinitely malleable by the tutor, like blank sheets for him to write on: this is the *tabula rasa* of the mind in Locke.[2] This was the mutilated materialist self that Kant tried so hard to restore deliberative life to, but ultimately, as we saw in chapter 3, only by injecting spontaneity into its core.

At the same time there was in Britain an important and quite distinct moral tradition, arising partly in reaction to Hobbes and Locke, and culminating in different ways in Hume and Smith, in which the touchstones were sympathy and benevolence, pity and friendship: conceptual equivalents of *agapê* and *caritas*, secular successors of the Christian love of one's neighbor (rather than of God Himself), and the key constituents of humanity in its happiest state. These were the true ingredients, said Shaftesbury, the leading proponent of the school, of the "wisdom of the heart." Our conscience is a kind of natural sense; virtue is a social pleasure. These "moral senses" are the ethical equivalents of the usual external senses, and are quasi-aesthetic, almost matters of taste. The virtuous man wills the general good in exercising his benevolence. Shaftesbury and his successor Francis Hutcheson thus also helped the *philosophes* in sowing the seeds of what was to become the utilitarian school of moral philosophy in Britain. But they too tried, like Kant, to re-insert some sort of living moral center into the eviscerated materialist self. Rousseau did too, injecting Shaftesburyan sentimentalism into the strange moral monads or nodes of the *philosophe* school to create a new Romantic self.

Roughly speaking, the first of these schools, or languages of the self, was what Wordsworth encountered when he read William Godwin's *Enquiry Concerning Political Justice*.³ The book was first published in February 1793, read by Wordsworth sometime between then and early 1794, and revised for its second edition by Godwin during 1795, at a time when he and Wordsworth were close acquaintances. The second language, or some version of it, was not what he wanted in his crisis. But it was more congenial to him; indeed this was both why it seemed inadequate now, and why he rebounded back into it afterwards.

Political Justice is the first true work of philosophical anarchism and one of the most celebrated books of its age. It "blazed as a sun in the firmament of reputation," said Hazlitt.⁴ Wordsworth himself seems much more likely, in the crucial book 10 passage we are talking about, as more explicitly in his other reflections on political philosophy in this period, to have been thinking primarily of Godwin, rather than of Rousseau or Thomas Paine, other natural allies in any fight against Burkean or anti-Revolutionary views. As for Godwin himself, Paine's *The Rights of Man* (1791–1792) and Émile were certainly among his key points of reference, along with Burke's own, satirical *Vindication of Natural Society* (1756). But he singles out Holbach and Helvétius for specific mention, alongside Rousseau, in his preface. *Political Justice* was seen by contemporaries as offering the first truly substantial and philosophical response to Burke's *Reflections*. Paine was regarded as relatively lightweight, though both then and later far more influential. He had also experienced the Revolution, including its jails, at much closer quarters than Wordsworth. Paine's tone is relatively sloganeering and combative, of the "Monarchy equals Ignorance, Republic equals Reason" type. His arguments (that the past is a burden not a resource, that constitutions can be drawn up from first principles, that freedom is a matter of will, that true civil rights grow out of natural rights, that all governments "un-make man") were all enduringly populist, but hardly an advance on Rousseau. Godwin's book, on the other hand, seemed both controversial and weighty. It is certainly long. Despite its studious and pedantic texture it also offers, like its chief antecedents, a radical theory of the self, and this, more than anything, was what both attracted and damaged Wordsworth.

The theory is set out clearly enough in three chapters: "The Characters of Men Originate in Their External Circumstances" (book 1, ch. 4), "The Voluntary Actions of Men Originate in Their Opinions" (book 1, ch. 5), and "Of Free Will and Necessity" (book 4, ch. 7). The central claim is that the "actions and dispositions of men . . . flow entirely from the operation of circumstances and events acting upon a faculty of receiving sensible impressions" (98). Circumstances operate as directly on the mind as they do on the character and behavior; "ideas are to the mind nearly what atoms are to the body" (104); "the human mind . . . is nothing else but a faculty of perception" (146). We could, given time and resources, lay out our ideas as clearly and sequentially as the periodic table. This impression of circumstances on his mind entirely "makes the man" (107).

And yet, crucially, despite all this determinist materialism, the human mind is "an intelligent agent." We act from "opinion" or "judgement," not "impulse." This judgment is based on some sense of *consequences* (119, 124). In fact this sense of consequences *is* what we call reason or understanding. Furthermore, reason or understanding "is susceptible of unlimited improvement" (135) as impressions multiply. We do not just *receive* our impressions, we *learn* from them, and the more of them there are, the more we can learn. "Thought is the medium through which the motions of the animal system are generally carried on" (363); our minds and their ideas in their movements may be just as much the product of external circumstances as billiard balls, but these are billiard balls that can *increasingly* foresee consequential (painful, painless) movement. And this foresight is progressive. "Sound reasoning and truth . . . must always be victorious over error . . . Truth is omnipotent . . . Man is perfectible . . . Man is a rational being" (140–41). To see the truth is to recognize it *as* truth, and so rationality implies perfectibility. Even though "man is in reality a passive, and not an active being" (354), he is "capable of exertion," of seeing which way truth and consequences will tend and, "tranquil and placid" in his knowledge that truth will be victorious, of simply *showing* them to others. "The genuine and wholesome state of mind is to be unloosed from shackles, and to expand every fibre of its frame, according to the independent and individual impressions of truth upon that mind" (548). Truth is "the object towards which the mind irresistibly advances" (794); "intellect has a perpetual tendency to proceed" (781–82).

Morally, the lesson we cumulatively and rationally learn is that virtuous behavior is closer to the natural order of things, and thus more productive of agreeable sensation, than vicious behavior. We also see that it is in our interest to apply this capacity for progressive understanding to promote the general good (351–53). The mind cannot freely originate or cause moral facts, but over time more and more minds can be made aware of how the moral world *is*, what it tends to, which is always *good*. The judging or reasoning principle in us applies especially to our ideas of benevolence and virtue (134). These are consequentialist considerations, "means of agreeable *sensation*" (379, emphasis added), not nuclear or spontaneous *concepts* (the polar opposite to the Kantian view). This picture of the mind and the moral universe is thus progressive and, in line with the usual paradox of philosophical radicalism, both materialist and rationalist. There is, finally, no need for political institutions; this is Godwin's anarchism. Such institutions impede our moral progress; the "auxiliaries" of Wordsworth's poem need only Reason and each other. Institutions embody custom and habit, which are regressive. "With what delight must every well-informed friend of mankind look forward to the auspicious period, the dissolution of political government, of that brute engine which has been the only perennial cause of the vices of mankind" (554).

Wordsworth says he had paid little attention in the past to these "wild theories," assuming that even in so far as they were true they would soon be made redundant by "events." But both events and his natural political intuitions had let him down. So he came to regard the theories not as wild but as "evidence / Safer, of universal application, such / As could not be impeached" (10.773, 789–90). A theory is attractive in such a case just because it is universal and so not subject to contingent events or idiosyncrasies. This had been the appeal of concepts and logic to philosophers ever since Socrates. *Evidentem* means something like "visibly egregious"; *impedica* (hence impeached) lies somewhere between "fettered" or "hobbled," and "impeded." The "evidence" of a theory is indeed unimpeachable; if it is logically consistent, it cannot be hobbled by facts or feelings. Theory is "safer" than practice because it is insulated from reality: exactly the opposite of a true scientific theory.

Here, then, are the two key excerpts from that all-important passage in which Wordsworth describes the attraction for him, and then the effect on him, of this failed Godwinian language of the self:

> This was the time when, all things tending fast
> To depravation, the philosophy
> That promised to abstract the hopes of man
> Out of his feelings, to be fixed thenceforth
> For ever in a purer element,
> Found ready welcome. Tempting region that
> For zeal to enter and refresh herself,
> Where passions had the privilege to work,
> And never hear the sound of their own names—
> But, speaking more in charity, the dream
> Was flattering to the young ingenuous mind
> Pleased with extremes, and not the least with that
> Which makes the human reason's naked self
> The object of its fervour. What delight!—
> How glorious!—in self-knowledge and self-rule
> To look through all the frailties of the world,
> And with a resolute mastery shaking off
> The accidents of nature, time and place,
> That make up the weak being of the past,
> Build social freedom on its only basis:
> The freedom of the individual mind,
> Which, to the blind restraint of general laws
> Superior, magisterially adopts
> One guide—the light of circumstances, flashed
> Upon an independent intellect.

> Thus I fared,
> Dragging all passions, notions, shapes of faith,
> Like culprits to the bar, suspiciously
> Calling the mind to establish in plain day

Her titles and her honours, now believing,
Now disbelieving, endlessly perplexed
With impulse, motive, right and wrong, the ground
Of moral obligation—what the rule,
And what the sanction—till, demanding proof,
And seeking it in everything, I lost
All feeling of conviction, and, in fine,
Sick, wearied out with contrarieties,
Yielded up moral questions in despair,
And for my future studies, as the sole
Employment of the inquiring faculty,
Turned towards mathematics, and their clear
And solid evidence. (10.805–29, 888–904)

The "philosophy / That promised to abstract the hopes of man / Out of his feelings" is Godwin's, as sketched earlier: that political man "by the very constitution of his nature" is "the subject of opinion," so that if "truth and reason when properly displayed give us a complete hold upon his choice," then "we have only to discover what form of civil society is conformable to reason" and encourage it to arrive (118); it will, of course, be one without "political government." The moral and political universe, just like the material one—in fact continuously with the material one—is laid out before the eye of reason so that to the benevolent and virtuous man or woman, and eventually to all men and women, the proper action will be evident. There is no place in this scheme for Kantian, Rousseauan, or Shaftesburyan spontaneity. It does, however, reflect Rousseau's view of social institutions. Godwin's anarchist paradise regained is the mirror image of Rousseau's natural paradise lost, or an alternative way to Rousseau's of regaining it.

But why should the poem regard this materialist, proto-utilitarian doctrine as most likely to appeal to a depraved mind? *Pravus*, incidentally, is "crooked" or "wrong" or "perverse": the diverted stream, the lapse, the turn, the single stride off the path into another region, the crooked change in the human timber. This depravity is literally what the double moral shock diverted Wordsworth into, and the diversion was into a final cul-de-sac, a terminal state of mind. If we are following him along the path of redemption in this book, then this is the lowest point in his descent into "sin." But why? After all, he and Godwin were both engaged in the same task: the pursuit of moral and political justice and virtue; the conversion of minds; the creation of a new political form. So why was this dry, temperate, understated book, this pedantic language, so destructive, so corrupting?

There are two reasons, and they interlock cruelly. First, through reading, and losing himself in, Godwin's version of philosophical radicalism, of the thin conceptual self, Wordsworth by implication accepted that he had lost, or disowned, the rich dynamic self he had briefly discovered in France. When Godwinism failed, he then also had to accept that he could never find an alternative form of life, never find *the* form of his life, in concepts, in that impoverished self. Once active politics had gone, Godwinism seemed to be the closest he could get to its goals; but he just could not *do* Godwinism. Maybe he could have done Burkeanism, but that seemed like the enemy. (He *was* doing it, in fact, more than he realized; this occluding or suppressing of an important part of himself must have contributed to his moral collapse.) So he had to find a richer replacement language, other than Burke's: a rich but still radical, still conceptual, moral language that was not philosophy.

But here was the second reason for despair: even that language, if he could find it, would still always and only be a substitute. So far all he knew was that he had no idea how to find it; and yet he must already have sensed that the form of life he had to find, that richer metaphorical form, would still have to be *in*formed by moral argument, since the agent self he had found and then so utterly lost still had to live, to work, in *some* way, even if only through words: or *he* might as well be a rock or stone or tree. The form had to be not just a form of *life*, a form of *beauty* and a form of *words*, but a form of *good* too, a plea for conversion. And yet this search for such a form would be endless, because even if he found it, it still could not be the same as what he had lost. Worse still, the better he did it, the more evident the substitution would be.

In the end Wordsworth did find a way to offer poetry as the needed form: not out of an interest in human lives, which he also could not do, but out of an interest in the only form of the good he *could* still attain—namely, a verbal and intellectual form. The failure of, first, his agent self, and then a conceptual or argument self intended to be its virtual substitute, was to force him to write a poetry of pleading, of conversion, of offering up his own life, in a kind of sacrifice, as *itself* the argument he could not sustain in philosophy, *about* a good he could not attain in life. The thread of sadness and loss running through all his work, as through almost no other English poet's, is drawn from this spool: that poetry itself was only for him a replacement for what he had lost, reminding him more with its every word that that was all it could be—and yet he had to write it, because it was the only thing that could save him, both from the awfulness of humanity and from himself. He had to be saved by something he also knew to be a failure, a second-best. He had truly found himself only as an agent, a dynamic, active, or purposive self, in the political realm. Then he lost that, and the very form he tried to regain it in was just the form that was least like it. In a way, that is the irony of all writing, but it was more painful in this case because the point of the writing was only to recapture the agency: not just to represent it, but to achieve in writing what he had failed to achieve in agency—as the radical philosophical writing had also failed. And this made poetry into something other than itself, something ameliorative, something quasi-redemptive. It proposed a rich metaphorized life instead of a thin conceptualized one, yes: but still in the service of an argument or agenda that could only impoverish and de-metaphorize both it and life. This was a corruption of poetry itself; *that* source had been soured and corrupted, too.[5]

So what this philosophy offered as a final promise turned out to be a final curse. The promise was *abstraction* of hope from feeling: exactly what the blissful dawn passage had rejected less than a hundred lines earlier. The proximity in the poem of one passage to its contrary crystallizes the contrast between experiences occurring many months or even years apart. Then, hope was an *exercise* of feeling, which was what made it live. Philosophy promised to preserve it conceptually, as "hope," which seemed better than losing *real* hope, but actually turned it into something dead—something precisely *fixed*: not plastic, not dynamic; a concept, not a lived feeling. By the time Wordsworth once again "dares to hope," in "Tintern Abbey," the hope is that poetry will redeem him from failed humanity, his own and others', and the exercise of *that* hope is the actual writing of the poetry in which it does this. But if abstraction is the bait, zeal is the poison. Zeal, as we saw earlier, is concept-worship, a fixation on "social freedom" or "liberty," or even "benevolence" and "virtue," experienced as the spontaneous emission of an inner god. In this purer element, the passions are the nameless workers, never spoken to, privileged even to be admitted to the sanctuary; zeal is the distinguished guest or owner, entering only to refresh herself. There is some hint that she may be Eve, tempted into the eating of this fruit. The naming of multiple passions, as we saw in the introduction to this book, is an important part of making life with concepts, although it is characteristic of Wordsworth to think that naming them is more important than letting them work. But at least he sees that poetry in some sense *works with* them, all of them, and that philosophic zeal is an antagonistic force (Keats had a more nuanced sense of this antagonism in *Lamia*).

The young ingenuous mind, so Wordsworth implies, is pleased with extremes, with the most outward appearances, *extremus* being the superlative form of *exterus*, "outward." Youth and openness are slow to see beyond the outside, are more excited by the edges than the center, are attracted to concepts just because of their "outwardness," their appearance of meaning, like tattoos on a body. His implication is that the nameless passions are what constitute the richer, deeper self, and that abstracted concepts merely "float"—there is some etymological connection with "flattering"—on the flattened surface. As we have seen, the trouble with the zealous emission of ruling concepts is that they are thought of as welling up from the mysterious deeps of the self—perhaps to float on its surface like globs of unassimilated crude oil. The point is that the homogeneous, passional texture or consistency is lost. Fervor is like zeal in its pursuit of an idea-object, and the idea here is that the reason *can* be a naked self, all "outer": that the self can be naked reason, made of bald concepts. The Godwinian idea, not just tempting but delightful, even "glorious" (the word drips with irony at the hubris involved), is that this naked being both knows and rules itself so completely that the whole world seems frail by comparison. Nature, time, and place are merely its accidental or contingent attributes, its "circumstances" (this is Godwin's key word; Wordsworth also uses "external accidents" at line 886).

These circumstances are easily mastered or magisterially ignored, reflecting the mind's power rather than impacting on its passivity. Godwin's argument is that the mind *is* its circumstances, but that it also comes to discern the shape of *all* circumstances, which are Truth, and thus master them. Burke, on the other hand, said that circumstances "give in reality to every political principle its distinguishing colour and discriminating effect. The circumstances are what render every civil and political scheme beneficial or noxious to mankind."[6] We do not master them by intellect. Instead they are what make the productions of the intellect real. The more Godwinian Wordsworth of 1794 may have exaggerated the independence of this intellect; the more Burkean Wordsworth of 1804 ironically points this out—but is still addicted to the idea of a mighty mind, magisterial and moral, rising up out of its circumstances. *The Prelude* holds all of this in tension. In the Godwinian view the being of the past, which is old circumstances, is weak once the mind has understood it. Consequences, perceptible to the reason, are what matter now. In the later Wordsworthian view the past is the sum of those fundamental circumstances that master *us*, or at least make us. The future, where consequences belong, is little more than an extension of the present.

It would be highly misleading, though, to think of Wordsworth as just "rejecting Godwin," switching models, at some time after 1795 but before 1798. The radical model, or language, of the self appealed to something enduring in him, even as he dismissed his youthful and fervent Godwinism. The very force of his revulsion bespeaks a kind of recognition. After all, the main "spots of time" passage, full of talk about our sense of the mind as lord and master, about the renovating virtue that is the confirmation of this sense, occurs at II.257–78, only shortly after the Godwin-rejecting passage we are looking at: and yet there is something highly Godwinian about the spots of time. They are, for one thing, *spots*: punctual, disseminating centers of meaning and virtue quite distinct from their surroundings—not blemishes, admittedly, but not like their surroundings either. They are of course spots of place too; their meaning lies as much in their *local* qualities as in their temporal *location*. As Geoffrey Hartman points out, the idea probably had its origin in the classical *genius loci*.[7] But a spot is not quite a genius; it *is* the place, not the deity of the place. And this place-time composite is incomparably more important, more charged with meaning than others. It gives meaning to everywhere else, not just itself. The spot of time is the *genius vitae*.[8]

The most famous and *genial* spot of time, in the sense that it most clearly gives birth to (*gignere*) Wordsworth's definitive and culminating recognition of the meaning of life, occurs in book 13, near the poem's end. Here too the light of circumstances flashes upon an independent intellect. Wordsworth and Jones (that other crucial *philos*, of whom so little is said) are climbing Mount Snowdon at night, in 1791. Suddenly the light of the moon "upon the turf / Fell like a flash" (13.39–40). An entire mountain landscape is revealed, a "circumstance most awful and sublime" that "Nature thus / Thrusts forth upon the senses" (13.76, 85–86). It "appeared to me," says Wordsworth, "the perfect image of a mighty mind" (13.69), a "genuine counterpart / And brother of the glorious faculty / Which higher minds bear with them as their own" (13.88–90). The whole passage, though already twice quoted in this book, still bears repeating:

> They need not extraordinary calls
> To rouze them—in a world of life they live,
> By sensible impressions not enthralled . . .
> Such minds are truly from the Deity,
> For they are powers; and hence the highest bliss
> That can be known is theirs—the consciousness
> Of whom they are . . .
> Hence truth in moral judgements; and delight
> That fails not, in the external universe.
>
> Oh, who is he that hath his whole life long
> Preserved, enlarged, this freedom in himself?—
> For this alone is genuine liberty. (13.101–22)

The echoes of the earlier Godwin passages in book 10 are remarkable, for all the differences of emphasis. In Godwin and book 10, circumstances flash upon a mind that then, magisterially, shakes itself free of them, rises above them (superior, higher), just by understanding them. In book 13, and in the whole *Prelude* project, the key "circumstances" are natural landscapes, perhaps with a single human figure in them, constitutive in their sublimity and awfulness of a counterpart mind, a mighty or higher one that again soars above them like a mountain, into highest bliss. This is not just political bliss now; it is an emotion arising from the self-recognizing act of consciousness transcending its original circumstances, just as "genuine" or conceptual liberty and free-dom transcend the dynamic kind Wordsworth had glimpsed in France. This is the consciousness of truth, judgment, and liberty (Godwin terms!). As Wordsworth goes on to say, in the poem's culminating pas-sage, this consciousness offers a transcendent perspective on the world of "circumstances," amounting to a higher or more "intellectual" kind of love, enabled in turn by a higher type of reason, or "reason in her most exalted mood." This superior reason is also known as Imagina-tion (166–70).

Surely this *is* Godwin: a sublimed Godwin. Even at its redemptive crescendo, Wordsworth's story bears traces, determinative traces, of the crisis just a few hundred lines earlier. The very doctrine of Imagina-tion is a glorified version of Godwin's doctrine of Reason. The mind's ascent into the sublime (the "exaltation" or making-higher of reason) recalls Godwin's irresistible march of intellect toward truth. Sadly, this new and "genuine" liberty (the word is exactly cognate with "ingenu-ous"), so zealously espoused, is more like Godwin's abstract concept than it is like the agency or exercise of 1792. Wordsworth's rejection of Godwin was in some ways more like an ingestion. The hated parasite remained in him, indeed altered him. Poetry was to replace philosophy, metaphor to displace (in fact to serve) concept, but in such a way as to retain the moral and political orientation that only philosophy seemed at first to offer, and that was all he had left of that brief glorious period of real political activity.[9]

When the final despair and depression arrive—Wordsworth is describing as if it happened in days or weeks a process that took years, and was only just resolved by the time of "Tintern Abbey"—pas-sions and shapes of faith (unformed or empty) seem not just name-less workers but culprits, declared guilty, ready to be sentenced by the arrogant reason in its unjust tribunal. Indeed now that conceptual zeal has been unleashed the mighty mind is even turning on itself, asking itself to prove everything. Wordsworth is expressing here a Romantic disgust with the whole tradition of skeptical philosophy since Des-cartes, who in this respect stands behind Bayle, Voltaire, and the *phi-losophes*: a tradition in which proof, suspicion, perplexity, and doubt become the only markers of genuine thought. This is the skepticism that, having expelled God, purports to seek a new ground for every-thing, especially morality, and yet accepts nothing *as* the final ground, since its own ground is precisely this endless seeking. Such an attitude must see morality, now ungrounded, just as a matter of obligation and thus of rules and sanctions, rather than as a matter of sympathy, love, or agency. Losing all feeling of conviction is realizing that one cannot *convict* the culprit or *convince* oneself (who is also the culprit). We are prosecutor, judge, and accused/convicted all at once, and to have "lost / All feeling" is the general state of the self. The weariness of contrariety lies in finding contraries everywhere without finding true progression: exactly Blake's point about reason without imagination. When moral questions are thus treated as if they were mathematical or evidential the result is despair, *dés-espoir*, the end of all hope, the last outcome of a process that began with treating hope as a concept, not an exercise. Existential despair is also consciousness of sin.

"Sick": this is Wordsworth's one-word summary of his condition in the 1805 text. He elaborated in the 1850 version (there in book 11), on one of the few occasions when his revision added anything substantial:

> This was the crisis of that strong disease,
> This the soul's last and lowest ebb; I drooped,
> Deeming our blessed reason of least use
> Where wanted most . . . (1850, 11.306-9)

In 1792 reason was of *most* use when wanted most. Then it was a part of active political thought. Now reason has skeptically turned itself into its own object (Kant warned against this), and is useless—until, that is, it can be blessed, become right reason, higher reason, imagination, not just an "inquiring faculty" occupied with "clear and solid evidence" (Kant thought he had achieved this, though by a different route). God-win is sublimed again. The crisis of moral disease or sickness, as in Bunyan and Milton, is despair. Despair is a state in which good seems to have no basis: the lowest skeptical state. As the 1850 text goes on to say (11.310-13), for a being who has no "test of good and evil," "will and choice" are mockeries, purely arbitrary impulses.

Utilitarianism is as much the culprit here as rationalism. Exactly the same sequence of joy, despair, and depression was also to afflict John Stuart Mill, thirty years later, before he followed Wordsworth himself down the track to recovery. Mill tells us in his own *Autobiography* that at the age of fifteen, some years younger than Wordsworth, he had found his cause. "From the winter of 1821, when I first read Bentham, . . . I had what might truly be called an object in life; to be a reformer of the world." But then one day, five years later,

> . . . it occurred to me to put the question directly to myself, "Suppose that all your objects in life were realized; that all the changes in institutions and opinions which you are looking forward to, could be completely effected at this very instant; would this be a great joy and happiness to you?" And an irrepressible self-consciousness distinctly answered, "No!" At this my heart sank within me: the whole foundation on which my life was constructed fell down.[10]

The joy Mill mentions is partly hypothetical, whereas Wordsworth's joy in France was entirely real. And yet their causes were the same. Both wanted to effect deep changes in institutions and opinions: to be reformers of the world. Mill had been assuming that his efforts were bringing him *some* happiness, at least, and no doubt they were. Wordsworth *knew* his were bringing him joy. But the foundations of both lives fell down, one when his cause was defeated in both action and argument, the other on realizing that the cause itself was not enough for him. The former returned to it only in a new mode of moral thought; the latter supplemented it in that same mode.

In both cases that new mode of moral thought, called poetry, is seen as medicinal, ameliorative of a diseased state of the soul: even redemptive, where the disease is felt as, or felt to be the result of, transgression or sin. They turned to the very same poems, in fact. Wordsworth wrote them, and Mill read them. They were "a medicine for my state of mind," he writes.

> In them I seemed to draw from a source of inward joy, of sympathetic and imaginative pleasure, which could be shared in by all human beings; which had no connexion with struggle or imperfection, but would be made richer by every improvement in the physical or social condition of mankind. From them I seemed to learn what would be the perennial sources of happiness, when all the greater evils of life shall have been removed.[11]

Mill is talking about the *Lyrical Ballads*, not *The Prelude*, but, after all, the *Ballads* were what Wordsworth wrote to cure his strong disease;

The Prelude, at least in these political books, is only where he tells us why he wrote them, just as Mill's own autobiography is where he tells us why he read them. Both men seem captured by the same notion: that poetry is a form of writing that accesses deep sources of joy. This joy is an almost abstracted emotion, a clear source accessible to all who dig for it, untainted by personal circumstances. But at the same time it is contingent in some way on social and political conditions. Something about the poetry arouses a political response even when its strongest effects are seen as post-political. Aren't the perennial sources of happiness simply perennial? Why would they become perennial only when the evils of life had been removed? The answer is that this is a kind of joy that is precisely post-political: it arises *out of* having passed *beyond* politics. This is exactly what the jaded young utilitarian reformer found in it, and it is exactly why Wordsworth wrote it. He gave up on reformist philosophy, but then wrote post-reformist poetry still colored by that motive.[12] He gave up on political redemption, but then turned to poetry to provide the same redemption.

The so-called "linguistic turn" in twentieth-century philosophy made the same mistake as Godwin and the early Mill: it was a turn to language, and especially a language of the self, that did not actually trust language, did not take it seriously. Wordsworth had seen all this in the course of his collapse. His recourse was to be to poetry, which of course is the form of language that takes language the most seriously. But he did not go, so to speak, "all the way" to poetry. He never took *it* completely seriously either, because he wanted it for something else— namely, to save him from all of the foregoing. Poetry had to succeed, finally, *in the same task*, not as itself but as a stand-in for something else, and, as we saw in "Tintern Abbey," it did not entirely succeed. Some of the failed language of the self he experimented with in the work of Godwin did creep into his poetry and travel back up to its source.

The final paragraphs of book 10 are addressed to Coleridge, but they refer also to Dorothy. They sound some of the same false notes as the final paragraph of "Tintern Abbey," addressed to Dorothy herself:

> Ah, then it was
> That thou, most precious friend, about this time
> First known to me, didst lend a living help
> To regulate my soul. And then it was

> That the belovèd woman in whose sight
> Those days were passed . . .
> Maintained for me a saving intercourse
> With my true self (for, though impaired, and changed
> Much, as it seemed, I was no further changed
> Than as a clouded, not a waning moon);
> She, in the midst of all, preserved me still
> A poet, made me seek beneath that name
> My office upon earth, and nowhere else. (10.904–20)

We have come full circle. The chronology is as unspecific as ever, but the lines conflate Wordsworth's reading of the second edition of *Political Justice* in 1796, his retirement to Racedown House with Dorothy in 1795, his first meetings with Coleridge, also in 1795, and the beginning of their real friendship in 1797. His "most precious friend" and his "dear, dear Friend" carry him with living help, an *exercise* of help, from the dreary intercourse of daily life to a saving intercourse with his true self. Regulating the soul, re-ordering it, recovering the soul of all his moral being, involves moderating the arrogant reason and remembering nature and the language of the sense, the simple "circumstances" that had made his life until France. From his friends he hears again the language of that former heart and mind, thought of here like the clouded and suddenly resurgent moon over Snowdon ("let the moon shine on thee," he prays for Dorothy in "Tintern Abbey"). He has changed much since first he "came among these hills"; but a shadow cast temporarily by clouds is not a loss of the sun's light as the moon turns away from it. He gives the credit to Dorothy for his whole vocation, suggesting that his function upon earth was not to be a politician or a political philosopher (the two things he tried to be in books 9–10) but to seek his office, his duty (*officium*), in poetry. Poetry is duty. It is subordinate, finally, to non-poetic ends: a mode of thought that *seeks* something other than itself. Once again we know Dorothy, and now Coleridge too, only in that they enabled Wordsworth to do his duty. He would do it only upon earth, and nowhere else: the place where in the end we find our happiness, or not at all. But this last echo of the blissful dawn passage is wistful as much as resolute. Wordsworth has an office now, instead of a country: it is "upon" earth, rather than being "the whole earth"; two friends, not "all of us." But it is what he has, now, and he is determined to make the most of it, to make its half-metaphorical, half-conceptual redemption as complete as the agential one he has lost, to find in it the spontaneous, quasi-religious annunciations and redemptions that replicate and displace the political and social bliss of that revolutionary dawn.

Conclusion to Chapters 4 and 5
The Failure of Political Redemption

In reading books 9 and 10 of *The Prelude*, these two chapters argue that in France, in 1792, Wordsworth discovered a kind of meaning in his life, a shape, a model of the self, which was quite new to him. It involved political making: participating in an active and collective exercise of power and creation. This was an apocalyptic or revelatory discovery, and it was a broad moral one, not just political. It taught him a new way of seeing himself in his relation to other people. The model had (to over-simplify) both Rousseauan and Burkean elements. The redemptive, "spontaneous" political concepts were Rousseau's; the sense of a habituated constructive practice was Burke's. The model also included, importantly but less crucially, a certain conception of God or Being as the ground of moral principles. This derived, if anywhere, from Locke and Milton.

The experiential foundations for this new discovery were laid in London, in book 7. The city is seen as a kind of Hell, but one where amelioration is possible. Wordsworth first saw social distress here as something he needed to *act* on, not just sympathize with. At the same time he saw himself not just as any beneficent agent, but as one of a special aristocratic group, uniquely free, powerful, and in touch with Being. His mission is really to save Man, not men. His power comes partly from a naturally egalitarian upbringing and disposition, partly from a deep or spontaneous source, a zeal.

He finds in France a new friend, Michel Beaupuy, who shows him this blissful world of political action. He sees Beaupuy as a revolutionary knight from the world of Romance, a political aristocrat who can manage the political world, the state, rather as a rider manages a horse. Wordsworth is his acolyte, but of course also the bard, whose story this is. Together the two of them offer a chivalric model of politics as service, which at its best offers a template for everyone, a whole people. But in Wordsworth's hands it too often hardens into a zealous elitism.

In any case, everything collapses when neither the evolving Revolution in France nor Wordsworth's fellow countrymen in England (a few young kindred spirits apart) turn out to share his vision or model of politics. Being so invested in it, he therefore feels turned inside out; he does not know himself any more. He even thinks he may have caused all this himself. In desperation he takes refuge in a particular language of politics and the self: a thin, radical language derived mainly from William Godwin. This is a last chance to vindicate conceptually what he has failed to achieve actively. But it too fails, because the model of the self it proposes actually damages him even further—critically, in fact.

He therefore turns in desperation to poetry, as a mode of moral thought, of *redemptive* moral thought, that avoids the thinness of the radical model and language of the self while retaining some of its reformist zeal. The problem with this strategy is that it prevents poetry from being all it can be. Poetry can never really be a substitute for the sense of political agency he experienced and then lost, but it will, in his hands, always carry the marks of this instrumentality. This is why his poetry appeals so strongly to such figures as John Stuart Mill, who appreciate its post-political flavor while remaining oblivious to its metaphorical and relational shortcomings.

Conclusion

Secular Redemption and the Modern Self

R edemption is not the whole of Christianity, but it is a crucial part, supplying perhaps its definitive metaphor ("He died to save us all"). Wordsworth is only one voice in English Romanticism, but arguably its most influential ("Bliss was it in that dawn to be alive"). There is much more to post-Enlightenment philosophy than Kant, but he more than anyone set its terms ("starry heavens above, moral law within").

The decline of Christian belief in the West, though far from total even there, let alone in other parts of the world, has left behind it a conceptual and affective space, felt as a need. Wordsworth and other Romantic poets, the English-speaking ones foremost among them, were possibly the first poets in history who, as early witnesses to a large-scale religious decline of this kind, felt that it was now their function to "save" or even redeem their fellow men and women by supplying this need. Kant was even more of a pioneer among philosophers in setting out to install at the center of the moral universe a new kind of faith, a philosophical faith in the good and free will.

Wordsworth's guiding stars were, first and fleetingly, political association; and then, more enduringly, forms of beauty, especially natural landscapes. Forms of beauty and forms of good had a quasi-religious aspect and a close connection to each other for Kant too; but at the center of his model of the redeemed self, and crucial for Wordsworth's as well, was the spontaneous individual will. Poet and philosopher alike wanted to redeem us: one of them, briefly, through politics; both of them through aesthetics and the spontaneous will; one from a terrible humanity, through nature; the other from mechanical nature, through the will.

These two great and influential writers were by no means unique in these beliefs and ambitions. Many philosophers and poets, then and since, though of course by no means all of them, have also believed that in the absence of God we now have to redeem ourselves, either from our own nature or from nature itself, either because the former is evil or because the latter is indifferent. Indeed for such writers this redeeming seems to be the most important thing that we have to do with our lives, and the most important thing they have to do in their work. We can discover how to live, they collectively seem to suggest (I am blending their ruling ideas), by seeing certain pleasing forms of nature or reason (or art, in later versions of this composite idea) as *good*. Forms of beauty become forms of good. By a mysterious and unpredictable alchemy, a spontaneous and inexplicable reflex, our wills are thus disposed to good action. Each of us can be reborn as a different kind of being, if only we will look long and deeply enough into the beautiful magic cavern of the self. Such writers think of themselves as having the best-equipped intelligences for this task, charging themselves with, or sacrificing themselves to, the duty of reporting back to the rest of us on what they have found. They have not usually approached this task in a spirit of conceit, but in some sense they have found themselves to be not just doing God's work, but also assuming his mantle. And we, as both their judges and their disciples, have tended to believe in them.

It seems to me that this belief in self-redemption by a wayward spirit of beauty, by a capricious and aestheticized will, was promoted in some form or other by many of the greatest thinkers of the modern era, from the 1780s to the 1960s, and is at the core of the dominant modern conception of the self in the West. It is, finally, the legacy of Rousseau: and it is an illusion, probably a dangerous one. We can wait forever outside the entrance to that cave, and even then what comes out may be a monster.

Yes, we need to know how to live, or to go on living; but meaning is not to be found within ourselves: only *between* ourselves. If we still have a memory or an imaginative understanding of redemption as a condition in which the burden of making us good or showing us how to live is borne by a divine version of ourselves, or a human version of God, then that simply shows us that we need to find our meanings outside the cave of the self: even outside the human world. For those who become or remain Christians this is no mere memory, of course. *They* are not living in a post-Christian world. Someone has still died for them, and they can get on with living, with just being human. As for the rest, they should be wary of any conception of a magic core, an inner divine self, a redemption by beautiful forms. Theirs is a community, not a communion, of more or less virtuous lives, each finding its place and meaning in and from and among and together with all the others. But even for some of them, perhaps, the Christian understanding of redemption may remain in their memories and imaginations, within their virtue community, as a reminder that there are some things we do not have to bear, and some we should not try to be. Sometimes knowing what we cannot do helps us do what we should. And knowing what none of us can be helps us all to accept what we are.

Afterword
The Intimations Ode

The poem's 1815 title, "Intimations of Immortality from Recollections of Early Childhood,"[1] more or less equates intimations with recollections. *Intus* is "within," and *intimus* is the deepest and most profound of inner things, the very core of the inner. These are messages from the core. But they are also "*from* Recollections": the core here *is* recollection. *Re-co-ligere*: binding-together-again. Religion and recollection are almost synonyms, and indeed for Wordsworth recollection *was* a religion, was *his* religion, especially when it was a recollection of childhood. Memory takes him to his deepest, which is to say earliest, self. And what he now finds there is immortality, "something that doth live" (132)—and lives forever. The promise of eternal life is to be found, glimpsed, in the earliest life of the mortal man or woman. Wordsworth's most famous and glorious poem tells us that we are to be redeemed by our own childhood.

There will be no more divine redemption, after all. In the end, that is the "something that is gone" (53). Celestial light and glory, radiance, the *jubilate agno* or jubilee of lambs, Heaven itself, the imperial palace, a world of bliss, the God who is our home: the Tree and single Field are negative signs, like the naked pool and burdened girl in *Prelude* 11, of the great and now eternal absence of those things (1–84). A visionary dreariness is the reflex of the visionary gleam, the thought of utter grief in the midst of universal joy. Nature can only be a foster-mother for any child so utterly orphaned, which is to say every child, now. All hope of *that* salvation, that redemption, is forever taken from us. Like the "four year's Darling of a pigmy size" (86) we must make do with our dream of human life, con whatever mortal part we must. Without that meaning-giving or value-adding prospect our whole vocation *is* just imitation; the grave *is* but a lonely bed.

And yet, with that familiar Wordsworthian rebound out of disappointment into reassurance, the "something that is gone" is somehow substituted by "something that doth live." What the child *did* see, did feel, redeems us from our dreary thoughts of the lonely grave. The capacity for blessing or benediction can return, even to a humanity no longer touched by divine grace. We *can* again be strong, we *can* find strength in what remains (24, 83). Here is the core of the entire Wordsworthian vocation, even the modern post-Christian conception of life, in all its glory and all its frailty. There is one human heart. It survives suffering and vicissitude. Faith in it transcends even death. Human sympathy is primal, foundational. As if to God, we give thanks and praise to our own obstinate refusal (144) to live just in a material world, to our own persisting instinct that there is a higher world, a deeper one: a value world.

In its crescendo, in the second half of the ninth stanza (151–70), with those variant odal lines working at the height of their contrastive power, as magnificent psalmic pentameters alternate with piercing short lines so that entire potential regular stanzas seem compressed into each turn, the poem tells us that the recollections themselves are the master light of all our *being* (*vide* 155, 157). They help us to bear even the prospect of eternal silence, by persuading us that eternity is actually constituted in the very brevity and apparent triviality of our brief noisy years, our still small voices. All our little moments are also imperishable truths, necessary parts of everything that is, droplets in the immortal sea. In remembering our own childhoods, and only in doing that, we will always remember this.

The post-Christian imagining of meaning and value has never been more powerfully or concisely articulated (whatever one's view of the unfortunate "best Philosopher" or "Mighty Prophet" effusions, 108–28: the kind of bathetic lapse that is somehow never far away from Wordsworth's most sublime passages). And what is absolutely intrinsic to its glory is also what makes it so poignantly frail. It throws away the very ladder it has climbed—for the texture of the feeling, the very strength itself that we are to find, is elegiac. We are, after all, "what remains behind" (183), when all that radiance has gone. "Remain" is *re-manere*. This is what it is to be post-Christian: after the time of immanence (*in-manere*) has passed, we are literally *remnants*. Tennyson was to feel this all over again in the next generation, when even foster-mother nature, "red in tooth and claw," deserted him: "we are not now that strength. . . ." And then Hegel, Wordsworth's exact contemporary, in the generation after Kant: the philosophic mind wakes only at dusk. Wordsworth's mind was always in this sense philosophical, even in his greatest poetry; the years had *always* brought the philosophic mind. Life is always what he looks *back* on; he is always a remnant of something that has passed, maybe something he never quite belonged to. As we have seen, that "something" for him actually was other people, as much as it was God. It was not just that he loved and lost, but that he never really knew how to love at all. So he has to find his redemption not in the messy, noisy richness, the obstinate community, of other lives, where in fact it would not even have been necessary to look for it, but in his own solitary childhood.

And one is tempted to think that this too has been the nightmare of modernity: the awful thought that each of us, indeed humanity *en masse*, faces the eternal silence alone—rather than the alternative that we all live noisily together, piping and playing, and that each of us, after all, *lives*, and lives *now*, rather than *then*, and is survived by others who also live. There is, surely, a time for elegy, a perspective of loss and even death; but surely, too, life in itself is not fundamentally elegiac.

It may, on the other hand, be fundamentally religious, where religion means such acceptance and celebration of the limits of life that enable life itself to be lived most richly. We do not have to redeem ourselves—or make ourselves. We are not God.

NOTES

Introduction

1   In saying any of this it is impossible not to be aware of the giant figure of
Nietzsche looking over one's shoulder. Ted Sadler, especially in the third
chapter, "Redemption and Life Affirmation," of his *Nietzsche: Truth and
Redemption*, offers an admirable account of the key role played by the concept of redemption in Nietzsche's work, showing how for him our relation
to truth is analogous to the Christian idea of our relation to God: how
we are "redeemed into truth" (Sadler 1995, 8). Sadler outlines Nietzsche's
quarrel with Schopenhauer's concept of redemption as a breaking free
of the tyranny of the will, breaking free of guilt at our very existence as
ego—but a breaking free into nothingness. For Nietzsche, says Sadler,
redemption is a coming home to oneself, a reinvesting of life with value, a
cleansing from *ressentiment*. In this picture Jesus, *contra* Paul, is the model
of a life directed against law and dogma, prompting us to think of how
one would have to live in order to feel as if one were in heaven (144). But
then, how deeply is Nietzsche's own thought imbued with the Christian
conception? How far is it even possible for him to throw away the lad-
ders he stands on? Giles Fraser argues that Nietzsche explores the ways
in which "the same basic instinct for redemption can be expressed in a
world without God" (*Redeeming Nietzsche: On the Piety of Unbelief* [London:
Routledge, 2002], 2); but as Alasdair MacIntyre suggests in the key chapter of *After Virtue* (ch. 9, "Nietzsche or Aristotle?," *After Virtue: A Study in
Moral Theory* [London: Duckworth, 1985]), and in many other places in
that book and others, Nietzsche's insistence that Enlightenment morality

fails to address the question, "what sort of person am I to become" (118) is far more congenial than his picture of the sort of person he would have us become. The very attempt to express a redemptive attitude "in a world without God" is just what turns it into something unprecedented and with possibly dangerous consequences. Nietzsche's word *Erlösung* is of course not literally the same as "redemption," but means a "setting loose," or as Leo Bersani puts it in his groundbreaking work on redemption in modern literature, "a kind of release of being" (*The Culture of Redemption* [Cambridge, Mass.: Harvard University Press, 1990], 98). The implications of this difference are quite far-reaching, it seems to me. "Release of being" implies a prior caging or imprisonment of some essentially free core: a Rousseauan model. Nietzsche may be right to attack the idea of a *sacrificial* redemptive aesthetic, as Bersani says (97), but in doing so he also jettisons the conserving or preserving aspect of redemption. The redemptive self attempts to save all of itself, all that it was, not to become a newly justified aesthetic phenomenon by simply dumping ballast. And the redeemed self is enabled to go on living in the world, not somehow be released from it.

2   A classic statement of the idea that many of our key moral concepts are the relics of a defunct system is G. E. M. Anscombe, "Modern Moral Philosophy," *Philosophy* 33, no. 124 (1958): 1–19. MacIntyre's *After Virtue* is among other things a powerful statement of this kind.

3   As Bersani puts it, on such a view art can "master the presumed raw material of experience in a manner that uniquely gives value to, perhaps even redeems, that experience" (*Culture of Redemption*, 1). But Bersani's just criticism of this view, that it tends to reduce art "to a kind of superior patching function" (1), or to the status of a handmaiden of philosophical truth in the task of correcting life and historical experience, is nevertheless heavily influenced by the example of Proust, whose redemptive aesthetic, contrary to Wordsworth's, was informed by art far more than by nature. A wild green landscape does not at all "master" experience in the way a musical phrase does; a poem about the landscape does not have the manifold insulating redemptiveness of a novel about the phrase. Charles Taylor's account of Proustian artistic redemption in his *Sources of the Self* is as usual highly pertinent: "the formally irretrievable past is recovered in its unity with the life yet to live, and all the 'wasted' time now has meaning, as the time of preparation for the work of the writer who will give shape to this unity" (*Sources of the Self: The Making of the Modern Identity* [Cambridge: Cambridge University Press, 1989], 51). Still, this is not really Wordsworth's position; Proust's conscious sense of redeeming the past

through writing could have been arrived at only after and as a result of the examples of such writers as Rousseau and Wordsworth, whose material was nature, not art, although in working that natural material they did produce art themselves, and thus began the tradition Proust belonged to. But redemption through producing art is not the same as redemption through consuming it.

4   A feature of the "redemptive aesthetic" that Bersani does not really consider, given his Proustian-Joycean presuppositions.

5   Nietzsche's was made simply of will, beyond good and evil; the model is not that different.

6   Edmund Burke, *Reflections on the Revolution in France*, ed. J. G. A. Pocock (Indianapolis: Hackett, 1987), 86. Other references in this introduction are to passages referenced fully in the relevant chapters of the book.

7   This view is related to but distinct from the Proustian aesthetic redemptiveness referred to in note 3.

8   Rousseau clearly stands behind this model.

9   The source of the Nietzschean "release of being" referred to in note 1.

10 Simon Haines, *Poetry and Philosophy from Homer to Rousseau: Romantic Souls, Realist Lives* (Basingstoke: Palgrave Macmillan, 2005).

Chapter 1

1   Cora Diamond, *The Realistic Spirit: Wittgenstein, Philosophy and the Mind* (Cambridge, Mass.: MIT Press, 1991), 262. See also Mark Johnson and George Lakoff, *Metaphors We Live By* (Chicago: University of Chicago Press, 1980), *passim*, and in much other work since. On life with *metaphors*, cognitive linguistics has done much since the 1980s to emphasize both literature's metaphoricity and metaphor's cognitive priority in all thought, without often linking the two points: literature is the primary form of metaphorical thought in language.

2   Including cognitive linguistics, for example.

3   See Haines, *Poetry and Philosophy*, 55–77; and Haines, "Iris Murdoch, the Ethical Turn and Literary Value," in *Iris Murdoch and Morality*, ed. Anne Rowe and Avril Horner (Basingstoke: Palgrave Macmillan, 2010), 91–94.

4   *The New Science* first appeared in 1725: see Giambattista Vico, *The New Science of Giambattista Vico*, trans. Thomas Goddard Bergin and Max Harold Fisch (Ithaca: Cornell University Press, 1984). For *The Four Ages of Poetry*, see Thomas Love Peacock, *The Works of Thomas Love Peacock*, ed. H. F. Brett-Smith and C. E. Jones (London: Constable, 1924–1934), 8:1–25.

5   A. D. Nuttall, *A Common Sky: Philosophy and the Literary Imagination* (London: Chatto & Windus for Sussex University Press, 1974), 126. Nuttall

wants to show that in its relative absence of metaphor Wordsworth's poetry is a very rare, almost unique, example of the primary imagination at work. But what this points toward (or so I want to claim in this book) is something like the death of poetry. I think Nuttall is close to saying this too, in different terms.

6 All references to the *Prelude*, unless otherwise indicated, are to the 1805 edition printed in William Wordsworth, *The Prelude, 1799, 1805, 1850*, ed. Jonathan Wordsworth, M. H. Abrams, and Stephen Gill (New York: W. W. Norton, 1979).

7 From the 1802 "Preface" to *Lyrical Ballads*: William Wordsworth, *William Wordsworth: The Oxford Authors*, ed. Stephen Gill (Oxford: Oxford University Press, 1984), 595. This is the edition of the "Preface" used unless otherwise cited.

8 William Hazlitt, "Mr Wordsworth," in *The Complete Works of William Hazlitt*, ed. P. P. Howe, vol. 11, *The Spirit of the Age* (1825; London: J. M. Dent & Sons, 1932), 87.

9 William Wordsworth, *The Prose Works of William Wordsworth*, ed. W. J. B. Owen and Jane Worthington Smyser (Oxford: Clarendon, 1974), 1:103. The *Essay* was never published by Wordsworth, but was probably written in the later part of 1798.

10 Wordsworth, "Preface," in *William Wordsworth*, 605.

11 Hazlitt, "On the Living Poets," in *The Complete Works of William Hazlitt*, ed. P. P. Howe, vol. 5, *Lectures on the English Poets* (1818; London: J. M. Dent & Sons, 1932), 163.

12 From a letter of October 27, 1818. John Keats, *Letters of John Keats*, ed. Robert Gittings (London: Oxford University Press, 1970), 157.

13 See Matthew Arnold, *Matthew Arnold's Essays in Criticism* (London: Dent & Dutton, 1964), 293–311 (his 1879 "Preface" to Wordsworth's poems); and F. R. Leavis, *Revaluation: Tradition and Development in English Poetry* (Harmondsworth: Penguin, 1967), 153 (for the quotation) and 130–54 (for the whole essay, "Wordsworth").

14 In "The Lost Leader": *The Poetical Works of Robert Browning*, 2 vols. (London: Smith, Elder, 1901; repr. Newcastle: Cambridge Scholars, 2012) 1:249.

15 David Bromwich, *Disowned by Memory: Wordsworth's Poetry of the 1790s* (Chicago: University of Chicago Press, 1998), 7.

16 Iris Murdoch, *The Sovereignty of Good* (London: Routledge, 1970), 58.

17 A. G Baumgarten, *Meditationes philosophicae de nonnullis ad poema pertinentibus* (1735), par. 1, cited in Wellek, René. *A History of Modern Criticism: 1750–1950*, vol. 1, *The Later Eighteenth Century* (London: Jonathan Cape, 1955), 145.

18 J. Wordsworth, *William Wordsworth*, 606.

19   Bromwich says acutely that "what Wordsworth cannot say about the revolution he will often consent to say about his childhood, and what he cannot say of childhood he will say of the revolution" (*Disowned by Memory*,
2). Something cannot be said, in either case: my own account of "Tintern
Abbey" tries to explore this.

Chapter 2

1   See Bromwich, *Disowned by Memory*, "Introduction" and, especially, chapter 3, "The French Revolution and 'Tintern Abbey,'" an essay much in my
mind in writing what follows, not least because it keeps so alive the mere
possibility of writing in this way about Wordsworth, or indeed poetry.
There has been too little criticism of this kind since. Note also Thomas
McFarland, *William Wordsworth: Intensity and Achievement* (Oxford: Clarendon, 1992), 25: "in every New Historical approach to literary matters that
I myself have seen, [the] masked core is a kind of coin whose obverse is an
unquestioning commitment to left-wing political understandings of the
human situation, and whose reverse is an inability to confront the quality
of the poem Wordsworth, or another poet, actually did write." One could
make a more general case about literary studies since the 1970s, perhaps,
by omitting "left-wing."

2   I have found the following accounts of the poem particularly helpful,
even those I radically disagreed with: Bromwich, *Disowned by Memory*,
69–91; Geoffrey H. Hartman, *Wordsworth's Poetry 1787–1814* (New Haven:
Yale University Press, 1964), 26–30; Marjorie Levinson, *Wordsworth's Great
Period Poems* (Cambridge: Cambridge University Press, 1986), 14–57; McFarland, *William Wordsworth*, 34–56; Nicholas Roe, *Wordsworth and Coleridge:
The Radical Years* (Oxford: Clarendon, 1988), 268–75. Stephen Gill's *William Wordsworth: A Life* (Oxford: Clarendon, 1989) was indispensable.

3   Wordsworth, *William Wordsworth*, 692.

4   I am mindful here of Hartman's comment that he has never seen this
note "entirely explained" (*Wordsworth's Poetry*, 27); maybe it has been since
then.

5   The text used is Wordsworth, *William Wordsworth*, 131–35.

6   I am thinking mainly of Levinson's *Wordsworth's Great Period Poems*, but
there have been many other recent studies of these and similar questions.

7   J. S. Mill, following Wordsworth's own lead in his various prefaces, may
after all have been closer to the truth of the poetry than many recent
commentators in drawing attention to its "culture of the feelings." J. S.
Mill, *Autobiography*, ed. Jack Stillinger (Oxford: Oxford University Press,
1969), 89.

8   Immanuel Kant, *Critique of Pure Reason*, trans. and ed. Paul Guyer and Allen W. Wood (Cambridge University Press, 1998), A125–26.

9   Let alone, as Bersani rightly says of Proust, in a work of art: see note 3 to the introduction.

10 This is the grain of truth in criticisms of Wordsworth's suppression of the political.

11 Wordsworth, "Preface," *William Wordsworth*, 599.

12 "Simon Lee," discussed in chapter 3.

13 Samuel Taylor Coleridge, *The Notebooks of Samuel Taylor Coleridge*, ed. Kathleen Coburn, vol. 1, *1794–1804*, Bollingen Series 50 (New York: Pantheon Books, 1957), 921.

14 The poem, says Bromwich (*Disowned by Memory*, 73), is "about the peace and rest that one can know only by a sublimation of remembered terror": an "*aesthetic* sublimation," furthermore. Bromwich is surely right to point out that "sublimation" here does *not*, as so many recent critics have argued, mean "the evasion of wordly politics" (74). So terror of what, exactly? Bromwich makes the just connection to *Prelude* 10 (the "unjust tribunals" passage): "Only one who felt himself somehow implicated in the regime of terror would resort to this particular tone of confession" (86). This seems exactly right to me.

15 From his "Note to the Ancient Mariner" in the 1800 edition: William Wordsworth and Samuel Taylor Coleridge, *Lyrical Ballads: Wordsworth and Coleridge*, ed. R. L. Brett and A. R. Jones (London: Methuen, 1965), 276.

16 Wordsworth and Coleridge, *Lyrical Ballads*, 277.

17 The Nietzschean and even the Proustian problem.

18 Frances Ferguson's perception that this "almost desperate reiteration" conveys "the poet's fear of losing yet another human passion" (*Wordsworth: Language as Counter-Spirit* [New Haven: Yale University Press, 1977], 146) is plausible, but perhaps insufficiently takes into account the contrast between its inarticulate sentimentality (*anyone* could say "I really really mean this, really") and the unique power of (much of) what has gone before.

19 Mill, *Autobiography*, 111–14, 145–50.

20 But see note 3 to the introduction. The redemptive force of nature is not the same as the redemptive force of art. Wordsworth consumed, so to speak, the former but produced the latter. Proust, by contrast, both consumed and produced the latter.

Chapter 3

1   René Descartes, *The Philosophical Works of Descartes*, trans. Elizabeth S. Haldane and G. R. T. Ross (Cambridge: Cambridge University Press, 1969), 1:175.

2   Jean-Jacques Rousseau, *Julie, ou La Nouvelle Héloïse* (Paris: Garnier-Flammarion, 1967), 529.

3   For a fuller version of this account of Rousseau see Haines, *Poetry and Philosophy*, ch. 8. Kant famously remarks at the second *Critique* that "Two things fill the mind with ever new and increasing admiration and awe, the more often and steadily we reflect upon them: *the starry heavens above me and the moral law within me*" (*Das moralische Gesetz in uns, der Gestirnte Himmel über uns*; Immanuel Kant, *Groundwork of the Metaphysic of Morals*, in *Practical Philosophy*, trans. and ed. Mary J. Gregor [Cambridge: Cambridge University Press, 1996], 271).

4   Footnote references to the first *Critique* (Kant, *Critique of Pure Reason*) have been kept to a minimum by using the conventional A and B citation method within the main text (modern editions present the two versions of the *Critique* as "A" and "B," interleaving but distinguishing them in the form of a single running text with two systems of marginal numbering). The two quoted judgments are from P. F. Strawson, *The Bounds of Sense: An Essay on Kant's "Critique of Pure Reason,"* (London: Methuen, 1975), 25; and A. C. Ewing, *A Short Commentary on Kant's "Critique of Pure Reason"* (Chicago: University of Chicago Press, 1967), 67. The structural analysis of the *Critique* in the following paragraphs is my own (including the chart!); but obviously anyone, especially an amateur, offering such an account of so complex a work is indebted beyond measure to earlier and much better analyses. In my case I found the following to be indispensable guides in making my way through the jungle: Henry E. Allison, *Kant's Transcendental Idealism* (New Haven: Yale University Press, 2004); Jonathan Bennett, *Kant's Analytic* (Cambridge: Cambridge University Press, 1966); Ewing, *Short Commentary*; Sebastian Gardner, *Routledge Philosophy Guidebook to Kant and the "Critique of Pure Reason"* (London: Routledge, 1999); Paul Guyer, "The Transcendental Deduction of the Categories," in *The Cambridge Companion to Kant*, ed. Paul Guyer (Cambridge: Cambridge University Press, 1992); Norman Kemp Smith, *A Commentary to Kant's "Critique of Pure Reason"* (Basingstoke: Palgrave Macmillan/St. Martin's, 2003); Roger Scruton, *Kant* (Oxford: Oxford University Press, 1982); Strawson, *Bounds of Sense*; Allen W. Wood, *Kant* (Oxford: Blackwell, 2005); and of course the comprehensive introduction and other explanatory material, including a glossary of German terms, provided by Guyer and Wood in Kant, *Critique of Pure Reason*.

5   Kant, *Critique of Pure Reason*, 226–44, 245–66.

6   Strawson, *Bounds of Sense*, 86.

7   A vocabulary that had disastrous consequences for philosophical clarity among Kant's numerous heirs from Hegel to Heidegger: including for Coleridge and *his* heirs, who were fewer but all wrote in English.

8 I found Terry Pinkard, *German Philosophy 1760–1860: The Legacy of Idealism* (Cambridge: Cambridge University Press, 2002), 19–44 and Andrew Bowie, *Aesthetics and Subjectivity: From Kant to Nietzsche* (Manchester: Manchester University Press, 2003), 16–48, and esp. 19–24 (from his chapter on Kant), indispensable in developing this short account of spontaneity in Kant. Also helpful was Robert B. Pippin, "Kant on the Spontaneity of Mind," *Canadian Journal of Philosophy* 17, no. 2 (1987): 449–76. The comprehensive study by Sgarbi (Marco Sgarbi, *Kant on Spontaneity* [London: Continuum, 2012]) has unfortunately appeared too recently for me to take it into account—a great pity. The topic is a burgeoning one, to say the least.

9 Kant, *Groundwork*, 82.

10 Kant, *Critique*, 484–89.

11 Kant, *Groundwork*, 63.

12 Immanuel Kant, *Critique of the Power of Judgment*, ed. Paul Guyer, trans. Paul Guyer and Eric Matthews (Cambridge: Cambridge University Press, 2000), 344.

13 Kant, *Critique of the Power of Judgment*, 147–48.

14 Kant, *Critique of the Power of Judgment*, 145.

15 Kant, *Critique of the Power of Judgment*, 91–92.

16 Kant, *Critique of the Power of Judgment*, 226–27.

17 Kant, *Critique of the Power of Judgment*, 333–38.

18 Page references to Kant's *Groundwork* appear in the text for the rest of this section.

19 Immanuel Kant, "Idea for a Universal History with a Cosmopolitan Purpose," in *Political Writings*, ed. Hans Reiss, trans. H. B. Nisbet (Cambridge: Cambridge University Press 1970), 46 (though the "crooked timber" translation is Isaiah Berlin's).

20 Immanuel Kant, *Critique of Practical Reason*, in *Practical Philosophy*, trans. and ed. Mary J. Gregor (Cambridge: Cambridge University Press, 1996), 163–64.

21 Immanuel Kant, *The Metaphysics of Morals*, in *Practical Philosophy*, trans. and ed. Mary J. Gregor (Cambridge: Cambridge University Press, 1996), 557.

22 Wordsworth, *William Wordsworth*, 598.

23 In the essay "Thoughts on Poetry and Its Varieties." 1833. In *The Collected Works of John Stuart Mill*, vol. 1, *Autobiography and Literary Essays*, 341–66. The Online Library of Liberty, Liberty Fund (no pagination).

24 Wordsworth, *William Wordsworth*, 598.

25 Shelley's phrase, from *A Defence of Poetry* (1821): *Shelley's Poetry and Prose*, selected and ed. Donald H. Reiman and Sharon Powers (New York: W. W. Norton, 1977), 482.

26 Gill, ed., *William Wordsworth*, 611.

27 Wordsworth, *William Wordsworth*, 130–31.

28 Wordsworth, *William Wordsworth*, 85–88.

29 Heather Glen mentions Southey's "Complaints of the Poor" in her fine account of "Simon Lee." Heather Glen, *Vision & Disenchantment: Blake's Songs and Wordsworth's "Lyrical Ballads"* (Cambridge: Cambridge University Press, 1983), 235.

30 Again Glen's account is rewarding. She speaks of the poem's tone as "never entirely free of condescension," and of its speaker as the only one in *Lyrical Ballads* who actually *acts* toward one of the less privileged—but notes that it is still about his private feelings first and foremost (Glen, *Vision & Disenchantment*, 236, 240).

31 Paul D. Sheats writes of this "powerful and liberating release of protective energy" (*The Making of Wordsworth's Poetry, 1795–1798* [Cambridge, Mass.: Harvard University Press, 1973] 192), as Glen notes (*Vision & Disenchantment*, 238). Bromwich (*Disowned by Memory*, 99) quotes Glen (237) on the blow as "an apt and powerful image for the unwitting ease of that paternalistic 'pity' which diminishes that which is to the suffering other impossible," and Bromwich himself notes that the poem is redescribing gratitude as a "vice," a "source of regret."

32 I am most grateful to Richard Lansdown for prompting me into thinking harder about this issue.

33 Wordsworth, *William Wordsworth*, 598–99.

34 Wordsworth, *William Wordsworth*, 599.

35 "The Old Cumberland Beggar," Wordsworth, *William Wordsworth*, 49–54, lines 81–83, 106–8, 114, 144–45. Also discussed in chapter 4's section, "Sources of Power." James K. Chandler's acute discussion of the poem (*Wordsworth's Second Nature: A Study of the Poetry and Politics* [Chicago: University of Chicago Press, 1984], 84–89) has been most influential in suggesting Wordsworth's practical Burkean political affiliations, but his sense of the poem's moral shortcomings, its liberal high-mindedness, seems more valuable to me.

36 Wordsworth, *William Wordsworth*, 140–42.

37 David Ferry's argument (*The Limits of Mortality: An Essay on Wordsworth's Major Poems* [Middletown, Conn.: Wesleyan University Press, 1959], 64) that Wordsworth "loves Emma in her grave more than he had loved her while alive," while part of a commendable reading, seems to me not to do full justice to this passage.

38 "Michael, A Pastoral Poem," also 1800: Wordsworth, *William Wordsworth*, 224–36. Lines quoted are 213, 474–75.

39 David Simpson (*Wordsworth's Historical Imagination: The Poetry of Displacement* [New York: Methuen, 1987], 141–49) finds that the poem "remains polemically efficient as a transcription of how the ideal rural economy might indeed operate for its inhabitants," while "One has no sense, reading this poem . . . of a local gentry taking over ownership of the landscape" (148). This is an idealized landscape, not an engaged one. At the same time the poem contains "some of the finest blank verse in the landscape" (141). It seems to me (as suggested in the first note to chapter 2) that its political qualities, overt or covert, are just what is *not* interesting about the poem, while the quality of its verse is just what Simpson is not interested in. His latest book on Wordsworth (David Simpson, *Wordsworth, Commodification and Social Concern: The Poetics of Modernity* [Cambridge: Cambridge University Press, 2009]) stakes its claim early on: "Reading Marx again after Derrida, and Wordsworth again after both, opens up a new way of understanding the historical affiliations between and determinations among spectral figures, commodities, factory time, machine labour, global war and poetic imagery" (4). But surely such understandings are far from new. Bromwich (*Disowned by Memory*, 154–62) offers another kind of account entirely, taking its characters as primary, while still being fully aware of the poem's status as social protest, as a "poem of independence justified" (171). But it seems to me he is rather *too* kind to the qualities of feeling manifested in the poem as a whole. Are Michael or Simon Lee primarily "people who continue to be themselves," as Bromwich says (172)? Or is it that their selves continue to be subservient in Wordsworth's mind to his own?

40 "Surprized by joy—impatient as the Wind," Wordsworth, *William Wordsworth*, 334.

41 References to *The Prelude* here, as throughout this book, are by book and line to the 1805 text in Wordsworth, *The Prelude, 1799, 1805, 1850*, unless otherwise indicated.

42 The text used, from the 1798 *Lyrical Ballads*, is the one printed in Brett and Jones, *Lyrical Ballads*, 9–35, with line numbers in parentheses, although in the section title I have substituted 1800's "Ancient Mariner" for the 1798 "Ancyent Marinere."

43 Samuel Taylor Coleridge, *Biographia Literaria* (1817), ch. 14, in *Samuel Taylor Coleridge: The Oxford Authors*, ed. H. J. Jackson (Oxford: Oxford University Press, 1985), 314.

44 Coleridge, *Biographia Literaria*, 314.

45 Samuel Taylor Coleridge, *Table Talk* (1835), in Jackson, *Samuel Taylor Coleridge*, 593–94.

46 The Blake quotations are from "The Divine Image" (lines 19–20) and "The Chimney Sweeper" (line 24); emphasis added. See *The Poetry and Prose of William Blake*, ed. David V. Erdman (New York: Doubleday, 1970), 10, 12–13.

47 Taylor, *Sources of the Self, passim.*

Chapter 4

1 Even if, unlike Proust's, say, its *material* is not art. See notes 1, 3, and 4 to the introduction.

2 James Chandler makes the valuable point that the "crisis . . . of poetic composition" enacted in book 1 of *The Prelude* "is congruent . . . with the crisis . . . of political morality" in books 9–11 (*Wordsworth's Second Nature*, 194). See also note 14.

3 I found Keith Hanley, *Wordsworth: A Poet's History* (Basingstoke: Palgrave/St. Martin's, 2001), chapter 3 ("Describing the Revolution") helpful in thinking about these two crucial books of the *Prelude*, although his focus is different from mine. Jonathan Wordsworth's *William Wordsworth: The Borders of Vision* (Oxford: Clarendon, 1982) is valuable, and so is the account in Hartman's *Wordsworth's Poetry* of the revolution books (242–51). Best of all is Gill, in both the magisterial *William Wordsworth: A Life* (44–79), on which I have heavily if silently relied throughout, and the excellent introduction in *The Prelude* (Cambridge: Cambridge University Press, 1991) (75–82). For Chandler, *Wordsworth's Second Nature*, see note 14.

4 Bromwich (*Disowned by Memory*, 10) writes that "neither the fictional story nor its real-life foundation is remotely suggestive of detachment." Not detachment, perhaps: but (it seems to me) a kind of incapacity nevertheless.

5 I am very much conscious, here and throughout the following chapters, of Nicholas Roe's closing remark in his *Wordsworth and Coleridge: The Radical Years*, that "it was failure that made Wordsworth a poet" (275).

6 *Discourse on Inequality*, note 15, in Jean-Jacques Rousseau, *Rousseau's Political Writings*, trans. Julia Conway Bondanella, ed. Alan Ritter (New York: W. W. Norton, 1988), 27.

7 Rousseau, *Discourse on Inequality*, 40–44.

8 Rousseau, *Discourse on Inequality*, 56.

9 Rousseau, *On Social Contract*, in *Political Writings*, 93, 95, 96, 98, 108.

10 Alexis de Tocqueville, *Democracy in America*, trans. Henry Reeve, ed. Phillips Bradley (New York: Vintage Books, 1945), 2:101.

11 Charles Louis de Secondat, Baron de Montesquieu, *Montesquieu: The Spirit of the Laws* (*L'Ésprit des Lois* 1748), trans. and ed. Anne M. Cohler, Basia

Carolyn Miller, and Harold Samuel Stone (Cambridge: Cambridge University Press, 1989), 310 (and see book 19 *passim*).

12 All *Prelude* references are to the 1805 text in Wordsworth, *The Prelude*, unless otherwise indicated.

13 For Locke references in this paragraph, see John Locke, *Two Treatises of Government*, ed. Peter Laslett (Cambridge: Cambridge University Press, 1988), 282, 331, 350, 357, 412; and *An Essay Concerning Human Understanding*, ed. Peter H. Nidditch (Oxford: Clarendon, 1975), 395.

14 From the *Defensio Secunda* (1654): Milton, John, *Paradise Lost*. Edited by Scott Elledge (New York: W. W. Norton, 1975), 302.

15 W. J. T. Mitchell, "Influence, Autobiography and Literary History: Rousseau's *Confessions* and Wordsworth's *The Prelude*," *ELH* 57, no. 3 (1990): 643–64.

16 Edmund Burke, *The Philosophy of Edmund Burke*, ed. Louis I. Bredvold and Ralph G. Ross (Ann Arbor: University of Michigan Press, 1967), 248–49.

17 Much of this discussion of Burke, and indeed much of these two chapters, covers ground expertly mapped out and indeed made his own by James Chandler, in his 1984 study of "Wordsworth's second nature." With great subtlety and in impressive detail Chandler traces Wordsworth's "involvement in the intellectual history of the French Revolution" (*Wordsworth's Second Nature*, xvii), and especially shows how his "ideological perspective" in the French books of *The Prelude* and elsewhere is "thoroughly Burkean" (32). I could not hope to emulate Chandler's scholarship but have benefited greatly from it. I suspect however that our accounts of what might be called the "limits of Wordsworth" arise from deeply differing perspectives on politics and the reading of poetry, not least in the central emphasis Chandler places on ideology.

18 Page references in parentheses are to Burke, *Reflections on the Revolution in France*.

19 Hans-Georg Gadamer, *Philosophical Hermeneutics*, trans. David E. Linge (Berkeley: University of California Press, 1976), 9.

20 Chandler makes it clear that for him Wordsworth's Burkeanism was something to be discovered anew or even for the first time.

21 The second and third chapters of Gill's *William Wordsworth: A Life* and, even more, "'Pretty Hot in It': Wordsworth and France, 1791–1792," the second chapter of Roe's *Wordsworth and Coleridge*, supplied me with a great deal of what I otherwise would sadly lack: a sense of the historical detail of these months in Wordsworth's life. I am much indebted to both.

22 John Milton, *Paradise Lost*, ed. Elledge, 86 (4.287–95).

23 Milton, *Paradise Lost*, 116, 119.

24 Murdoch, *The Sovereignty of Good*, 80.

25 Milton, *Paradise Lost*, 8, 12.

26 Milton, *Paradise Lost*, 13.

27 Milton, *Paradise Lost*, 246.

28 See Wordsworth, *The Prelude*, 8. The "spots of time" passages with the reflection on them occur at the start of this early version.

29 See also chapter 3's section, "The Tangled Root of 'Simon Lee.'"

30 Bromwich, *Disowned by Memory*, 23–43, has a fine account of "The Old Cumberland Beggar," pointing out that neither sympathy nor gratitude is Wordsworth's business in the poem, but that the old man is purely "seen from the outside" (41). The tension between protest against a social system and protest against spiritual loss incurred by welfare policy is the poem's point. It is the second protest I find more audible. See also note 34 to chapter 3, and Chandler, *Wordsworth's Second Nature*, 84–89.

31 Burke, *Reflections*, 37.

32 Burke, *Reflections*, 39.

33 Editors' note, Wordsworth, *The Prelude*, 162. Chandler's account of Wordsworth and Rousseauan education theory (Chandler, *Wordsworth's Second Nature*, ch. 5) is illuminating.

34 This is from "Mr Wordsworth" again: Hazlitt, 87.

35 Chandler's key phrase, though not quite in his sense.

36 For a very different account of these passages, see Chandler, *Wordsworth's Second Nature*, 203–6.

37 Burke, *Reflections*, xxxii–xxxiii.

38 Burke, *Reflections*, 149.

Chapter 5

1 See also on this passage J. Wordsworth, *William Wordsworth*, 268–69.

2 For a somewhat fuller account of this picture of the Enlightenment self, see Haines, *Poetry and Philosophy*, 151–54. Chandler, *Wordsworth's Second Nature*, ch. 9, is a useful exposition of the role of the more derivative French ideologues, especially Destutt de Tracy, coiner of the term "ideology," in influencing Wordsworth.

3 The text used here is William Godwin, *Enquiry Concerning Political Justice, and Its Influence on Modern Morals and Happiness* (Penguin Books: Harmondsworth, 1985); all page references in parentheses are to this edition. Useful commentary on *Political Justice* and on Wordsworth's relation to it and to Godwin is to be found in John P. Clark, *The Philosophical Anarchism of William Godwin* (Princeton: Princeton University Press, 1977), especially part 1; and Mary Jacobus, *Tradition and Experiment in Wordsworth's*

"Lyrical Ballads" (1798) (Oxford: Clarendon, 1976), ch. 1: "The Godwinian Background." J. Wordsworth, *William Wordsworth*, ch. 8 ("Versions of the Fall"), has a valuable account of Wordsworth's acquaintance with Godwin. Celeste Langan, *Romantic Vagrancy: Wordsworth and the Simulation of Freedom* (Cambridge: Cambridge University Press, 1995), 175–81, proposes interestingly that "Godwin's political theory figures in Wordsworth's text most prominently when *The Prelude* . . . is least apparently political"—that Godwin is "a formal model for the aesthetic experiment of *The Prelude*" in so far as "the poem's unifying 'method'" *is* "its politics" (175). But see note 1 to chapter 2.

4　From "William Godwin," Hazlitt, *Complete Works*, 11:16.

5　See note 5 to chapter 4. Roe remarks with an acuteness backed up by his entire study that Wordsworth's poetry arose out of political failure (Roe, *Wordsworth and Coleridge*, 275). My study claims only to takes this insight a step further (a big step, I admit!), by saying that in some sense this "failure" was transmitted into the poetry itself.

6　Burke, *Reflections*, 7.

7　Hartman, *Wordsworth's Poetry*, 212.

8　I am uncomfortably conscious of the brevity of this account when compared with some recent scholarly interpretations, such as David Ellis' (*Wordsworth, Freud and the Spots of Time: Interpretation in "The Prelude"* [Cambridge: Cambridge University Press, 1985]): a whole book on the psychology of the "spots of time" (disagreement with Hartman, *Wordsworth's Poetry*, is a key point of departure for this book). Jonathan Wordsworth's "Spots of Time and Sources of Power" (Wordsworth, *William Wordsworth*, chapter 3) is still a foundational account.

9　Paul Hamilton (*Wordsworth* [Brighton: Harvester, 1986], 121) comments shrewdly that "the implication of poetic and revolutionary sympathies in each other ceases [i.e., in book 10] to be a political embarrassment and becomes an alibi." But "embarrassment" perhaps hardly does justice to Wordsworth's deep and conflicted feelings about those transgressions, against poetry especially, which required such an alibi.

10　Mill, *Autobiography*, 80–81.

11　Mill, *Autobiography*, 89.

12　His "deepest fear is that his ambition to change the world may succeed for himself at a price to nature," writes Bromwich (*Disowned by Memory*, 2)—but perhaps at an even greater price to poetry itself. See note 5.

Conclusion

1   The "Ode" was composed between 1802 and 1804 and first published in 1807 simply as "Ode." It was given the fuller title in the 1815 edition of Wordsworth's collected poems. For text used here see Gill, ed., *William Wordsworth*, 297–302 (where the 1807 version is used). I have not printed the poem here, but the reader might find it helpful to have it to hand. Line numbers are given in parentheses.

BIBLIOGRAPHY

Allison, Henry E. *Kant's Transcendental Idealism*. New Haven: Yale University Press, 2004.

Anscombe, G. E. M. "Modern Moral Philosophy." *Philosophy* 33, no. 124 (1958): 1–19.

Arnold, Matthew. *Matthew Arnold's Essays in Criticism*. London: Dent & Dutton, 1964.

Bennett, Jonathan. *Kant's Analytic*. Cambridge: Cambridge University Press, 1966.

Bersani, Leo. *The Culture of Redemption*. Cambridge, Mass.: Harvard University Press, 1990.

Blake, William, *The Poetry and Prose of William Blake*. Edited by David V. Erdman. New York: Doubleday, 1970.

Bloom, Harold, ed. *William Wordsworth*. Bloom's Literary Criticism. New York: Infobase, 2009.

Bowie, Andrew. *Aesthetics and Subjectivity: From Kant to Nietzsche*. 1990. Manchester: Manchester University Press, 2003.

Bromwich, David. *Disowned by Memory: Wordsworth's Poetry of the 1790s*. Chicago: University of Chicago Press, 1998.

Browning, Robert, *The Poetical Works of Robert Browning*, 2 vols. London: Smith, Elder, 1901; repr. Newcastle: Cambridge Scholars, 2012.

Burke, Edmund. *The Philosophy of Edmund Burke*. Edited by Louis I. Bredvold and Ralph G. Ross. Ann Arbor: University of Michigan Press, 1967.

———. *Reflections on the Revolution in France*. Edited by J. G. A. Pocock. Indianapolis: Hackett, 1987.

Chandler, James K. *Wordsworth's Second Nature: A Study of the Poetry and Politics*. Chicago: University of Chicago Press, 1984.

Clark, John P. *The Philosophical Anarchism of William Godwin*. Princeton: Princeton University Press, 1977.

Coleridge, Samuel Taylor. *The Notebooks of Samuel Taylor Coleridge*. Vol. 1, *1794–1804*. Edited by Kathleen Coburn. Bollingen Series 50. New York: Pantheon Books, 1957.

———. *Samuel Taylor Coleridge: The Oxford Authors*. Edited by H. J. Jackson. Oxford: Oxford University Press, 1985.

Descartes, René. *The Philosophical Works of Descartes*. Translated by Elizabeth S. Haldane and G. R. T. Ross. 2 vols. Cambridge: Cambridge University Press, 1969.

Diamond, Cora. *The Realistic Spirit: Wittgenstein, Philosophy and the Mind*. Cambridge, Mass.: MIT Press, 1991.

Ellis, David. *Wordsworth, Freud and the Spots of Time: Interpretation in "The Prelude."* Cambridge: Cambridge University Press, 1985.

Ewing, A. C. *A Short Commentary on Kant's "Critique of Pure Reason."* 1938. Chicago: University of Chicago Press, 1967.

Ferguson, Frances. *Wordsworth: Language as Counter-Spirit*. New Haven: Yale University Press, 1977.

Ferry, David. *The Limits of Mortality: An Essay on Wordsworth's Major Poems*. Middletown, Conn.: Wesleyan University Press, 1959.

Fraser, Giles. *Redeeming Nietzsche: On the Piety of Unbelief*. London: Routledge, 2002.

Gadamer, Hans-Georg. *Philosophical Hermeneutics*. Translated by David E. Linge. Berkeley: University of California Press, 1976.

Gardner, Sebastian. *Routledge Philosophy Guidebook to Kant and the "Critique of Pure Reason."* London: Routledge, 1999.

Gill, Stephen. *The Prelude*. Cambridge: Cambridge University Press, 1991.

———. *William Wordsworth: A Life*. Oxford: Clarendon, 1989.

Glen, Heather. *Vision & Disenchantment: Blake's Songs and Wordsworth's "Lyrical Ballads."* Cambridge: Cambridge University Press, 1983.

Godwin, William. *Enquiry Concerning Political Justice, and Its Influence on Modern Morals and Happiness*. Harmondsworth: Penguin Books, 1985.

Guyer, Paul. "The Transcendental Deduction of the Categories." In *The Cambridge Companion to Kant*, edited by Paul Guyer, 123–60. Cambridge: Cambridge University Press, 1992.

Haines, Simon. "English Bards and German Sages." In *English Now: Selected Papers from the 20th IAUPE Conference*, edited by Marianne Thormahlen, 72–82. Lund: Centre for Languages and Literature, 2008.

———. "Iris Murdoch, the Ethical Turn and Literary Value." In *Iris Murdoch and Morality*, edited by Anne Rowe and Avril Horner, 87–100. Basingstoke: Palgrave Macmillan, 2010.

———. *Poetry and Philosophy from Homer to Rousseau: Romantic Souls, Realist Lives*. Basingstoke: Palgrave Macmillan, 2005.

Hamilton, Paul. *Wordsworth*. Brighton: Harvester, 1986.

Hanley, Keith. *Wordsworth: A Poet's History*. Basingstoke: Palgrave/St. Martin's, 2001.

Hartman, Geoffrey H. *Wordsworth's Poetry 1787–1814*. New Haven: Yale University Press, 1964.

Hazlitt, William. *The Complete Works of William Hazlitt*. Edited by P. P. Howe. 21 vols. London: J. M. Dent & Sons, 1932.

Jacobus, Mary. "The Godwinian Background." Chap. 1 in *Tradition and Experiment in Wordsworth's "Lyrical Ballads" (1798)*. Oxford: Clarendon, 1976.

Johnson, Mark, and George Lakoff. *Metaphors We Live By*. Chicago: University of Chicago Press, 1980.

Kant, Immanuel. *Political Writings*. Edited by Hans Reiss. Translated by H. B. Nisbet. Cambridge: Cambridge University Press, 1970.

———. *Critique of Practical Reason*, in *Practical Philosophy*. Translated and edited by Mary J. Gregor, 133–272. Cambridge: Cambridge University Press, 1996.

———. *Groundwork of the Metaphysic of Morals*, in *Practical Philosophy*, 37–108.

———. *The Metaphysics of Morals*, in *Practical Philosophy*, 353–603.

———. *Critique of Pure Reason*. Translated and edited by Paul Guyer and Allen W. Wood. Cambridge: Cambridge University Press, 1998.

————. *Critique of the Power of Judgment*. Edited by Paul Guyer. Translated by Paul Guyer and Eric Matthews. Cambridge: Cambridge University Press, 2000.

Keats, John. *Letters of John Keats*. Edited by Robert Gittings. London: Oxford University Press, 1970.

Kemp Smith, Norman. *A Commentary to Kant's "Critique of Pure Reason"* (1918). Basingstoke: Palgrave Macmillan/St. Martin's, 2003.

Langan, Celeste. *Romantic Vagrancy: Wordsworth and the Simulation of Freedom*. Cambridge: Cambridge University Press, 1995.

Leavis, F. R. *Revaluation: Tradition and Development in English Poetry*. Harmondsworth: Penguin, 1967.

Levinson, Marjorie. *Wordsworth's Great Period Poems*. Cambridge: Cambridge University Press, 1986.

Locke, John. *An Essay Concerning Human Understanding*. Edited by Peter H. Nidditch. Oxford: Clarendon, 1975.

————. *Two Treatises of Government*. Edited by Peter Laslett. Cambridge: Cambridge University Press, 1988.

MacIntyre, Alasdair. *After Virtue: A Study in Moral Theory*. London: Duckworth, 1985.

McFarland, Thomas. *William Wordsworth: Intensity and Achievement*. Oxford: Clarendon, 1992.

Mill, John Stuart. *Autobiography*. 1873. Edited by Jack Stillinger. Oxford: Oxford University Press, 1969.

————. "Thoughts on Poetry and Its Varieties." 1833. In *Autobiography and Literary Essays*. Vol. 1 of *The Collected Works of John Stuart Mill*, 341–66. The Online Library of Liberty, Liberty Fund.

Milton, John. *Paradise Lost*. Edited by Scott Elledge. New York: W. W. Norton, 1975.

Mitchell, W. J. T., "Influence, Autobiography and Literary History: Rousseau's *Confessions* and Wordsworth's *The Prelude*." *ELH* 57, no. 3 (1990): 643–64.

Montesquieu, Charles Louis de Secondat, Baron de. *Montesquieu: The Spirit of the Laws* (*L'Ésprit des Lois*, 1748). Translated and edited by Anne M. Cohler, Basia Carolyn Miller, and Harold Samuel Stone. Cambridge: Cambridge University Press, 1989.

Murdoch, Iris. *The Sovereignty of Good*. London: Routledge, 1970.

Nuttall, A. D. *A Common Sky: Philosophy and the Literary Imagination*. London: Chatto & Windus for Sussex University Press, 1974.

Oxford English Dictionary (*OED*).

Peacock, Thomas Love. *The Works of Thomas Love Peacock*. Edited by H. F. Brett-Smith and C. E. Jones. 10 vols. London: Constable, 1924–1934.

Pinkard, Terry. *German Philosophy 1760–1860: The Legacy of Idealism*. Cambridge: Cambridge University Press, 2002.

Pippin, Robert B. "Kant on the Spontaneity of Mind." *Canadian Journal of Philosophy* 17, no. 2 (1987): 449–76.

Roe, Nicholas. *Wordsworth and Coleridge: The Radical Years*. Oxford: Clarendon, 1988.

Rousseau, Jean-Jacques. *Julie, ou La Nouvelle Héloïse*. 1761. Paris: Garnier-Flammarion, 1967.

———. *Rousseau's Political Writings*. Translated by Julia Conway Bondanella. Edited by Alan Ritter. New York: W. W. Norton, 1988.

Sadler, Ted. *Nietzsche: Truth and Redemption*. London: Athlone, 1995.

Scruton, Roger. *Kant*. Oxford: Oxford University Press, 1982.

Sgarbi, Marco. *Kant on Spontaneity*. London: Continuum, 2012.

Sheats, Paul D. *The Making of Wordsworth's Poetry, 1795–1798*. Cambridge, Mass.: Harvard University Press, 1973.

Shelley, Percy B. *Shelley's Poetry and Prose*, selected and ed. Donald H. Reiman and Sharon Powers, New York: W. W. Norton, 1977.

Simpson, David. *Wordsworth, Commodification and Social Concern: The Poetics of Modernity*. Cambridge: Cambridge University Press, 2009.

———. *Wordsworth's Historical Imagination: The Poetry of Displacement*. New York: Methuen, 1987.

Strawson, P. F. *The Bounds of Sense: An Essay on Kant's "Critique of Pure Reason."* 1966. London: Methuen, 1975.

Taylor, Charles. *Sources of the Self: The Making of the Modern Identity*. Cambridge: Cambridge University Press, 1989.

Tocqueville, Alexis de. *Democracy in America*. Translated by Henry Reeve. Edited by Phillips Bradley. 2 vols. New York: Vintage Books, 1945.

Vico, Giambattista. *The New Science of Giambattista Vico*. 1948. Translated by Thomas Goddard Bergin and Max Harold Fisch. Ithaca: Cornell University Press, 1984.

Wellek, René. *A History of Modern Criticism: 1750–1950*. Vol. 1, *The Later Eighteenth Century*. London: Jonathan Cape, 1955.

Wood, Allen W. *Kant*. Oxford: Blackwell, 2005.

Wordsworth, Jonathan. *William Wordsworth: The Borders of Vision*. Oxford: Clarendon, 1982.

Wordsworth, William. *The Prose Works of William Wordsworth*. Edited by W. J. B. Owen and Jane Worthington Smyser. 3 vols. Oxford: Clarendon, 1974.

———. *The Prelude, 1799, 1805, 1850*. Edited by Jonathan Wordsworth, M. H. Abrams, and Stephen Gill. New York: W. W. Norton, 1979. (All references are to the 1805 text unless otherwise indicated.)

———. *William Wordsworth: The Oxford Authors*. Edited by Stephen Gill. Oxford: Oxford University Press, 1984.

Wordsworth, William and Samuel Taylor Coleridge. *Lyrical Ballads: Wordsworth and Coleridge*. Edited by R. L. Brett and A. R. Jones. London: Methuen, 1965.

INDEX

absolution (absolve), 6, 17, 70, 75, 140
Achtung, 96, 98–99
aesthetic (-ism, -ization), 7–9, 11,
  18, 33–34, 43, 46–48, 50, 52, 55–57,
  65–66, 79, 82, 84, 96, 101, 155–56,
  160, 164–66, 168, 173, 197, 216,
  222n1, 223n8, 234n3; *aisthêsis*, 25, 33,
  47, 54; *see also* Kant, "Transcendental Aesthetic"
Allison, Henry E., 227n4
Anscombe, G. E. M., 222n2
Aquinas, Thomas, 18, 25, 33, 52, 99,
  168, 193
aretê, 51
Aristotle, 18, 25, 91, 221n1
Arnold, Matthew, 32, 66, 224n13
Augustine, St., 18, 27, 35, 75, 91, 99,
  101, 131, 165
Austen, Jane, 18, 22, 29, 33, 52, 57;
  Northanger Abbey, 52; *Persuasion*, 22,
  33, 52, 57

Baumgarten, A. G., 33, 224n17
Bayle, Pierre, 27, 194, 208
Beaupuy, Michel, 15, 141–42, 144, 164,
  171–80, 183, 187, 192, 213

Being, 9, 12, 16, 38, 56, 65, 135–36, 153,
  156, 170–71, 213
Bennett, Jonathan, 227n4
Bentham, Jeremy, 131, 210
Beowulf, 69
Bergson, Henri, 80
Berlin, Isaiah, 228n19
Bersani, Leo, 222–23nn1, 3
Bible, The, 153; Old Testament, 173;
  Genesis, 102; John, 152–53; Luke,
  167; Matthew, 167; Psalms, 65, 67
Blake, William, 28–29, 33–34, 126,
  157, 176, 189, 209, 229n29, 231n46;
  Songs, 28–29
bless (-ing, -ed), 13, 38, 46, 49, 52–53,
  55–56, 68–69, 128–30, 152–53, 183,
  189, 209, 218
Bonaparte, Napoleon, 178
Bondanella, Julia Conway, 231n6
Boswell, James, *Life of Johnson*, 4
Bowie, Andrew, 228n8
Bredvold, Louis I., 232n16
Brett, R. L., 226n15, 230n42
Bromwich, David, 33, 224n15,
  225nn1–2, 226n14, 229n31, 230n39,
  231n4, 233n30, 234n12

Browning, Robert, 33, 58, 224n14
Burke, Edmund, 13–15, 43, 55, 142,
　144–50, 154, 158, 166, 168–69, 174,
　176, 178, 182, 191, 193, 196, 198, 203,
　206, 213, 223n6, 229n35, 232nn16–18,
　20, 233nn31–32, 37–38, 234n6; *Reflec-
　tions*, 145–49, 198, 223n6, 232n18,
　233nn37–38, 234n6
Byron, George Gordon, Lord, 29,
　52, 59, 101, 112, 178; *Childe Harold's
　Pilgrimage*, 52

Cabanis, Pierre, 197
Chandler, James, 229n35, 231nn2–3,
　232nn17, 20, 233nn30, 35, 2
Christian (-ity), 1–6, 12, 18–19, 28, 45,
　57, 65, 72, 74, 92, 97, 114, 125–26,
　129, 137, 143, 153, 165, 197, 215,
　217–19, 221n1; post-C, 1–5, 18–19, 45,
　57, 65, 72, 92, 165, 217–19
Cicero, 135
Clark, John P., 233n3
Coburn, Kathleen, 226n13
Coleridge, Samuel Taylor, 11, 13, 17,
　29, 32, 56, 59–61, 80, 90, 104, 110,
　124–30, 134, 171, 174, 191, 211–12,
　226nn13, 15–16, 227n7, 230nn42–45,
　231n5, 232n21, 234n5; *Aids to Reflec-
　tion*, 13; "Ancient Mariner," 60–61,
　74, 124–30, 226n15, 230n42; *Bio-
　graphia Literaria*, 1124, 230nn43–44
concept (-ion, -ual, -ualism), 1, 3–8,
　10–11, 13, 16–19, 21–29, 31–35, 39–43,
　45, 47–48, 51–56, 62, 65–67, 70–71,
　73, 75–91, 93–101, 106–7, 124, 126,
　130–31, 133, 135–36, 139–44, 147–51,
　153, 163, 166–68, 178–80, 183, 189,
　194–97, 200, 203–5, 208–9, 213–18,
　221n1, 222n2
Condillac, Etienne, 197

Dante, 18, 23, 27, 44, 54, 159, 162
Darwin, Charles, 193
Derrida, Jacques, 25, 230n39

Descartes, René (Cartesian), 18, 24,
　26–28, 35, 39, 41–42, 75–76, 80, 97,
　140, 196, 208, 226n1
de Tracy, Destutt, 233n2
Diamond, Cora, 22, 223n1

Edgeworth, Maria, 29, 172
Eliot, T. S., 18, 54, 61, 66; *Prufrock*, 61,
　66; *Waste Land*, 54
Elledge, Scott, 232nn14, 22
Ellis, David, 234n8
Enlightenment, the, 3, 19, 28, 52–55,
　77, 91, 131, 159, 196, 215, 221, 233
Erdman, David V., 231n46
eudaimonia, 8, 51–52
Ewing, A. C., 227n4

faith, 1–2, 11, 27, 32, 34–35, 43, 68–69,
　72, 76, 82, 91, 95, 97, 103, 133, 150,
　157, 159, 171, 176, 192–94, 201, 208,
　215, 218
Ferguson, Frances, 226n18
Ferry, David, 229n37
Fichte, J. G., 103
forgive (-ness), 2, 7, 76
forms: of beauty, 8, 18, 32–33, 38, 43,
　45–47, 49, 55–57, 60–62, 64–67, 70,
　96, 155, 158, 160, 170, 215–16; of
　good, 18, 32, 38, 57, 64, 70, 73, 96,
　155–56, 215–16; of life, 65
Foucault, Michel, 25
Fraser, Giles, 221n1
freedom, 10–11, 73, 75, 90, 93–95,
　97–98, 100–103, 130, 140, 142, 146,
　148, 157–58, 174–75, 198, 201, 204,
　207, 208, 234n3
Freud, Sigmund, 35, 234n8

Gadamer, Hans-Georg, 91, 149, 232n19
Galileo, 131
Gardner, Sebastian, 227n4
Gill, Stephen, 224n7, 225n2, 229n26,
　231n3, 232n21, 235n1
Gittings, Robert, 224n12

Glen, Heather, 229nn29–31
God, 1, 5, 7–11, 13–14, 16, 18, 24, 26–28, 38, 45, 46, 56–58, 65–66, 71, 75–77, 81–82, 92, 95–97, 99, 102–3, 114–15, 117, 123, 125–26, 129, 131, 136, 138, 141–43, 152–56, 158–60, 162–63, 165–66, 170, 182, 197, 209, 213, 216–19, 221–22n1
god (-s), 38, 55, 61, 66, 91, 129, 158–59, 167, 205
Godwin, William, 13, 16–17, 31, 33, 149–50, 198–211, 214, 233–34nn3–4; *Political Justice*, 198–211, 233–34nn3–4
grace, 1–2, 5, 11–13, 18, 23, 35, 55, 64, 76–77, 114–15, 120, 129, 138, 156–57, 165, 218
gratitude, 2, 49, 64, 113–15, 117, 122, 124, 130, 229n31, 233n30
Gregor, Mary J., 227n3, 228nn20, 21
Guyer, Paul, 226n8, 227n4, 228n12

habeas corpus, 180
Haines, Simon, 223n10, 3, 227n3, 233n2
Haldane, Elizabeth S., 226n1
Hamann, J. G., 103
Hamilton, Paul, 234n9
Hanley, Keith, 231n3
Harrington, James, 142
Hartley, David, 31, 197
Hartman, Geoffrey, 32, 206, 225n2, 231n3, 234nn7–8
Hazlitt, William, 15, 29–30, 32, 38, 173–74, 198, 224nn8, 11, 233n34
Heaney, Seamus, 29
hêdonê, 14
Hegel, G. W. F. (Hegelian), 4, 13, 24, 26, 103, 126, 189, 196, 219, 227n7
Heidegger, Martin, 4, 18, 227n7
Helvétius, Claude, 197–98
Herder, J. G., 103
Hobbes, Thomas, 27–28, 166, 196–97
Holbach, Baron d', 197–98

Hooker, Richard, 142
Horace, 38, 135
Horner, Avril, 223n3
Hume, David, 4, 18, 25, 27, 39, 41–42, 75–78, 80, 82, 84, 87, 197
Husserl, Edmund, 80
Hutcheson, Francis, 33, 52, 197
Huxley, Thomas, *Brave New World*, 140

Jackson, H. J., 230nn43, 45
Jacobus, Mary, 234n3
James, William, 80
Jesus Christ, 1–4, 18, 19, 28, 152–53, 221n1
Johnson, Mark, 223n1
Johnson, Samuel, 30
Jones, A. R., 226n15, 230n42
Jones, Robert, 151, 161, 207
justice (in-), 3, 24, 76, 136, 141–43, 145, 147, 183, 192, 194, 212

Kant, Immanuel, 4, 9–14, 16–17, 19, 24, 37, 39, 41–42, 45, 58, 66, 73–103, 106, 121, 126, 127, 130–31, 144, 148, 150, 157–59, 162, 166, 168–69, 175, 197–98, 200, 202, 209, 215, 219, 226n8, 227nn3–7, 228nn8–21; *Critique of Judgment*, 92, 96–97, 228nn12–17, 240; *Critique of Practical Reason*, 11, 92, 98, 228n20; *Critique of Pure Reason*, 10–11, 73, 77–97, 226n8, 227nn4–5; *Groundwork*, 92, 97–101, 227n4, 228nn9, 11, 18; *Metaphysics of Morals*, 100, 228n21; spontaneity in, 9–11, 17, 73, 86, 88–95, 101–3; "Third Antinomy," 73, 90, 92, 94, 97, 100–101; "Transcendental Aesthetic," 79–82, 87; "Transcendental Deduction," 10, 77–96; "Transcendental Logic," 81–82
Keats, John, 18, 29, 32, 54, 66, 205, 224n12; *Lamia*, 205; "Ode to a Nightingale," 54

Kemp Smith, Norman, 227n4
Kierkegaard, Søren, 4, 12, 103, 196

Lakoff, George, 223n1
La Mettrie, Julien, 197
landscape, 7–8, 14, 40–50, 52, 56,
    59–63, 66–67, 69–70, 122, 165, 170,
    188, 207, 215, 222, 230
Langan, Celeste, 234n3
language: life with, 22, 27, 29, 35;
    materialist/reductive, 16, 31, 196,
    203, 214; as redemptive, 4–7, 26–27,
    35, 38; of the self, 16, 137, 197–98,
    201, 206, 211, 214
Lansdown, Richard, 229n32
Laslett, Peter, 232n13
Leavis, F. R., 32, 224n13
Le Brun, Charles, 151
Leibniz, G. W. von, 75–77, 81–82
Levinson, Marjorie, 225n2
Linge, David E., 232n19
Locke, John, 14, 26, 47, 50–51, 61, 80,
    84, 141–44, 149–50, 153, 155–56, 168–
    69, 196–97, 213, 232n13; Essay, 142–43,
    232n13, Second Treatise, 142, 232n13
Luther, Martin, 18, 77, 101, 131

Machiavelli, Niccolo, 18
MacIntyre, Alasdair, 221–22nn1–2
Marcus Aurelius, 135
Mark, St., 3–4, 6, 18, 28
Marx, Karl, 24, 35, 196, 230n39
Matthews, Eric, 228n12
McFarland, Thomas, 225n1
metaphor, 6–10, 18–19, 21–29, 31–33,
    37, 40, 42–45, 48–53, 55, 61–67, 71,
    91–92, 98, 102, 106–7, 130, 142–43,
    147, 149–50, 160, 164, 174, 178, 180,
    182, 188, 193–94, 203–4, 208, 213–15,
    223n1, 224n5
Mill, J. S., 17, 70, 105–7, 168, 209–
    11, 214, 225n7, 226n19, 228n23,
    234nn10–11; Autobiography, 70, 210,
    225n7, 226n19, 234nn10–11

Miller, Carolyn, 232n11
Milton, John, 3, 14, 18, 23, 28, 30, 32,
    34, 38, 54, 65, 114–15, 136, 141–44,
    149, 156–59, 173–75, 183, 209, 213,
    232nn14, 22, 233nn23, 25–27; Adam,
    65, 143, 156, 158, 162–63; Areo-
    pagitica, 143; Defensio Secunda,
    143, 232n14; Paradise Lost, 65, 114,
    137, 143, 158, 161–62, 183, 185, 202,
    232nn14, 22, 233nn23, 25–27; Satan,
    23, 28, 114, 129, 137, 143, 147, 159,
    160, 162
Mitchell, W. J. T., 143, 232n15
Montesquieu, C. L. de S., Baron de,
    141–42, 231–32n11
Moore, G. E., 34
Murdoch, Iris, 33–34, 158, 223n3,
    224n16, 233n24

nature, Nature, 10–11, 14, 16, 18–19,
    32, 38–39, 42, 52, 56, 58, 61–71,
    76–77, 84, 88–91, 93–105, 107, 122,
    124, 131, 136, 139–46, 154–56, 158,
    161–63, 165–66, 170–74, 182, 193–94,
    201–2, 205, 207, 212, 216, 218, 219,
    222–23n3, 226n20, 234n12
Newton, Isaac, 131
Nidditch, Peter H., 232n13
Nietzsche, Friedrich, 4, 18, 35, 103,
    196, 221–22n1, 223nn5, 9, 226n17,
    228n8
Nisbet, H. B., 228n19
noêsis, 47, 54
Nuttall, A. D., 29, 223–24n5

Orwell, George, Nineteen Eighty-Four,
    140
Overton, Richard, 142
Owen, W. J. B., 224n9

Paine, Thomas, 144, 198
Paul, St., 3, 6, 18, 23, 28, 101, 131, 165,
    221
Peacock, Thomas Love, 27, 223n4

Percy, Bishop, 110; "Chevy Chase," 110; "Lucy and Colin," 110; "Margaret's Ghost," 110; *Reliques*, 110, 126; "Sir Patrick Spens," 110, 126

philosophy, 6, 11, 16, 18, 24‒27, 29‒31, 33, 35, 71, 73‒75, 78, 80, 85‒86, 90‒91, 103, 130‒31, 134‒35, 144, 158, 173‒74, 176, 178, 195, 198, 201, 208, 211, 215, 222n2, 227n7

Pietism, 92

Pindar, 38, 44

Pinkard, Terry, 228n8

Pinocchio, 103, 114

Pippin, Robert B., 228n8

Plato (-nism, -nist), 3‒4, 18, 24, 47, 56, 73, 154, 166, 178, 182

Pocock, J. G. A., 178, 223n

poetry, 6‒9, 15‒18, 21‒35, 38‒40, 42, 45, 48, 51‒53, 60‒63, 65, 69‒72, 74, 91, 103‒7, 117, 124, 130, 133, 135‒36, 149‒51, 164, 172‒74, 177, 191, 195‒96, 203‒6, 208, 210‒12, 214, 219, 224n5, 225nn1, 7, 232n17, 234nn5, 9, 12

Powers, Sharon, 228n25

Proust, Marcel, 80, 222‒23n3, 223n4, 226nn9, 17, 20

Radcliffe, Ann, 29

Redeemer, 1‒2, 5, 13, 14, 114, 123

redemption (-ist, redemptiveness, redeemer), 1‒9, 11‒13, 17‒19, 71, 113, 115, 120, 123, 127, 129‒31, 133‒36, 149, 162, 183, 187, 189, 202, 211, 213, 215‒17, 219, 221‒22n1, 222‒23n3; aesthetic, 7, 9; political, 7; secular, 7, 9, 12, 14, 18, 30, 215; and spontaneity, 7, 130‒31

Reiman, Donald H., 228n25

Reiss, Hans, 228n19

Ritter, Alan, 231n6

restoration (restoring), 1, 5‒8, 37 42‒46, 56, 64, 69, 160, 181

Robespierre, Maximilien, 185, 193

Roe, Nicholas, 225n2, 231n5, 232n21, 234n5

romance, 14‒15, 123, 171‒78, 180, 183, 186, 213

Romanticism, 3, 13, 19, 21, 26, 133, 159, 215

Ross, G. R. T., 226n1

Ross, Ralph G., 232n16

Rousseau, Jean-Jacques, 4, 9, 13‒17, 27, 35, 39, 50, 74‒77, 99, 136‒44, 149‒50, 152‒54, 158, 165‒66, 169‒70, 172, 174‒76, 178, 183‒84, 193, 197‒99, 202, 213, 216, 222n1, 227nn3, 8, 231nn6‒9, 232n15, 233n33, 239‒41; *amour-propre, amour de soi*, 136; *Confessions*, 4, 35, 75‒76, 140, 143‒44, 234n15, 240; *Discourses*, 136‒38, 231nn6‒9; *Emile*, 75, 140, 144, 172, 197‒98; *La Nouvelle Héloïse*, 75, 227n2; *Savoyard Vicar*, 76, 153; *Social Contract*, 136‒41, 143‒44, 231n9

Rowe, Anne, 223n3

sacrifice, 1‒5, 7, 11, 13, 55, 59, 69, 128‒29, 177, 204

Sadler, Ted, 221n1

saving, salvation, 1‒2, 5, 7, 11‒12, 17, 19, 26, 30, 35, 51, 59, 65, 71, 76, 94‒95, 101, 103, 123, 125‒26, 128‒29, 130, 135, 160, 163, 165, 174, 178, 183, 186, 204, 211, 213, 215, 218, 222n1

Schelling, F. W. J., 103

Schleiermacher, Friedrich, 103

Schopenhauer, Arthur, 103

Scott, Sir Walter, 29, 232

Scruton, Roger, 227n4

Sgarbi, Marco, 228n8

Shaftesbury, 3rd Earl of, 31, 33, 52, 197‒98, 202

Sheats, Paul D., 229n31

self, the, 2‒6, 9‒11, 13‒19, 23‒24, 26, 37, 41‒42, 44, 49‒52, 54, 56, 59, 61‒62, 64, 74‒78, 81‒83, 85‒103, 113,

116, 123, 127, 128–31, 133, 136–40, 142–44, 148–50, 157, 164–68, 170–71, 177, 179, 183, 186–89, 192, 195–99, 210, 203–6, 209, 211–17, 222n1, 233n2; concept, punctual, Romantic, 3, 9, 18, 23–24, 137, 198, 203; Humean, 76–77; Kantian, 24, 74, 103; modern, 17–19, 74, 85, 215; Rousseauan, 50, 76, 140

sentiment (-al, -ality, -alism), 50, 52, 54, 75–77, 101, 105–6, 115, 121, 126, 134, 136, 138–39, 144, 146, 150, 168, 170, 180, 186, 188–89, 192, 194, 197–98, 221n1, 226n18

Shakespeare, William, 18, 173–74; *King Lear*, 48; *Othello*, 21–22, 33; *Measure for Measure*, 23; *The Merchant of Venice*, 5

Shelley, P. B., 29, 32, 40, 54, 56, 112, 176, 228n25; "Defence of Poetry," 228n25; "Hymn to Intellectual Beauty," 56; "Ode to the West Wind," 54

Simpson, David, 230n39

sin, 1–2, 4–5, 7, 9, 11–14, 16, 19, 44, 62, 69, 71, 76, 115, 131, 134, 136–41, 162, 193, 209, 210

Smyser, Jane Worthington, 224n9

Socrates, 3–4, 91, 200

Spenser, Edmund, 144, 171, 179; *Faerie Queene*, 23, 173; "Red Crosse Knight," 174, 177

Spinoza, Baruch de, 75, 77

spontaneity (spontaneous/ly), 7, 9–13, 17–18, 73–74, 77, 86, 88–95, 98, 101–3, 105–7, 113–15, 117, 120–25, 128–30, 133, 141, 148–49, 152–53, 164–65, 167, 174, 182, 188, 197, 200, 202, 205, 213, 216, 228n8; *see also* Kant, redemption

Stillinger, Jack, 225n7

Stone, Harold Samuel, 232n11

Strawson, Peter, 85, 227nn4, 6

sublime (sublimity), 13, 42–44, 46, 54–55, 57–58, 60, 62–66, 69, 96, 104–5, 123, 161–62, 190, 207–9, 219

Taylor, Charles, 130, 222n3, 231n47

Tennyson, Alfred, Lord, 193, 219

Thompson, E. P., 32

Thucydides, 25

Tocqueville, Alexis de, 140, 142, 231n10

Vallon, Annette, 15, 121, 164

value, 7–9, 12, 21, 24–25, 37–38, 42–43, 47–48, 51, 55, 65, 97, 105–6, 110, 112, 137, 197, 218–20, 221n1, 222n3

Vauvenargues, 197

Vernunft, 81

Verstand, 82

Vico, Giambattista, 27–28, 182, 196, 223n4

Virgil, 18, 27, 91, 101; *Aeneid*, 23, 90–91, 99, 161–62

Voltaire, 4, 27, 196, 208

Walpole, Horace, 29

Watts, Isaac, 126

will, the (free, good, general), 7, 12, 14–15, 42, 45, 75, 77, 81–82, 91, 96–101, 103, 106, 117, 125, 129, 133, 138–39, 142, 150, 153, 157–58, 175–76, 178, 182–83, 197–99, 208, 215–16, 221n1

Winstanley, Gerrard, 142

Wittgenstein, Ludwig, 4, 18, 25, 81, 91, 196, 223n1

Wood, Allen W., 226n8, 227n4

Wordsworth, Catherine, 121

Wordsworth, Dorothy, 17, 59, 69–70, 104, 123, 134, 171, 211–12

Wordsworth, Jonathan, 224nn6, 18, 231n3, 233n1, 234nn3, 8

Wordsworth, William: "Anecdote for Fathers," 115–16; *Convention of*

Cintra, 143, 149; *Essay on Morals*, 30–32; *Excursion*, 32; "Immortality Ode," 44, 173, 193, 217–19, 235n1; *Letter to the Bishop of Llandaff*, 143, 149, 177; *Letter to a Member of the National Assembly*, 144; "'Lucy' poems," 134–35; *Lyrical Ballads*, 38–39, 60, 74, 105, 117, 122, 167, 210, 226n15, 229n29, 230n42, 234n3; "Michael," 12, 121–22, 143, 229n38, 230n39; "Old Cumberland Beggar," 14, 40, 104, 117, 167–69, 180, 229n35, 233n30; "Preface" to *Lyrical Ballads*, 103, 105–7, 113, 116–17, 198, 224nn7, 10, 13, 225n7, 226n11; *Prelude*, 12–13, 15, 30, 32, 40, 42, 59, 62, 67, 69, 74, 117, 120, 122–24, 134–36, 142–44, 149–97, 200–214, 224n6, 230n41, 231nn3–5, 232nn12, 17, 21, 233nn28, 33, 234nn8–9, 12; *Prelude* book 5, 172–74; *Prelude* book 6,

161; *Prelude* book 7, 213; *Prelude* book 8, 159–63; *Prelude*, book 9, 165–72, 174–84, 212–13; *Prelude* book 10, 185–96, 200–209 211–13; *Prelude* book 11, 218; *Prelude* book 11 (1850), 209; *Prelude* book 13, 207; "Simon Lee," 12, 38, 40, 74, 104, 107–17, 119–22, 124–27, 169, 175, 180, 226n12, 229n29, 230n39, 233n29; "Surprized by Joy," 121; "Tables Turned," 107; "Tintern Abbey," 7–10, 17, 31, 35, 37–73, 88, 105–97, 114, 116–17, 120, 123–24, 134–35, 151, 155, 168, 170, 178, 189–90, 192, 204, 208, 211–12, 225nn19, 1–6; "Two April Mornings, The," 12, 117–21, 134; "We Are Seven," 115–16

zeal (-ot, -otry, -ous), 14–15, 68, 70, 164, 166–67, 169–71, 177–80, 186, 193, 196, 201, 204–5, 208, 213–14